A Hand Always Above
My Shoulder

A Hand Always Above My Shoulder

By Howard Conn

— *A journey through philosophy, oriental mysticism and the Bible toward a Christian Universalism*

— *An Unseen Providence guiding the rejuvenation of a metropolitan parish*

— *The amazing fitting together of the pieces in a nonconformist ministry*

— *A demurrer from church mergers and the vision of a wider ecumenism*

Aberfoyle Press
5804 Oak Lane
Edina, Minnesota 55436

Library of Congress Catalog Card Number: 90-84941
International Standard Book Number: 0-962-7764-1-6

Printed in the United States of America

CONTENTS

Chapter 1. The Expanding Wonders of Existence   1

Chapter 2. Growing Up   7

Chapter 3. The Harvard Year   25

Chapter 4. Seminary Days   35

Chapter 5. Thoughts of a Seminarian   49

Chapter 6. My First Job   59

Chapter 7. Great Barrington Years   65

Chapter 8. From the Berkshires to Minneapolis   81

Chapter 9. A New Era: A Time of Testing   95

Chapter 10. Gathering Momentum   109

Chapter 11. The First Building Program   135

Chapter 12. The Plymouth Chapel   145

Chapter 13. Securing Room to Expand   157

Chapter 14. Creating an Endowment Fund   177

Chapter 15. Our India Family   187

Chapter 16. Neighborhood Involvement   211

Chapter 17. The Social Action Controversy   219

Chapter 18. The Merger Controversy   229

Chapter 19. Continuing Denominational Relations   245

Chapter 20. Ecumenism   253

Chapter 21. Retirement Years   265

Epilogue   275

THE HOWARD CONN WINDOW
Depicted on Cover

To mark the fiftieth anniversary of his ordination (June 15, 1986), Plymouth Church of Minneapolis dedicated a stained glass window to commemorate the thirty-two-year pastorate of Dr. Howard Conn, from 1944 to 1976. The window was designed by Crosby Willet of the Willet Stained Glass Studios of Philadelphia. It is based on a sermon, "A Faith to Match the Universe," which tells of Dr. Conn's spiritual pilgrimage.

While a college freshman he had a conversion experience through Plato which changed the direction of his life from the law to philosophy. The right panel represents his interest in philosophy rather than theology. The left panel suggests the influence of oriental mysticism, which came from his study at Harvard of the Hindu Upanishads and from his love for the writings of Rabindranath Tagore, the Bengali poet. New Testament studies at Yale Divinity School made central the ministry of the historical Jesus. The central panel shows our Master giving the Sermon on the Mount, which is the focal point for a universal approach. Dr. Conn's definition of pure religion is inscribed in a ribbon surrounding the beautiful blue central circle: "Religion is a response of adoration, thanksgiving and trust which a person makes to the Unseen; out of the belief that at the center of the universe is a Being of intelligence, purpose and love with whom we seek to be in harmony."

Above these three major panels is a lovely depiction of the majestic sweep of the universe, our planet earth moving in rhythmic pattern among the celestial bodies.

At the top of the window are six symbols. First, the Mayflower, symbolic of Dr. Conn's long devotion to historic Congregationalism; then the pomegranate, whose successive layers one penetrates to the unseen essence; the Hand of God, which ever guides us; the dove of the Holy Spirit, which descends into each soul; Plato's image of the Cave; and the Wings of the Morning on which our spirits soar to communion with the Eternal.

In the lower section are three other characteristics of Dr. Conn's ministry: his warm friendliness, his administrative and building skills, and his clear, intellectual yet forceful preaching. The Plymouth Chapel is his dream, for which he commissioned Mr. Willet's father, Henry Lee Willet, to design the sixteen windows to celebrate the Seasons of the Christian Year.

Across the lower lancet is one of the oldest and most universal of prayers, from the Upanishads:

> From the unreal lead me to the real
> From darkness lead me to light
> From death lead me to immortality.

ACKNOWLEDGMENTS

I hold in grateful remembrance all the persons in the congregations I have served. They encouraged and supported me through years of growth. Their friendships and affections enriched our pastoral relations and made possible the joy we shared in churches that are caring communities. Without them my ministry would not have been effective.

I want to acknowledge the presence and participation of my former wife Viola Mann Conn in the events recorded in this volume. Through thirty-four years of marriage she contributed significantly to my career. We shared the same religious perspective. We both loved people and our congregations. Beyond parish affairs she took an active role in several community organizations.

Several persons helped me in the preparation of this book. Connie Keller read each chapter along the way and made helpful suggestions. Miriam Hanson supervised the details of publication and chaired a trustee committee to oversee the project. The actual manufacturing of the book has been done with patience and care by Meg Colwell, a fourth-generation Plymouthite from a family of printers. The editing and typesetting is the careful work of Barbara Field, a professional book editor.

In addition to these, I am grateful to the Solstad-deForest family for support and encouragement.

Special tribute must be paid to Grieg Aspnes, whose enquiring mind and artistic sensitivities responded to my philosophical outlook. As a professional librarian with Cargill Incorporated, he undertook the task of going through my carefully kept twelve file drawers of sermon envelopes. He made a catalog of my sermons from 1936 to 1988, listing dates, titles and texts. Through a project supported by the Plymouth trustees, he had all the manuscripts put on microfilm so that anyone in the future can read what I thought at various stages in my ministry. This truly was a labor of love by Grieg Aspnes, and I am indeed appreciative.

In the text all references to God assumes a Spirit that combines both male and female attributes, and use of the pronoun "he" or "him" referring to Deity intends to be inclusive of both.

Howard Conn
Minneapolis
September 1990

1

The Expanding Wonders of Existence

MY FATHER WAS A LAWYER, and he wanted me to become one, too. He said, "I have enough wills in my safe to keep you on easy street the rest of your life."

In my early years that seemed a good prospect. I was interested in politics and world affairs, and one of my dreams was someday to become a United States senator. Most of the members of that select debate society are lawyers, so law school seemed an appropriate preparation for such a career. As I shall explain later in the story, the major interests during my youth seemed to indicate that I would indeed follow my father's profession.

But something happened along the way, and events did not turn out according to my earliest expectations. In the midst of a philosophy class during my freshman college year, I experienced a "conversion" as real as that of St. Paul on the Damascus Road. I hesitate to use that term because mine was devoid of the theological trappings associated with the Biblical account, but it was similar to Paul's in that it turned my life toward a new direction. Mine was an illumination in which I suddenly became aware of values more basic than legal rulings and of truths more precious for daily living than the conventions in which I had been raised. From that moment I knew my mission was not to extricate people from legal tangles but to awaken them to an awareness of the wonders of a meaningful life to which all of us are heirs. I knew that I wanted to be a college professor or a nonconformist minister to make the Great Tradition in Philosophy a lively backdrop for everyday living.

I believe that this transition from one goal to another was more than a shift in my own personal choice. The revelation as it came to me at the moment and as I have reflected on it over the decades has about it the feel of guidance by a power greater than myself. We commonly use the term *divine guidance* for such leadings, and I do accept this if we can lift the term into a fuller context than that of narrow sectarian theology. A phrase from the poetry of Robert Browning best suggests my experience.

In June of 1861—the month in which his wife Elizabeth Barrett Browning died and ended one of the great love-marriages of history—Robert Browning was rummaging among the crowded stalls that to this day line the square of San Lorenzo in Florence. He came across an old yellow book, part print, part manuscript, then two centuries old, which was the account of a 1698 murder trial in Rome. This seemingly chance discovery became a decisive moment in his life, as during the next six years he transformed the facts of this account into the masterpiece of his career, *The Ring and the Book*. In the opening pages of this dramatic work, he gives a vivid account of that June morning.

> I found this book,
> Gave a lira for it, eightpence English just,
> (Mark the predestination!) when a Hand,
> Always above my shoulder, pushed me once,
> One day still fierce 'mid many a day struck calm,
> Across a Square in Florence, crammed with booths,
> Buzzing and blaze, noontide and market-time,
> Toward Baccio's marble . . .

Robert Browning believed that his life had been quietly but steadily led by a "Hand Always Above My Shoulder." This is a helpful phrase to remember. It has none of the dramatic thunder of God speaking out of whirlwinds nor of miracles that violate the natural order. Rather, it reminds us that there is a pattern to life larger than we may at first comprehend, and that a benevolent and caring Deity brings together circumstances to make for a glorious whole.

This has been my faith substantiated through seventy years of experience in which my life has developed more beautifully than I myself could have planned. Like any human being I have had numerous specific goals and wishes, some of which were attained and some of which were not. In all of these gains and losses, however, something better has come to pass, and earlier experiences which seemed to happen by chance have later become significant strands in the total tapestry of my life. I am convinced that my pilgrimage is not the result of my wisdom, cleverness or endeavors—though I worked hard and enjoyed my tasks—but of a Hand Always Above My Shoulder who knew the goal long before I was aware of it and guided me toward its realization.

The secret is to be open and responsive. In this latter part of the twentieth century, society has succumbed to the cult of the movers and the shakers. We envy the wealthy and we emulate the powerful. We want to push our way to the top. Through the media we hear of successful persons who have forced their way to pinnacles. What we do not know is that often these achievers later fall by overplaying their own cleverness. Nor do the media reporters realize that some who have attained success did so by responding to guided inspiration more than by plunging ahead on their own.

Our own perspective is the key to what happens to us. Are we open or are we closed? Are we humble or are we arrogant? Hard realists or sympathetic listeners? Cynical or optimistic? Are we factual or imaginative? Religious or atheistic? Satisfied with ourselves or willing to learn? If we are religious, is our faith confined to the dogma of an institution, or are we open to the leadings of a universal Presence.

It is highly important that we develop a perspective that will keep us growing. The Hand Always Above Our Shoulder has marvelous designs for creation, but the degree to which these designs will be fulfilled depends on whether we are open and responsive. The Beatitudes which Jesus gave in the Sermon on the Mount are more than beautiful sentiment or authoritative commands. They are descriptive of the basic attitudes that enable us to be in harmony with the cosmic plan.

We need a philosophy of life that encourages us to develop these attitudes and that provides the stamina to persevere through obstacles and crises. I believe that such a philosophy is a religious one, sensitive to the guidance of the Spirit. I believe that it is a religious outlook much more universal than traditional Christianity, for the institutionalized church has all too often abandoned the open, spiritual, compassionate teachings of Jesus for insistence on a creed that focuses on him rather than on his attitudes.

The story of how I came to this universal faith and what it produced in my ministry is what I want to tell. Often I say that I am first a Platonist, second a Hindu mystic, and third a Christian, for that is the order in which I was exposed to the insights of great world teachers. All three of these outlooks I find blended into a harmonious whole. We do not have to choose sects nor brand ourselves with one label or another. What the Lord of Life asks is that we be responsive to the Hand Always Above Our Shoulder.

We need not be scholars or technical philosophers to grasp this. It is desirable, however, that we cleanse ourselves from the preconceptions with which we have been conditioned by traditional religious parlance. Multitudes of people accept the dogma of orthodox preachments because they think they ought to. They may have grown up in small towns across the country in which the only churches are evangelical or orthodox, in which the preachers vie with one another in proclaiming the dire consequences of damnation. They accept as literal and true whatever text the minister quotes, because it is in the Scripture. They have no comprehension of the origin and diversity of the Bible. They are intimidated by concrete images of God, Christ, Satan, sin, heaven and hell. They never realize that spiritual values refer to truths and feelings that are seldom literal but are expressed through metaphors and images. The proper religious vision belongs more to art than to objective history. That vision is part of the Mystery in which we find our deepest satisfaction.

Rather than look for the vision in dogmatic stereotypes, I suggest that we begin with our own experience. Each of us has some inkling of who we are. Our pilgrimage is to find our true self through the guidance of wise teachers who will not intrude upon us with extravagant claims, but who out of their own journey will help us to understand ours. Because I learned from such teachers, my satisfaction has come from trying to share with fellow pilgrims the wonder and the mystery that can be exciting.

In our own experience, we know that the two basic realities are ourselves and the universe in which we live. Each of us is a distinct person, each with unique possibilities. We have the right to choose, and within certain limits to make our own decisions. The possibilities within us are more numerous than we may at first suppose. Through the process of education and the contacts of experience, we begin to discover interests and talents that were not earlier evident. Our first assumptions may not reveal the truest measure of our potential.

The Greeks call it *entelechy*, the essence or force within that directs life in its development. We are born with a certain drive that shapes our destiny. The acorn contains the seed that causes it to grow into an oak tree rather than a cedar or eucalyptus. Modern geneticists speak of the DNA as containing the blueprint for individual development. We humans contain multiple factors that affect our destiny, and free will enables us to make choices among them. Whatever we do must somehow be an expression of possibilities latent within us. Psychologists have devised tests to help us see our temperamental traits and hidden interests. These enable us to know ourselves better and to function more happily. The innate capacities that early aroused my interest in becoming a lawyer contained other elements that offered more excitement through the choice to become a minister.

While we have these personal capacities which make us distinct and unique, we as individuals are at the same time part of a larger whole. We belong to a universe, the totality of all that exists. This universe is a vibrant meaningful whole. The religious affirmation is that this totality is indeed a system that is coherent and dependable. There are forces and principles which operate in orderly fashion. Were this not the case, no science would be possible, no knowledge would be attainable, and no experience would relate to any other experience. Everything would be chaos.

In order for any one of us to function, the uniqueness of our capacities must operate within the enormous framework of the universe. We have choices to make and talents to develop that center within ourselves, but this personalism is only part of our life history. Our personal development is set within a cosmic development. We are created and shaped by that cosmos, so that happiness results from harmony between ourselves and the universe. We listen, we reflect, we respond to a reality greater than ourselves. As our personal instincts become tempered and harmonized with the cosmic overdrive, we feel ourselves led and supported in a mysterious way that no words can explain.

We who are religious call this cosmic force "God." By this we recognize that the totality in which we operate is not haphazard, is not capricious, and is not chaotic. It is a meaningful whole; and that whole is an entity in which intelligence, purpose and love are of the essence. This essence is God—so magnificent, so infinite, so luminous, so loving beyond anything we mortals can possibly fathom. God is mystery. God is wonder. God is Beinghood. God is love, and in him we live and move and have our being.

This is the ultimate religious affirmation. It is universal, and has been made by people of all generations, all eras, all lands. The particularities that we may want to say about this Deity become the details of the historic religions, such as Judaism, Hinduism, Taoism and Christianity. Whatever the details, the basic insight is the relationship between my personal self and the Cosmic Overself.

When I establish this relationship, a sense of awe arises in me, and all my journey becomes an adventure of wonder and beauty. I feel a Hand Always Above My Shoulder, and life develops in marvelous ways. Life becomes a daily miracle, not because God intervenes to violate the natural course of events, but because I have been open and receptive to the miraculous possibilities in my path.

This is the framework of my life. I have been very fortunate and am deeply grateful. Exciting things happened in my ministry at Plymouth Congregational Church of Minneapolis, and I was privileged to serve among wonderful people. I want to show how one step led to another.

Above all, my purpose is to indicate that much of this excitement happened not by me but to me. The pattern was larger than I envisaged, and events fitted together better than I could have planned. Divine guidance has been a reality for me, and it can be for anyone who responds to the Hand Always Above Our Shoulder.

2

Growing Up

HEALTH SPECIALISTS OFTEN MAKE the facetious comment that the crucial decision in a person's life is the selection of parents, because hereditary factors affect one's physical traits for all the years. This is not a choice that any of us can make. Our parents have made it for us. They provide not only our biological inheritance, but also the atmosphere in which we develop. We can look back upon our early home life and see the beginnings of what has matured.

My sister and I are fortunate to have grown up in a loving, stable home. Our parents were in their late thirties and early forties when we were born, so we were cherished as the fulfillment of their dream to have a happy, normal home life. Our parents were frugal and lived comfortably but without ostentation. Neither my sister nor I in our younger years were conscious of the affluence our father's law practice provided. We were raised with conventional values and motivated to be achievers in whatever we did. Above all, we were expected to behave properly at all times. I think that I inwardly rebelled against such strict standards of propriety because many of my memories of childhood are of incidents in which I disagreed with my parents, though outwardly I acted like a "good boy." The pattern of my life has been one of inward rebellion and preference for nonconformity, while at the same time outwardly practicing the conventions that win public approval. The question has always been, How far can I go in my individuality and still be accepted?

Behind the houses on our block was an open field that fronted on a trolley line. One day an advertising man came to the house to ask my mother if he could put a huge sign on the back fence that read "Welcome Stranger," the name of a movie about to open. In return for this favor he offered free passes to the theater. My mother declined the offer. As the family sat at supper and each of us told about the day's happenings, I related this incident and finished with the comment, "If we could have free passes to the movies I would let them put up a banner even if it read 'Go to hell!'" This was far beyond family acceptance! None of us indulged in any kind of swearing. My father was horrified and ordered me to my room for the evening.

The family social life centered in the church, though it was such a liberal religious atmosphere that we knew none of the piety usually connected with religion. We had no prayers in the home and no mention of sin. We had strict moral conduct in conformity with the standards of decent people, but this had no overtones of damnation or eternal punishment. Religion was a warm, friendly feeling of trust and goodwill. I am proud to be a birthright Congregationalist, as both my parents came from this liberal, nonconformist group, which traces its heritage back to the Pilgrims. In fact, they met in the First Congregational Church of Fresno, and the fellowship of this congregation was an extended family.

My mother was born Anna May Peabbles to a family of truck farmers who grew fruits and vegetables on Cape Elizabeth, near Portland, Maine. She had an older brother who married, carried on the farm work and was road commissioner for the area. Also she had a married sister who lived in the city. As the youngest she was left at home to take care of her father after her mother's death. For fifteen years she was a music teacher, riding into the city with a small cart and pony to give piano lessons to a large circle of pupils. She was thrifty, saving her money for the dream that she might someday be free from this limited area in which her family seemed bound.

In 1907, when she was thirty-four, the opportunity came. Her father had recently died, so she no longer had obligations at home. An older woman acquaintance was going to California to spend some time in Fresno, and my mother asked to accompany here. For a young woman to embark on such travels alone would have appeared unseemly in those days, but with an older companion it was acceptable. I do not recall from the stories my mother told why Fresno was the point of destination, for it seems an unlikely one! It must have been that the older woman had friends or relatives with whom she wished to spend some time.

The pair arrived by train and rented lodgings. The first two Sundays my mother went to the Episcopal church with her companion. On the third week she said, "I have been to church with you these past two Sundays, but, if you don't mind, this time I would like to go to mine." The other not only consented, but offered to come also, because "No one at the Episcopal church has spoken to us on either of these Sundays."

The two ladies went to the Congregational church. My father was the usher who showed them to a pew. My mother must have caught his fancy, for after the service he introduced himself and asked if he might call some evening. This was the beginning of a romance and a devotion that lasted until my father's death in 1934. They were married in Santa Cruz on July 4, 1909. From the beginning, their life was centered around the Congregational church in Fresno, and it was natural for this to be the focal point also for my sister and me. It was a small but friendly church composed of people who were active in community affairs, many of them being educators.

As for theology, there really was none. The minister during all my boyhood days was Dr. Thomas T. Giffen, a lovable, warm-hearted man. He was a graduate of Pomona College, very liberal in his thinking. Of course I cannot recall any of his sermons, but I know that the atmosphere was free and open. We had no creed. After I began to consider the ministry, I remember being a bit disturbed on going home that in the baptismal service there was no reference to the Trinity, but the infants were baptized into the good life. Jesus was our friend who showed us the way in which to walk. I recall no element of transcendence. The church was a friendly center where we met each week with people close to us. It was an enjoyable, supportive place for congenial companions.

My father was a serious man with dignified manner, a quiet private person for whom my mother's outgoing sociability was a happy balance. His parents were Scotch-Irish from near Belfast. Grandfather James Conn first came to this country as a young man. He crossed the continent in a covered wagon caravan as part of the rush to find gold in northern California. He returned to Ireland and married his sweetheart. On a visit to that country, I found the record of their marriage in the Belfast archives. They found passage on a ship and came to California around Cape Horn and up the South American coast. They found no gold in the mining town where they settled, and where my father was born in 1869. They soon moved down to the San Joaquin Valley to become ranchers. From my aunt I learned that James Conn had a philosophical turn of mind, and as a member of a neighborhood periodical club preferred such thoughtful journals as *Harper's* and the *Atlantic Monthly*.

My father had a keen mind and enrolled at the University of California in Berkeley. He found the academic process too slow for his ambitious spirit. He dropped out, read law on the side, studied with a judge, and was admitted to the bar. He was a practicing attorney in Fresno from the mid-nineties until he was forced to retire by illness in 1929. He was a cautious, conservative type who concentrated on probate and title work. Each evening he sat at home reading the *Daily Abstract Report*. He had a retentive memory, so he kept abreast of real estate developments within the county and was looked to for title searches before the day of abstract companies. He was highly regarded in the city, and served as president of the Board of Education.

He was not athletic nor a country-club sport. He was fond of walking, and generally walked between home and office, a distance of at least two miles. As I grew older and went downtown to the library or the movies, I often walked home with him. He was good to his family. Each year he took a month to six-week vacation, renting a house at Pacific Grove on the Monterey coast or taking us on a motor trip to Yellowstone or the Canadian Rockies.

I admired my father, and it was natural that I fell into the assumption that I would follow in his footsteps as a lawyer. In my early years that seemed a good prospect. Politics and world affairs fascinated me, and the law seemed the proper avenue for such pursuits.

One of the oldest clubs in Fresno was the High School Senate, composed of about thirty boys who met each Friday night under the supervision of a faculty teacher who was called the president of the United States. On admission each boy was given a state to represent. Back in the twenties youth activities were much more restrained than in recent years. We did not have so many alluring attractions. The meetings of the Senate were conducted according to strict parliamentary rules, and within this framework we had great fun. We had to know our Robert's Rules of Order. In lively discussions over current issues, we challenged one another in forensic maneuvers. This was excellent training. Many of the public officials and lawyers of the community developed their aptitudes and sharpened their skills through participation in the Fresno High School Senate.

Public speaking was one of my early interests, and I was on the high school debate team. In three years of competition I never lost a debate. Later at Stanford I had a similar experience, being captain in my senior year. Being active in school and college debating is an exceedingly formative experience. Beyond giving one confidence in platform appearances, it has an even greater benefit in teaching the participant to study and to prepare. I learned easily because I was doing something I wanted to do, not just meeting a classroom assignment. I learned how to use the public library, how to be imaginative in seeking leads, how to skim quickly through long technical documents, how to select the key quotation that would illumine the argument. These skills would have helped me as a lawyer, but they turned out to be equally good training for the preparation of carefully crafted sermons.

Because I like people and got along well with others, I developed another talent which seemed to indicate politics as a likely field. I was a good vote-getter. In both junior and senior high school, I became president of nearly every group or club to which I belonged. We had a spirited campaign in which I was elected president of the student body at Fresno High.

I recall one time when voter popularity led to a failure. Our high school French teacher thought we might enjoy doing a play. She made the mistake of allowing the class members to choose the cast, and I was quickly voted to the role of the principal male character. I was never good at foreign languages, and even through years of travel have never made any effort to master them. Neither do I possess any talents as an actor. The result of this election doomed the project. After a few rehearsals, the distraught teacher wisely decided that the players were unsuited for the parts, and so abandoned the play.

Another of my youthful endeavors that turned out to be a useful preparation for my later career was the editing of a newspaper. To call my simple beginnings a "newspaper" is to credit it beyond its deserving, yet it was the embryo of a life-long interest in writing. In my grammar school days, my father brought home from his law office a typewriter that he was replacing. I often wonder what prompted him to do this, whether he had any notion of what it would mean for my younger sister and me. Both of us began to use the machine. Neither of us ever took any lesson in typing, but we quickly picked it up on our own. We developed our own techniques, and have been using them through a lifetime. I can type as fast as most office workers, and through the years, even with a secretary, I have done most of my own typing. I prefer to do this because I am so accustomed to working over a machine that I cannot think or compose clearly in any other way. Dictating for me is not the same thing at all.

With a typewriter at home, another mode of expression opened. In my grammar school days I began writing a one-sheet paper, which I posted on a large frame background nailed to a post in our backyard arbor. It reported family and neighborhood news, but was made up largely of editorials that gave my views on political events. The readers were only myself and my parents, but the paper provided the fun and the discipline of expressing myself cogently and briefly.

Each hobby that a person develops leads to another, so that the labyrinth of human interests becomes ever more involved. I was an avid reader, and one summer a librarian directed me to *The Americanization of Edward Bok.* He tells how he began collecting autographs of famous people. This sparked an idea in my mind.

I was keenly interested in world affairs. Inasmuch as I was also writing this neighborhood newspaper for backyard consumption my imagination took another leap to conceive of an honorary board of directors! I selected the twenty persons whom I most admired and placed them on this august body. It mattered not that they were unaware of this distinction. I could make up comments from them and arrange for their elections and resignations! My father was in his forties when I was born and had long wanted a son. Hence he took special pride in my development, and kept in a file the typed copies of my paper as they came down from the arbor board after a week or a fortnight.

The changes I frequently made in the membership of this honorary board became a record of the shifts in my own ideals and interests. Most of the early names were of political figures. They indicated my preference for Republicans over Democrats, for internationalists over isolationists, for independents over conventionalists. As I got into high school and then the first year of college, the list of honorees began to show more writers, religious leaders and philosophers. After I left Fresno in 1929 the lists and the paper ceased.

This list became a link with Edward Bok's experience of autograph collecting. When I published my first printed edition for wider circulation, I sent copies to the honorary directors. The results were quite impressive. I received brief but kindly notes from several, such as William Howard Taft and Charles Evans Hughes. These encouraged me to more general requests for autographs, a hobby I pursued during my three years at Stanford.

In 1928 I graduated from high school just as I was turning seventeen. Since neither of my parents was a college graduate, we had not given serious consideration to my entrance into a university. I think it was always assumed that both my sister and I would go to Stanford, which we did, she being in the last class of the famous "Five Hundred." During my high school years, my father had taken me each fall to the big game between Stanford and the University of California. This surprises me as I reflect upon it, since I have no recollection of him as a sports enthusiast. His motive must have been to direct my attention toward Stanford.

In the summer of my graduation from high school, we found that it was too late to make application to Stanford. In those days schools did not have career counselors, and we obtained no advice on such matters. My mother said afterward that if she had had five children she might have known what to do for the fifth!

The alternative was to enroll at Fresno State College for my

freshman year. This was an excellent institution, now the University
of California at Fresno in the state's educational hierarchy. The
retired president had been our next-door neighbor during my school
years. Quite a number of the professors were members of our
church, as were many public school teachers. The Congregational
church was very much at the heart of the intellectual and cultural
community. The minister's wife and my father were both long-time
members of the school board, and my mother served a term as president of the Scholia Club, a social and study organization composed
of wives of men in education.

My freshman year at Fresno State proved to be a good one, for it
was then that the decisive change of direction took place. As I was
considering what classes to take, my mother suggested that I take a
course from Dr. Edward V. Tenney, an attractive, able, younger man
who was professor of philosophy. Since my mother was not college-
educated, I do not think she had any clear idea as to the subject matter of philosophy, but her suggestion was prompted by the fact that
Dr. Tenney was a highly regarded member of our church. In her loving way she guided me better than she realized! That year I took
debating and was on the college debate team, but my four principal
courses were taken under very able teachers, all of whom were
members of the Congregational church: Philosophy under Dr.
Tenney, American History under Mitchell P. Briggs, European
History under Dean Hubert Phillips, and French under a Swiss
named Maiers.

Dr. Tenney was a Jungian and an Idealist, an extremely creative
thinker. He chose to remain at Fresno State throughout his long
career rather than accept other offers from better-known institutions.
I owe a great deal to him and regret that I did not continue my contacts with him, but after 1929 I was seldom in Fresno for any length
of time. From him I learned a basic distinction that has been important in my thinking throughout my career—the difference between
experience and *experiencing*.

The source of most of our knowledge is experience. We may use
reason to interpret our experiences, but seldom do we spin theories
that are far removed from actual happenings. Plato, who dramatized
the life of reason, used his dialogues to reflect upon illustrations that
everyone could appreciate from their own daily living. We employ

the term *experience* constantly in our discussions to refer to what we know at first hand. Such usage, however, employs *experience* as a noun referring to an event that has happened to us and has already taken place. We make experience an object at which we can look or upon which we can reflect.

This misses the dynamism of what experience is all about. It is we—with all the sensations of feeling, seeing, evaluating, appreciating—who are involved in the experiencing of the moment, who give the content to what later we objectify by the term *experience*. The true self is always the subject who does the *experiencing* rather than the object whose *experience* we talk about.

Often through the years I have invited friends at a party or a congregation in celebration to be consciously aware of what they are feeling at the moment, to realize that they are vibrantly involved in a dynamic act in which they are subjects or persons participating. To do so is to catch the *experiencing* in such a way that may give flavor when later they refer to it as an *experience*. When I stood at the rear of the aisle to commence the processional at the dedication of the Plymouth Chapel at Ahmednagar College in 1962, I realized that this was one of the high moments of my life. I tried to make every part of me vibrate to its thrill, so that in later years the remembrance of this event would conjure up some of the emotional feelings that made it significant. The identical group of persons in a gathering will never be assembled again, nor will the same event ever repeat itself. Life and time are constantly moving forward like the thousands of frames snapped by a motion picture camera. But the significance of the multitudinous frames of a person's life is held together by the experiencing self. It is this experiencing vitality that in some mysterious way constitutes the soul.

This gets a bit ahead of my story, but permits me to suggest the lasting influence of my one year with Dr. Tenney. During the first semester in the philosophy class I was fairly bewildered. The terminology, the outlook, the questions were quite different than those of the practical issues of politics and world history. I recall that Dr. Tenney told us of Plato's theory that knowledge is illumination that comes suddenly. It is not a matter of degree. Either we understand or we do not. It was in this philosophy class that the illumination came which completely turned me around.

It was sparked by Plato's Myth of the Cave given in the seventh book of the *Republic*. We are like people living in a cave chained to benches turned inward toward the back wall. Behind us is a large fire burning. Between our backs and the fire are people moving on a stage. We never see these actors, but watch the reflections which they cast upon the wall. Since these shadows are all that we ever see, we assume that they are the real world. If someone were to remove our chains, turn us around and show us the true people, we would be so dazzled by the light that we would at first deny their reality. Only after adjustment would we come to appreciate how much clearer and more vital they are than the shadows which they cast.

Reality, says Plato, is like that. Reality consists of archetypes or heavenly models that are perfect and abiding. They are the forms God uses in fashioning the created world. All the objects we see about us are imperfect copies of these models. A lamp is a lamp or a tree a tree because each such particular participates in or reflects the perfection of the ideal. There is thus an eternal realm that is the measure of true beauty, true goodness, true friendship, true whatever. We mortals are like people chained toward the shadows on the cave wall. We assume that the material objects we see and the human judgments we make are the truth about existence. We are not aware of their imperfections and approximations, but are content to live out our days in the manipulation of what are little more than shadows of real values.

This insight hit me with tremendous force. I saw my life and everything around me in new perspective. I was like the prisoner turned to the opening in the cave rather than to the back wall. I can only describe it as a conversion experience that changed the course of my life from one path to another.

If there be a noumenal world—one whose essence is *nous*, or mind, centered in the overarching mind of a cosmic value-force—then that is the realm of utmost importance. We humans are the evolving creations of the noumenal world. We stray, we err, we deviate, but our primary objective should be to harmonize our judgments and actions with the divine prototype. Happiness and abundance lie in this direction.

Hence the study of philosophy and the pursuit of wisdom appeared to me as the most exciting challenge. Psychologists will say that somehow I was born with an intuitive, artistic nature that made me respond to this possibility. I think this is probably so. There are many temperaments among people, and only a small number respond to the mystic, intuitive leadings of the spirit. Much later in life I took the Myers-Briggs temperament test, which showed clearly that I am among the twelve percent of the total population who have introvert-intuitive-feeling-judgment factors in that combination—INFJ. In my youth I was not aware of such testing, and my illumination seemed a natural response to Platonic insight.

Politics and law center around the judgments and decisions of society. They deal with what men and women decide. Laws are not necessarily correct or true to the archetypal value. What is considered right and wrong differs between civilizations and generations, for such judgments are made by fragile human beings influenced by various factors. Congress passes laws permitting or prohibiting certain acts of conduct, but such laws determine what is legal rather than what is right. I could not see myself spending a lifetime arguing about legalities when philosophy offered the far more exciting prospect of leading people to appreciate what is divinely true. I therefore told my parents that I did not wish to become a lawyer but wanted instead to become a philosophy professor at the college level.

I should explain that when I speak of appreciating what is "divinely true" I am in no sense referring to religious orthodoxy or any form of institutional authoritarianism. I am a nonconformist by instinct. A philosopher must always be humble, as Socrates was. The Delphic Oracle pronounced him to be the wisest man. After puzzling over this statement, Socrates came to the conclusions that his wisdom consisted in his recognition of how much he did not know. Seers have written their books, their poems, their dramas out of the illumination that has come to them; but they have recognized their insights as tentative approximations of the true, the beautiful and the good. They ardently offer the finest they can grasp, but the wise never claim the ultimate. No human has seen God at any time.

There will be varying responses to the Platonic insight. A few persons choose to become ascetics who spurn the material world entirely in order to give unswerving attention to spiritual values. I am not of this type whatsoever. I enjoy material comforts and like to be surrounded by beautiful objects. I recognize that this creates a tension. One of my most searching sermons was under the title, "Living a Spiritual Life in a Material World." I am convinced that God understands the problem. A God who puts us in a world of lovely lakes, towering mountains and mighty oceans must surely intend for us to appreciate the natural environment. We are to enter into life rather than withdraw from it. A mystic can be fascinated by the surrounding wonders, seeing in them a transcendent reality that gives a meaning far deeper than sensual pleasure.

During my freshman year at Fresno State, I applied to Stanford University and was admitted for the sophomore year. I enrolled in September 1929. As I look back nearly sixty years later, it is a shock to recall that during my three years tuition was ninety-nine dollars a quarter. Room and board were one hundred fifty dollars for each period, making the cost of a Stanford education less than a thousand dollars a year!

At the outset of my Stanford years, a striking "happening" occurred that was to influence my education. It seemed to occur quite by accident and yet is still another experience that I feel was directed by a Hand Always Above My Shoulder. Each quarter the university published a "time schedule" listing all the courses given according to hours and days. From this schedule a student would select his own program to be approved by his advisor, with an eye toward meeting the requirements for graduation. On my first day of registration, I readily picked three courses that seemed essential and that totaled twelve units. Even in those days the advisors were largely graduate students rather than senior ranking faculty members. Mine looked at my list, then consulted the time schedule to find an offering that would fit the open eleven o'clock hour Monday-Wednesday-Friday on my chart. "Here is a course in the classical literature department on Herodotus. I think that would be a good choice for you."

I had never heard of Herodotus. Over the years I have often wondered whether my advisor had either! I knew nothing about the classical literature department and had not intended to be there. The young instructor made this choice because the time slot was open, and this way he could fulfill his responsibility for another of his assignees. Yet it proved to have consequences beyond my grasp at the moment. This was a strong department at Stanford which offered in the English language many courses in Greek literature and culture. I was so fascinated by Ernest Whitney Martin's course on Herodotus that I went on to other offerings, and actually graduated three years later with a minor in classical literature. I took Greek Epic, Greek Tragedy, Greek Mythology, New Testament Literature. Some of these were given by the scholar Augustus Taber Murray, some of whose translations are published in the Loeb Classical Library. He was also a moving lecturer and a saintly character who had been among the original faculty chosen by David Starr Jordan. My years at Stanford coincided with the presidency of Herbert Hoover, revered by all of us because he had been in the first entering class when the university was founded. He was a Quaker and for two years of his term had brought Dr. Murray to minister to the Friends Meeting in Washington.

This chance introduction to Greek thought had a profound influence on my development. I had been redirected in my freshman year through Plato, and now I was not only going on into philosophy but was also gaining a deeper perspective into the foremost ancient culture. Herodotus is called "the father of history," for he was the first to record a major event that occurred five centuries before the Christian Era. He developed the style of writing common to that ancient period. He was not the factual reporter to record dates and details, but the artist who related anecdotes and told stories that illumined the character of the persons involved. He saw the wide sweep of history, and interpreted the significance of these movements. At Stanford I had the opportunity to become familiar with Greek thought processes, which became one of the major factors in western civilization. When later at Yale I was to study both the Old and New Testaments, I could approach these as Hebrew counterparts in that ancient world. I could see that they too tell history through myths and stories. This is quite a different perspective from that of most seminarians, who come out of evangelical backgrounds in which they regard the Bible as a holy revelation from God. They lack the wider vision to see the Greeks and the Hebrews alike as ancient pilgrims seeking to understand human experience. I often think that laypersons in a Bible study class ought to be required first to read Herodotus before starting Scripture!

The Greeks early recognized the essentials of moral character and gave us the values we cherish. It is scant wonder that they were the developers of democracy. One of the memorable experiences of these college days was reading Sophocles' *Antigone*, that masterpiece of Greek drama which tells the story of two sisters, Antigone and Ismene, whose brother is killed in an attack on the city of Thebes. The tyrant on the throne decrees that the body of this youth must not be given burial but be left to rot in disgrace. Antigone tells her sister that love for their brother bids them defy the law and give him proper burial. The other sister is afraid to disobey the law, and Antigone alone does what she believes is right. When she is discovered, brought before the king, and asked why she has done what she knows is against the law, she replies:

> Because it was not Zeus who ordered it;
> Nor justice, dweller with the Nether God,
> Gave such a law to men; nor did I deem
> Your ordinance of so much binding force,
> As that a mortal man could overbear
> The unchangeable unwritten code of Heaven.
> This is not of today and yesterday,
> But lives forever, having origin
> Whence no man knows.

This is the same appeal to a universal moral order that I had heard a year earlier from Plato and that prompted me to seek a career in obedience to that order rather than to human laws. This has been a bedrock of my independence throughout my life.

Later I was to read in the Book of Acts the thrilling story of Peter and John brought before the Sanhedrin and commanded no longer to preach the gospel of Jesus Christ. Boldly Peter answered, "We must obey God rather than men," and dared to continue his witness. Martin Luther's defiant cry to his accusers within the Church—"Here I stand"—comes from the same insight. In our own country's annals Henry David Thoreau and Martin Luther King were to exemplify similar civil disobedience. This is a perennial theme running through all civilizations, but I heard it from the Greeks before I heard it from the Christians. Since I was introduced to the Greeks by two seemingly chance happenings, surely it was the Hand Always Above My Shoulder guiding me.

The philosophy department was small, having three professors, few majors and not many students. In my class I think there were fourteen majors. In the class ahead of me was Lawrence A. Kimpton, who succeeded Robert Maynard Hutchins as chancellor of the University of Chicago. The teachers were excellent, and I think I got a good grounding. The chairman of the department was a wise and distinguished gentlemen, Henry Waldgrave Stuart. He was a poor lecturer, but in seminars was excellent. One could follow him thinking aloud and appreciate his wisdom.

His principal insight, which I branded "Stuart Ethics" and carried with me to graduate school, fitted well into the pattern visible in my life of being guided beyond my own ability. Stuart held that we make moral judgments on the basis of what we already know, using standards that we have previously accepted. These, however, are not ethical choices. They are factual determinations based on how a particular situation meets a norm.

A typical illustration of his is the decision to vote in a certain way. Suppose I am asked by a friend to support a candidate who is a socialist. My instincts and my historical perspective tell me that socialist principles lead to disaster, and so my moral judgment is that I cannot vote for this candidate. But what if I have a high regard for the friend who has made the suggestion? What if I trust his insight? Or what if I know that this particular candidate is indeed a superb individual, or feel that he has been misunderstood, or remember that he acted responsibly in some past situation? These questions introduce two new factors into my decision: that of taking the recommendation of a trusted third party, and that of being sympathetic with someone from whose ideas I differ. These questions challenge me to some risk taking in which I may not depend upon my previous understandings, but may choose to decide upon the recommendation of another or out of sympathy, which is a feeling and not an intellectual idea. To take the risk and act upon these impulses becomes an ethical situation because I have introduced two human factors into my otherwise moral rigidities.

Such a concept may be hard to grasp, and may even seem dangerous. Yet as I went on to seminary a few years later and studied the ministry of Jesus as recorded in the New Testament, I began to see that Dr. Stuart's ethics were really Jesus' ethics. There is no indication that Jesus persuaded anybody by logical argument. His was the appeal of a strong personality that moved men and women to change their ways. He walked by the lakeshore and said, "Follow me." He said to Zaccheus, "Come down out of the tree, for today salvation has come to your house." He reprimanded the crowd by saying, "Let him that is without sin cast the first stone." In incident after incident, Jesus invited persons to turn their lives around, to act in ways contrary to their previous patterns. To respond meant not to continue as had formerly seemed proper, but to take the risk of stepping out on his invitation to discover a better way.

This is what was developing as my life's adventure. Dr. Stuart was giving an intellectual formulation to the innovativeness that was unfolding exciting opportunities for me. My earliest years had indicated law and politics as the path to follow, but the conversion through Plato, then the Greek classics through Herodotus, and now Dr. Stuart's ethics, all were showing me to yield to a Hand Always Above My Shoulder, guiding me better than I knew.

I did very well academically at Stanford. I was elected to Phi Beta Kappa in my junior year and was to graduate "with great distinction." I am an achiever and feel that I would have succeeded in whatever career endeavor I had undertaken. I feel good about myself and expect to reach my goals. However, I have no competitive instinct. I do not like games and am not particularly interested in who wins in spectator sports.

By the time I was finishing Stanford, I was clear in my mind that I wanted to go on for a doctorate in philosophy in order that I might teach this subject at the college level. I was eager to share with others the insights that had come to mean so much to me. I felt that we live in an intelligible universe in which the Creator has blessed us with exciting possibilities. My parents really did not understand this but were always very supportive. When I explained to my father that when we look at a chair we cannot be certain what it is that we really see, whether the object is a focal point of sensations, whether it be material substance or the manifestation of an idea, he considered it nonsense. He wondered why he had paid money for his son to get an education like that, and he was certain that it would have been better for me to follow my original plan to become a lawyer.

Unfortunately, my father developed Parkinson's disease in 1929 just as I was going to Stanford. This was a severe blow to his pride and to his sense of achievement. When the ailment was diagnosed, he went to the library to read all he could about it. He was overwhelmed by the prognosis and became despondent. He gave up his law office and stayed at home. He went down hill fast, which for him was probably preferable to many years of lingering illness. My mother was a marvelous woman who could rise to every situation. She took excellent care of Father. She wanted the best for my sister and me. She told us that our lives were before us, whereas she had had a happy marriage. We should get on with our education, while she would look after Father. Wilma entered Stanford in 1932, the fall after my graduation.

A word should be said about our financial situation. My father was a prudent man and my mother was equally thrifty. Out of his legal practice he had fairly substantial earnings for those days. We were not wealthy but comfortable. As a conservative person, my father had not invested in the stock market, but had put his savings into farm mortgages and municipal bonds. While the price of these declined sharply in the depression to add to my father's despondency, most continued to pay interest. Only a few went into default. Hence our assets were not greatly diminished, and our family came through the depression of the thirties without any financial hardships. My mother had previously left all business matters to Father, but she did exceedingly well in managing finances.

Each year the San Francisco Harvard Club gave a scholarship to Harvard Graduate School to one Stanford senior and one Berkeley senior. No one from the Stanford philosophy department had ever received this award, and Dr. Stuart said that I should make application. In 1932 Harvard had the foremost department in the country, and was still basking in the light of such luminaries as Josiah Royce, George Santayana, William James, Charles S. Peirce, Alfred North Whitehead and William Earnest Hocking. I did apply for the scholarship, and my mother said that if I received the award I could go east. A short time later the chairman of the Stanford faculty committee called me to his office. He said the committee considered that I had the highest credentials among the applicants but was troubled because I had stated in response to a question that I had financial resources so that I could go to Harvard without the scholarship. What did this mean? I told him the situation, that I wanted to seek a doctorate in philosophy, that I wanted to study with Dr. Hocking, and that Dr. Stuart felt I had earned this recognition. However, my parents could pay my expenses. If the committee decided to give the award to another, I would understand. He seemed sympathetic but said such a situation had never before arisen. The next week the committee met again and awarded me the scholarship. This was a happy finale to my undergraduate years.

3

The Harvard Year

IN THE FALL OF 1932, I WENT EAST to Boston to begin study in the philosophy department of the Harvard Graduate School. For a boy raised conservatively in a small California town, it was to be the most momentous year of my life. New horizons in art, music and culture were opened, and my world greatly expanded. A Hand Always Above My Shoulder was to lead me to the second major discovery in my spiritual pilgrimage. As Stanford had introduced me to Greek philosophy, so Harvard unexpectedly brought me to philosophic Hinduism.

It was an exhilarating year because somehow I did not feel pressured but enjoyed the freedom to explore new interests. Home was now a continent away, and I was on my own to a degree not felt before. The students with whom I associated had broader interests than those I had previously known. Though I had gone to the theater a few times in San Francisco, those were but occasional recreational outings, whereas Boston housed major productions which were on their way to Broadway or had already achieved success. Here I could see the magic of Katherine Cornell and the Lunts. I became so excited by the theater as a form of communication that I said to my father one morning that next summer that I wished I could be a drama critic. His immediate response was, "You know that is out of the question." My remark was only a passing one, as I had no intention of embarking on such a career, but that exchange between my father and me has remained in memory as a symbol of the gulf between the world in which I was raised and that which I discovered in Boston.

There was music. I have never had special training in this area and cannot claim a deep understanding of music, but down Massachusetts Avenue from Harvard Square was Symphony Hall. There I heard a great orchestra in concert. Ever since I have enjoyed the symphonic classics.

Art has been a major interest in my career. In my senior year at Stanford, I took three quarters in Art History that introduced me to the masters from Giotto onward. This course, which was chosen as an elective after department requirements had been fulfilled, has proven more useful through the years than most college subjects. I am a strong believer that education should familiarize us with broad areas and thus open possibilities that we can follow as avocations throughout our lives. One of my hobbies is visiting the major museums of the world. I am not an expert, but I can walk through these, understand how the various schools relate, and recognize the works of the masters. In Boston were the Fogg, Mrs. Gardner's Fenway Court, and the Museum of Fine Arts. All of these are rich storehouses, and I continue to return to them on every visit. In the park entrance to the Fine Arts Museum is an equestrian statue which for me epitomizes life's quest. It is called "Appeal to the Great Spirit." An American Indian seated on his horse with arms outstretched and head upraised suggests the humility open to receive all that is good and worthwhile, and the confidence that the universal Source will share the bounty.

And there was great preaching in the Boston area. Most frequently I attended the First Congregational Church on the Cambridge Common, where Raymond Calkins gave simple, straightforward Biblical sermons that made Jesus relevant. Once a month John Haynes Holmes came from New York's Community Church to give eloquent sermon-lectures at Symphony Hall. I found him courageous and fascinating. He was of the stature of William Ellery Channing and Theodore Parker, who a century earlier had addressed great Boston crowds. To the Harvard Church came the famous pulpiteers from New York. There I heard Harry Emerson Fosdick repeat his celebrated "My Debt to the Unknown Soldier." At

Old South Church at Copley Square was Russell Henry Stafford, whom later I came to know quite well and whose committal service I conducted at Lakewood Cemetery in Minneapolis. It was one feast after another to hear these preachers, and, though at the time I had not made the conscious choice to enter the ministry, they must have been working as yeast in my subconscious.

Though I was three thousand miles from home I was not bereft of family influence. The churches of the Northern California Congregational Conference had fairly close ties. Our family was active in church matters, as I have indicated. Each summer the young people went to a week-long assembly at the stunning conference grounds on the Monterey coast at Asilomar. The ministers taught morning courses and came to know us. The pastor at the Stockton Church was Hugh Vernon White, a saintly man and brilliant scholar who was later to become Professor of Theology at the Pacific School of Religion in Berkeley and to be recognized as one of the finest teachers in that difficult field. In 1932 Dr. White was appointed philosophical consultant to the American Board of Commissioners of Foreign Missions, the overseas arm of Congregationalism and the oldest foreign mission board in the United States. It had been founded out of the Haystack Meeting at Williams College in 1804. Thus the fall that I went east to Boston was the same time that the White family moved from California to Brookline, Massachusetts. They had two children slightly younger than me, Malcolm and Barbara. Since we had known one another in the west, the Whites opened their home to me on many occasions, and I had two friends with whom to go to the theater, musicals and other events.

I lived in Perkins Hall, a dormitory for graduate students. My roommate was Charles Archelaus Steele, an English major from Texarkana, Arkansas. We had two rooms, one for sleeping and one for study. We went our separate ways, but he was a congenial person who made my living situation pleasant. There was no dining room, and the residents went out for meals. This was in the depth of the depression, during which Roosevelt closed the banks in February of 1933. In terms of prices in the eighties, everything was unbelievably cheap. I took my meals largely at a boardinghouse over on Mass Avenue, at which dinners were seventy-five cents, with a ten percent discount when one purchased a ten-dollar coupon book. For splurging there was a fine restaurant at Harvard Square, where dinners cost a dollar. In the spring the representative of a Boston tailor came through the dorm offering three-piece garments for twenty-five dollars. From him I ordered my first tailor-made suit!

One of the nice touches I recall was that President Abbott Lawrence Lowell invited students who could not go home for the holidays to a reception at his home on Christmas Eve. During the evening Harvard's popular English professor, Charles Townsend Copeland, gave some readings from his collection in *The Copeland Reader*. This hospitality gave a warmth to the Harvard atmosphere. I tried to attend morning chapel on those weekdays when President Lowell was to lead. This was the last year of that distinguished Bostonian's presidency, for in the spring announcement was made of the selection of James Bryant Conant to be his successor.

My choice of Harvard for graduate work was not only because its philosophy department had a long history of distinction, but particularly for the opportunity to study with William Ernest Hocking. He was the foremost representative of the long line of Idealists for whom mind is the essence of reality, and whose monumental volume, *The Meaning of God in Human Experience,* is a contemporary expression of that view. In the fall of 1932, Professor Hocking returned from a sabbatical during which he chaired a Rockefeller Committee to study the effect of Christian foreign missions on Asian countries. The commission was comprised of an excellent panel of American churchpeople. The findings were that the work of Christian missionaries in medical, educational and social institutions had had a profound impact upon the Orient. It had brought a new appreciation of the worth of human life and had advanced programs to help multitudes of people. The report suggested that mission efforts be continued with emphasis upon the cross-fertilization of culture between East and West. These findings were published in a small book entitled *Rethinking Missions*, which was immediately attacked by evangelical Christians as a betrayal of Christ's commission that his disciples go out and baptize all nations. The International Missionary Council set about to counteract the Hocking report through an Assembly at Madras in 1938.

I took a year's course in metaphysics with Professor Hocking. It was an inspiration to listen as he sat at his desk and lectured in a soft, quiet voice but firm manner. Metaphysics is the study of the nature of reality and is concerned with the first principles that explain the origin and structure of the world. It speaks of being-hood, of what is basically real. The Great Tradition in Philosophy, which began with Plato, relates to this issue. The recognition of this problem through Plato's Myth of the Cave is what turned my life around in my freshman year. Ever since, I have felt that this is the primary question of life. My criticism of most preaching is that it does not rest upon a metaphysical foundation but accepts a dogma about Jesus which the early church promulgated from the writings of Paul. Too few ministers have a metaphysical view of the universe, and hence do not see life in its total perspective. To be sure, Christianity offers a world view, but it is one based on Biblical assumptions rather than metaphysical analysis. Theologians do develop a world view that makes way for the unique manifestation of divinity in Christ, but I regard this as an accommodation to justify revelation.

A specific point at which the Hand Always Above My Shoulder was guiding me was in a seminar on Asian Religions with Professor Hocking. There were but a few in the group, and he assigned to each the writing of a thesis paper on a specific sacred book. He directed me to the Hindu Upanishads. Of these I knew nothing at the time, but through this seemingly arbitrary assignment my world view was introduced to its second major component.

Hinduism is one of the oldest of the world religions. Its intellectual foundation rests upon the writings of ancient seers who around the fifth century before the Christian Era expressed their view that the real universe is a single entity whose unity is centered in Mind or Idea. Most of these writers were unknown, as were those who put together the early historical books of the Old Testament. Brahma is the name given to the Supreme Deity whose purpose and will sustain creation. Brahma is not a specific personage around whom legends can be built, as the Greek Zeus or the Hebrew Yahweh. He is Personhood or Beinghood in its essence and can be described cognitively only in negatives:

> What is soundless, touchless, formless, imperishable,
> Likewise tasteless, constant, odorless,
> Without beginning, without end, higher than the great.
> —*Katha Upanishad 3:15*

Brahma (God) is *ind*, the basic reality in which all particulars inhere. To a westerner this may at first seem to render the Deity meaningless as an abstraction, but to the Hindu mystic it elevates reality by making it above and beyond all particularities that attach to the deities we humans like to describe as glorified reflections of ourselves. Brahma is everything. Because he is glorious beyond description, so is life glorious. The pains, the enmities, the shortcomings we experience are illusions that will disappear when we gain perfect understanding.

The Hindu seers are mystics who feel the union of all human creatures with ultimate reality. They teach the harmonizing of the finite with the Infinite, the losing of self in the universal Self. "As rivers run to the ocean and are lost in its bounty, so the self seeks its true existence in the ocean of Beinghood."

The favorite illustration is given in the Brihad-Aranyaka, one of the thirteen principal Upanishads, as part of the education of the pupil Yanavalkya. The youth is asked to open a pomegranate and tell what he sees. "Seeds." Open that, and what do you see? "A kernel." Break that open and what do you have? "Nothing." "*Tat, tvam asi!*" "That art thou!" The invisible essence of the world is identical with the invisible essence of the Self. It is the same reality that runs throughout creation. Wisdom comes from penetrating beyond all the separate appearances of things to the ultimate reality where kinship rests.

Like all religions, Hinduism has had many schools of thought during the generations. We may criticize rituals in which temple worshippers burn incense and lay floral petals on altars, but such acts are comparable to ceremonial forms of all religions. We ought not compare the highest expressions of our faith with the more primitive practices of others. Evaluations should be made at comparable levels. Philosophical Hinduism was given its classical expression in the ninth century A.D. by Sankara's Advaita Vedanta. From this period comes the Bhagavad Gita, which does for Hinduism something akin to what the New Testament does for Christianity.

With the coming of Christianity to India a modern rebirth occurred. Ram Mohun Roy (1772–1833) founded Brahma Samaj, which was a defense against both the Hindu extremists and the Western missionaries. A century later came a true renaissance with Sri Ramakrishna (1836–1886). His disciple, Swami Vivekananda (1863–1902), established centers in the United States.

My own contemporary interest in Hinduism comes through Rabindranath Tagore (1861–1941), one of the great mystic poets of the world. His concern was not with institutional religion but as a writer and teacher to convey the spirit of unity between man and God. At Santinikathen near where Buddha had his enlightenment, Tagore built a school whose gracious ways provided an element in the passive resistance movement of Mahatma Gandhi. In 1910 he published *Gitanjali*, Songs of Joy, a collection of lovely hymn poems of a mystic who knows that his life is one with the universe. At the heart of creation is the King who bestows blessings upon all humankind. For this volume he was awarded the Nobel Prize for literature, the first non-Westerner to receive such an honor.

Gitanjali carries the same powerful affirmation as does the Book of Psalms in Judaism. Both are songs of trust and joy because one has come to know the Creator.

As a young student interested in law and politics I was guided by the Hand Always Above My Shoulder, first at Stanford to a conversation that oriented me toward Platonic philosophy, and next at Harvard to an appreciation of the mysticism of India. The whole culture of that subcontinent came alive to me. What I did not know even then was that this new interest was only the unexpected first strand among many that over the next forty years were to bring me closer to the country, culture and people of India.

When I say that I am a Hindu mystic I mean that the Upanishad teaching of the identity of the individual self with the Universal Reality is a vital element of my faith. I do not subscribe to the notion that the material world is an illusion, but I recognize that the abiding realities are those of mind and spirit rather than the material goods that we accumulate and hoard. Multitudes of people are enslaved by physical sensations to a lifetime pursuit of physical pleasures, material wealth, and ruthless competition. They become citadels protecting themselves, viewing others as potential enemies, and cutting themselves off from the life-giving flow of the spirit, which brings generosity, love, compassion, strength, joy. Hindu mystics like Tagore have hearts swelling in song out of appreciation for the bounty of creation. To open to the universe is to experience the love from whom all blessings flow.

The department sponsored a Philosophy Club, which met one afternoon a month and to which outstanding persons in the discipline were brought to lecture. It was at these gatherings that I heard James Bissett Pratt of Williams College and Arthur O. Lovejoy from Johns Hopkins. From the latter I heard a magnanimous statement that made a lasting impression. In the question period after his lecture, one of the students probed to one of the critical issues in Idealism and asked Professor Lovejoy how he dealt with this weakness in his position. I do not recall what the technical question was, but I was thrilled by the response. Instead of giving an erudite defense, Lovejoy acknowledged that this was a vulnerable point but declared that it was a price he was willing to pay for what in its totality seemed to him the most satisfactory theory. No system is perfect, else there would be near-unanimous acceptance of it. Each alternative has its own particular vulnerability, and we must decide which we are willing to accept in order to develop a philosophy that on balance seems to us most satisfying. I was impressed with the candor and openness of this distinguished thinker. He indicated a tolerance and a humility which lead to magnificence and make possible rational discussion. He was echoing the words of Plato, who in the *Phaedo* said that no one can claim that reality is precisely as he has described it, but that life becomes worthwhile when lived on the assumption that his outlook is as near the truth as one can come.

Experiences like this led to the shift in my career expectations. I had gone to Harvard with the intent to obtain a doctorate degree and become a college professor. The freedom and exhilaration I experienced that year in the Cambridge area contrasted with the technical details in which most of the graduate students seemed engrossed. Also, academically one of my courses was Mathematical Logic, a field of growing importance but far removed from reality. It is a field pioneered by Bertrand Russell, in which mathematical relationships are developed based on various hypotheses that are taken as starting points. In the years that were to follow, the study of philosophy through the influence of Wittgenstein's Logical Positivism veered considerably from its traditional quest for meaning. These trends indicated that an academic career devoted to technical points was not for me. Under such auspices the study of philosophy was becoming more of an intellectual game than a quest for significance. I was attracted to philosophy because it offered a world view to serve as a backdrop for daily living. I wanted to share with men and women the enrichment that I believe a spirit-oriented insight can bring to the joys and sorrows, the problems and frustrations, the hopes and challenges that we encounter throughout a lifetime.

This sharing I can better do as a minister than as a college teacher. I need not argue about technicalities nor dwell on details of history. I can paint a broad picture of the rich and abundant life always open and available. My motivation for entering the ministry had very little to do with Biblical history nor with any theological message of salvation. To proclaim Jesus or any New Testament message was not my purpose. I saw life as the poets, the dramatists, the seers had pictured it, and I wanted to convey this vision not as a course in a four-year college career but as a week-by-week inspiration to people caught up in the traumas and dilemmas of daily living. At this point my formative years in a liberal Congregational church came to the fore. I recalled that our hometown minister, Tom Giffen, had held out as an attraction to his calling that a pastor in such a setting has the privilege of speaking each Sunday about something close to his heart and mind. This is what I wanted to do.

In the thirties Yale Divinity School seemed the outstanding seminary, and so I applied and was accepted for entrance in the fall quarter of 1933. The year at Harvard had been an expansive adventure. It had liberated me from the provincialism in which I had been raised, and it had clarified my vision as to the way in which I could best fulfill these hopes. I am ever grateful to Harvard for its refining process, but it sent me to Yale for my next adventure.

4

Seminary Days

IN THE FALL OF 1933, I JOURNEYED by train to New Haven to begin my seminary training at Yale Divinity School. Even though I did not fully realize at the time the significance of this step, it was to open the third major influence in my spiritual pilgrimage. It was also to develop one of my deepest loyalties, that to Yale, and to begin a comradeship with the men of our class that has grown even more meaningful through a half century of ministry.

This was only the second year that the Divinity School had occupied its new campus at the crest of Prospect Street Hill. The buildings were fresh and clean. The setting is serene and beautiful, reminiscent of the Puritan tradition of New England. The architecture is Georgian Colonial, forming a U-shape around a spacious lawn that rises from the street level. At the top are the clean lines of the chapel with its white tower, entered at the second floor level from wrought iron staircases in a gracious curve on either side. Coming out toward the street and connected to the classroom area by arched walkways are the residential houses, four on each side. These are named after Congregational clergymen whose distinguished careers were associated with the university. Among those celebrated are Nathaniel Taylor, Jonathan Edwards, Samuel Hopkins and David Brainerd. For nearly two centuries of often heated theological debate, Yale was generally associated with the more conservative elements as contrasted with the liberalism of Harvard, but by the early 1900s its faculty was thoroughly modern in outlook.

In that September of 1933, fifty-five of us entered Yale Divinity School. In those days very few were married. We were a diverse group from all parts of the country and from many denominations. Though the school is Congregational in its roots, it has long welcomed students from all church groups. For some decades it had been recognized as one of the most liberal and scholarly seminaries, with a faculty of renowned scholars. In our class there were more Methodists than any other single background. This in part was attributable to the presence of southerners who, with a vision of social justice, chose to come north to a liberal school rather than attend the church-controlled seminaries of the south. This was a brave choice on their part, for when they returned to their native areas they were viewed with some suspicion by their more conservative contemporaries.

I was fortunate in being assigned a room in Taylor House, for this turned out to be a collection of the more vivacious and playful students. We were a cross-section of the three-year classes, and developed a congenial comraderie that erupted at various times in public displays that amused if not annoyed the residents of other houses. We had frequent late-night parties in which we mimicked members of the faculty and produced skits of a humorous nature. We displayed our Taylor House loyalties by arranging occasionally to be seated at the head tables in the refectory, usually reserved for more formal events when faculty were present for special days. One of the snapshots from those days cherished by my daughters catches the playfulness of our group. Three of us are seated on the dormitory steps holding a banner that reads, "For God, for Country, and for Yale." Clark Poling is lifting a stein, Roger Squire holds a dagger, and I am pointing upward to the heavens. After being immersed in all the seriousness of traditional theology, six of us Taylorites formed a society to parody traditions, which we called "Birdus Sanctus," the symbol of which was to raise the left hand with three fingers folded and index and thumb erect. One day on the lawn in front of the chapel, we persuaded one of the professors to join us for a snapshot with arms raised for the Birdus Sanctus!

In my eight years of college training, I was fortunate to pass six of those in two colleges that observed the honor system during examinations. I come to my independence and my disdain of authority not only by temperament but also by training. The motto of Stanford University is *"De Luft der Freihart Wert!"*—"The Winds of Freedom Blow." No instructors were present when we were taking tests, but each of us signed at the end of our papers, "No unpermitted aid given or received." Only Harvard had classroom monitors. At YDS we took our exams in classrooms without supervision. Another of our Taylor House antics was to strive to be ahead of the class in finishing our exam papers. As any of us arose and put our papers on the front desk, we exclaimed, "Taylor House One, Taylor House Two," as the case might be. It often happened that Roger Squire and I were leaders in this race. Roger was one of our most charming, the clown of our class. He had a brilliant mind and a winning personality. He was a Methodist, and had a distinguished ministry at Red Bank, New Jersey. A very promising career was cut short when he died of a heart attack. At the Fiftieth Reunion of YDS '36, his widow presented the school with a check for $700,000 to establish a chair in Pastoral Counseling in memory of Roger. After his death she had inherited money from her father, who had invented a manufacturing device. This generous gift is a fitting tribute to one of our best.

My closest friend during seminary days—and perhaps the person for whom I have had the deepest affection in my lifetime—was Clark Vandersall Poling. Clark was the youngest son of Dr. Daniel A. Poling, the distinguished clergyman who was at one time minister of Marble Collegiate Church on New York's Fifth Avenue, editor of the *Christian Herald* and successor to founder Francis Clark as president of World Christian Endeavor. He thus came from fine religious traditions. He had an older brother, Daniel K., who also has had an outstanding career in the Reformed Church. Clark's mother had died earlier, and his father then married a woman of deep sensitivity and rich culture. The family included four daughters and these two sons. I was privileged to be a part of this loving family circle on many occasions, and spent one Christmas holiday in the wintry setting of the Poling family farm at Deering, New Hampshire.

Clark was educated in the traditions of the Reformed Church of America, which goes back to the early Dutch settlers on Manhattan. He attended Hope College in Michigan, and later Rutgers. Yet he was a mystic like myself. We read poetry together, such as the writings of Rabindranath Tagore and Houston Peterson's *A Book of Sonnet Sequences*. We particularly delighted in the works of the Irish mystic, George William Russell, who wrote under the pseudonym of "A.E." A favorite was his book, *The Avatars*. Avatars are spiritual beings who come to earth "trailing clouds of glory," who remember that they are souls whose homeland is beyond and whose destiny is once again to dwell in eternal realms. At our best we are avatars, sensitive and appreciative of things intangible. To Clark and me, these feelings and aspirations were more important than the historic traditions in which we were being trained.

Our friendship began from a specific incident. The two-story residential houses were connected by one-story rooms across an open court, which paralleled the arched walkways on either side of the campus lawns. I was assigned the room facing this open court and to the left of the main doorway to Taylor House. Thus anyone entering our dormitory had to pass by my door. Just beyond mine was another one-story room facing a little-used driveway and a grove of trees. The occupant of that room for my first two years was John Oliver Nelson, who later served on the faculty and founded Kirkridge. I was fortunate to have as a neighbor a gentleman of unusual culture and erudition, from whom I learned a great deal. It was he who introduced me to the *Saturday Review of Literature*, which I came to read regularly through the editorships of Henry Seidel Canby and Norman Cousins. When Jack graduated in 1935, I transferred from my front single room to his rear one.

I had a small portable radio that first year. This was a luxury which few others had. During the World Series, which came early in our association as students, several of the fellows gathered in my room to listen to the ball game. In the midst of it I asked them to leave because I wanted to study. A few evenings later Clark Poling came down to my room to ask me a question about one of our courses. As he later related, he contrived this excuse in order to become better acquainted. A person who could dismiss a group listening to a World Series game must indeed be an intellect worth knowing! It was out of this rather strange beginning that our friendship formed, and we became inseparable during our three years at Yale. We later attended each other's ordination and the installation in our first parishes.

Out of this friendship came a lesson that I am glad to have learned early. Dr. Poling elaborates on this in his book written after Clark's death, *Your Daddy Did Not Die*. I was attracted to Clark because I thought he had the most contagious smile and most attractive personality of anyone I knew. I wished that I could be like him. At the same moment I was wishing this, he was viewing me as having the most brilliant mind that he had encountered. We each admired the other for a different aspect, and thus discovered that each of us had a gift to be developed. We did not need to envy or covet the other's strength, for each had a worth of his own. The most important friendship of my life was founded on this realization. Through the years I have met many people who are my superiors in various capacities, but from my relations with Clark I have remembered not to try to imitate them but to be my own self. Each of us has a worth that is distinctive and precious.

Clark became minister of the First Reformed Church of Schenectady, New York. He was married June 21, 1938, to Elizabeth Jung, whom he had courted and idolized. They enjoyed four golden years of life and ministry together in that parish, during which their son, named after his father but called "Corky," was born in the summer of 1940. It was for him that Dr. Poling wrote the above-mentioned book.

After Pearl Harbor in December of 1941, Clark was one of two out of the forty-seven men of our class to volunteer for army chaplaincy. During the pacifist era of the thirties, all of us had signed pledges never to go to war, but that atmosphere was shattered by the tragedy of December 7. Clark did not want to fight, and he was never really happy in the military, but he felt that it was a duty of his generation to enlist.

During our seminary days Clark had been impressed by the story of the three men whom King Nebuchadnezzar had thrown into the fiery furnace for refusing his command to worship him. To the king's astonishment, when he looked into the flames he saw not only the three Jews walking without hurt in the midst of the fire, but a fourth also who was like the Son of God (Daniel 3). Clark often referred to this imagery to suggest the presence of the Invisible Companion.

After his training and commissioning, Clark was sent overseas on the troopship *Dorchester*, which was torpedoed in the North Sea in the early morning hours of February 3, 1943. His sacrificial death has become one of the legends in our nation's history. He was one of the four chaplains—a Jew, a Roman Catholic and two Protestants—who gave their lifebelts to enlisted men when there were not enough to go around. They stood on the deck that night as the *Dorchester* sank into icy waters. It was a heroic sacrifice and a great loss. I am sure Clark would have become one of the religious leaders of our time. He had all the charm and exuberance of his father, but a mind more widely encompassing and a spirit more openly inclusive.

On the night before the *Dorchester* sailed, Clark wrote a letter to his father in which he referred to the fiery furnace imagery. "Apparently I am headed for a blind alley, but, Dad, if when I get there, I find one other man, then there will be three of us."

These words have come to be for me the symbol of our friendship and of the ministry we both loved and shared. In my ministry at Plymouth Church Minneapolis, and in the four interim pastorates I have taken since retirement, I have begun with a first sermon entitled, "Two Must Face a Third." I have told the story of our friendship, of Clark's sacrifice, and of his closing words. In all human relationships—be it marriage, parenting, minister and congregation, employer and employee, neighbor and neighbor—two persons entering need to recognize that they are in the presence of a Third, the Invisible Eternal God whose steadfastness, righteousness and love provide the backdrop for all that is said and done.

Though my closest companion during seminary days was Clark Poling, I had happy associations with many classmates. Through the years my friendship with them has been undiminished, and my respect for their accomplishments has grown. All of us are indebted to the outstanding members of the faculty who taught and inspired us. Quite a number were recognized as premier scholars in their field, while at the same time being excellent lecturers and teachers. To six I particularly owe a great deal for the training I received.

Perhaps the most brilliant lecturer I encountered through eight years of college was Roland H. Bainton, Titus Street Professor of Church History. The Reformation was his period of expertise. He had a lovely home in Woodbridge, some distance out from New

Haven. He usually bicycled between home and school. Sometimes he would bring his bicycle into the classroom if his arrival was at the last minute before the hour. He had a rich sense of the dramatic, and was in great demand as a lecturer all over the country. He never used a note, but could quote extensively from sources. He could relate the thought of a character to colorful incidents in the person's life. His lectures on Abelard and Eloise, on Erasmus, on Luther and his wife Katy, were classics which drew more than those enrolled in his course. At the dedication of our Fine Arts Center at Plymouth in 1967 I had him come to give his Erasmus portrait.

Roly Bainton was a careful scholar who authored many books and papers, but he was also a warm human being with many interests. He and his gracious wife Ruth kept friendships with scores of students long after they had gone to their own fields of endeavor. When my wife and I built a new house in Darien, they brought their two youngest children to spend the night as first occupants of the guest bedroom. Inasmuch as Martin Luther was his specialty, the Lutherans adopted him as one of their celebrities. He came frequently to Minneapolis and made appearances at Plymouth Church. His mischievous pen sketches, made while sitting at meetings, were coveted by those fortunate enough to attract his attention. Roland Bainton was a Congregationalist with strong Quaker leanings. He was a pacifist who wrote many pamphlets for that cause and carefully researched the history of that strand within the Christian Church. It is safe to say that he probably had more friends among Yale Divinity School alumni than any other professor.

A brilliant star on the faculty was Robert Calhoun, in my day the professor of philosophy but who later developed more interest in theology. Bob Calhoun had been a prodigy at Carleton College in Northfield, Minnesota, where he achieved one of the highest academic records of any student in that institution's history. He, too, was a brilliant lecturer who could expound on intricate intellectual issues with scarcely a note. Because of health problems, he lacked the charm and humor of Bainton, but his care and accuracy were always evident. He was tall, spare and distinguished in appearance, but his body could not sustain the intensity of his intellect. He had limited hearing and wore a strong hearing aid. In his classes on the history of philosophy, which were large because we recognized that we were in the presence of a genius, one could interrupt by raising a hand. Calhoun would come down into the row where the student was sitting, stand before him and hear the question. Always he responded with kindness yet earnestness.

Because I was a philosophy major all eight years of my academic life, I had the privilege of frequent associations with Bob Calhoun. I had several seminar courses from him. Relations were fairly formal, never casual. Yet of all the teachers I have known, in small groups or face-to-face conversation, he had an uncanny ability to stimulate a student to think. In philosophy one is not dealing with facts, dates or figures but with ideas, reasonings, arguments. Calhoun could ask a question in such a way as to draw from me thoughts that I never knew I had. Here was a teacher in the true Socratic tradition.

H. Richard Niebuhr was professor of ethics, a member of a distinguished clergy family that has left a mark on American religious thought that will always be remembered. I regard him as a more profound and wider-ranging thinker than his elder brother Reinhold. His books on *The Kingdom of God in America, Christ and Culture,* and *Radical Monotheism* established seminal points in my own religious development. He, too, lectured with few notes. He was not as fluent as Bainton or Calhoun, but was quite deliberate in his manner. From him we recognized that we were not getting oft-repeated lectures but fresh reflections on some current event, some play he had seen or book he had read. He held up these current interests to ethical norms. As we sat in his classroom we could observe a keen mind at work. Niebuhr's legacy to us was the awareness that Christian principles are always relevant and need to be interpreted at their deepest level rather than in the popular cliches of the day. One of his last contributions was in *The Christian Century* series on "How My Mind Has Changed," in which he affirmed the need for ever-recurring reformation. Some of the popular movements during his lifetime had not produced the fruits they had promised. We must always reexamine, reform, and renew our basic insights lest they become lost in the quagmire of inadequate expressions.

The fourth of my special mentors was the dean of the Divinity School, Luther A. Weigle. He was a superb administrator who combined erudition, scholarship in his particular field of the psychology of religion, and a keen perception of people. He had been dean of Carleton College before being called to Yale. He was chairman of the committee of thirty-two scholars who from 1937 to 1951 prepared the Revised Standard Version of the Bible. This was a tremendous task in itself. He also chaired the committee that laid out the structure of the National Council of Churches as that body emerged out of the older Federal Council. He was a dynamic individual whose presence was felt wherever he went. His analytical skills enabled him to cut through to the core of an issue, and his wise judgment enabled him to bring people together to effect a program.

Our homiletics professor was Halford E. Luccock. With a Methodist background he was very much a down-to-earth person who, with a somewhat raspy voice, was one of the most effective and popular preachers of his day. He had a rare sense of humor that enabled him to take incidents recorded in the daily press and relate them to a larger perspective in such a way as to expose their incongruity. Every few sentences of his lectures and sermons produced a laugh, but each time he had his listeners amused he followed immediately with an incisive comment that hit squarely between the eyes. He used contemporary stories and events to drive home a message. For many years he wrote a weekly column for *The Christian Century* under the pen name of Simeon Stylites in which his humor penetrated the foibles of church life. The reference was to the celebrated fifth-century ascetic who attained sainthood through the then exalted posture of spending his life sitting atop a high pillar. Hal Luccock taught us to read with observant minds, and to see the subtle connections that often lie beneath the surface. His warm humanity made him a good friend as well as an inspiring teacher. He mingled freely with the students and was a sympathetic listener.

One of our assignments was to plan a set of sermon themes for the four Sundays of Advent. One classmate came up with a list for an entire year. In his droll manner Professor Luccock commended the man for his organizational skill and far-sighted planning, but tempered his enthusiasm with the query, "But what would you do, if, by some chance, in mid-year you suddenly came up with a fresh idea?"

In addition to the Divinity School faculty, another Yale professor had a lasting influence on me. He was William Lyon Phelps, by that time retired from the English department. Phelps was the country's leading authority on Robert Browning, and a much beloved teacher because he was a colorful figure who knew how to dramatize his work. He was a devoted Christian layman in the American Baptist fellowship. Each year he was invited to address the divinity students at a packed chapel. I recall his oft-repeated admonition that if we told our people that to follow our advice would enrich their lives, we would have few followers; but if we told them that to disregard our preaching was to risk the fires of damnation, we would attract large congregations. Each year for fifteen weeks, Billy Phelps gave a popular lecture in the sanctuary of the First Baptist Church from 4:30 to 5:45 on Tuesday afternoons. Tickets were minimal, and several hundred people attended. The topic was a portion of Browning's poetry, but the sessions began with delightful commentaries on whatever he had been doing the previous days. As a raconteur he was a superb artist. Though I love poetry, I had never taken a formal course in English literature at Stanford, so what I know I have picked up as I have gone along. It was a treat to have this scholar and popularizer bring Browning to life for me, and I regard these Tuesday lectures to have been a valuable part of my Yale education. Over the years in my ministry I have taught many courses in adult education, most of them concerning the Bible. However, the subject that I have done more than any other, perhaps eight times, is *The Ring and the Book*. I find this one of the greatest Christian poems in the English language, with an astounding perception of human character.

The concern that Dean Weigle had for his students is shown in the way in which he influenced my life at the time of graduation and through the years. I had taken a course from him on the psychology of religion, but his interest in us went beyond the classroom. In a quiet way he knew the students, saw our possibilities, and dealt with us in a firm yet kindly fashion. I cannot recall any single incident during our three years through which he would have had the chance to evaluate me, but by the time of graduation he was my strongest advocate.

At that point it was suggested that I go for one year to teach English at Doshisha University at Kyoto, Japan. The missionary who held that post wanted to come back to the States for a furlough, and a temporary replacement was needed. The suggestion was made by Hugh Vernon White of the American Board, who had just returned from a trip to Japan. As my graduation approached, he suggested that Doshisha would be an interesting year for me. He pointed out that I could afford to go, and that I had no wife or family ties to hold me back. To teach English in a foreign college was not something I had anticipated, but I thought I ought to give the offer some consideration.

I went to see Kenneth Latourette, whose monumental *History of the Expansion of Christianity* is the classic for the growth of the missionary movement around the world. He would know Doshisha. Dr. Latourette was the epitome of a scholar, a bachelor who lived in one of the dormitories, who followed a strict regime of so much reading, so much writing, so much translating each day. He was a kindly soul whom we privately referred to as our "Uncle Ken," but he lived more in history than in daily events. He listened politely to my story, and offered the opinion that it would be an interesting and enriching experience to live for a year in Japan.

Then I went to see Dean Weigle and laid the suggestion before him. He did not hesitate for a moment. He told me that I should not consider such an offer. "You are going to be one of the great preachers of your generation, and had better get on with it. If you go to Japan, you might like it. You may be tempted to stay on a few more years. Then your life will lose its focus. You are meant to be a minister, and that is the work to which you should go."

For the next decade while he was still dean, he recommended me for several positions which I think at the time were beyond my capabilities. One of these was the chaplaincy of West Point!

In 1947, after I had been three years at Plymouth, he offered me a full professorship to come back to the Divinity School, in what would have been his last appointment before retirement. John Schroeder had been teaching homiletics but was going down the hill to the religion department of the university and to be master of one of the colleges. Our beloved and inspiring Halford E. Luccock would retire in another year, and I was being groomed to be the teacher of preaching.

This was a flattering offer, and a tempting one. I received letters from several of my former professors, urging me to accept and welcoming me back. Yale Divinity School had been and is one of my great affections, so that the thought of being there was enticing. A Hand Always Above My Shoulder, however, led to the strong conviction that this was not the true path before me. Several factors went into the declining of this generous offer.

First, I did not think I was the equal of the giants by whom I had been taught, and I did not want to be a weak member of a strong faculty. Next, I had reservations as to whether homiletics can truly be taught. A good preacher is born, not made, with instincts and directives that are innate. Probably a teacher can instill discipline, suggest techniques, and improve delivery. He may keep a person from being a bore in the pulpit, but this does not get to the essence of good preaching. I think I have a homiletic mind. I sense what are effective phrases, what are good illustrations, what is logical, what carries an emotional impact. I learned part of this through the training I got in debate at high school and college, when one has to sift through a lot of material to find what really communicates. Many people think that I am a scholar and a wide reader. Actually, I am neither. Reading for the sake of reading is not a pleasure for me. I would rather be walking through woods or fields. But when I do read, I can spot what will be effective in my job of communicating. I have tray upon tray of five- by eight-inch cards that carry poems, quotations and illustrations. And I have the good sense to use but a few of these in constructing a sermon. I have confidence in my own preaching, but have doubts that I could helpfully train another person.

The main reason for declining the offer was the feeling that this was not what the Lord wanted me to do. I was well into my ministry at Plymouth, the church was coming back from its discouragement, large classes of members were joining. We were in the midst of our first building project, an education wing and a lovely chapel. I loved my work, and was happy every day in what I was doing. New possibilities loomed. I felt it would be a mistake to transfer from what I felt was my God-directed work to another task in which I did not feel comfortable.

I think my decision was a wise one. I went on in a ministry that continued to grow, in a fellowship with people with whom we shared a mutual love and trust, with whom we built a strong church that could be a national leader in resisting several popular trends in churchmanship. Had I gone to New Haven, I would have become a minority voice in matters of social action and in movements toward organic church union. This would have been uncomfortable for me, and possibly embarrassing to the university. I think the Hand Always Above My Shoulder had led me to the proper arena for my ministry.

As we came to the end of our senior year, my classmates elected me to be the permanent officer of our group. As secretary, it became my responsibility and privilege to keep alive the warm fellowship we had developed over our three years together. Each graduating class elects a secretary, but most of these do very little. I realized that when we scattered we would lose our kinship if from the beginning we did not keep contact. So each spring I sent a mimeographed request to each man asking for a letter telling of professional and family activities. Often I posed a question on which they could offer comments. As the replies came back, they were copied onto stencils, mimeographed and gathered into a booklet of forty to fifty pages. This was quite a chore. My wife Viola and I did all the work for the first eight years, but after going to Plymouth Church I had secretaries who could do a lot of the manual work. The men responded well, and for the first twenty-five years we did not miss an annual newsletter. After that period we went to five-year intervals. This was a joyous task because our YDS fellowship has meant a great deal to me over the years.

Our men have done well. We have given meaningful ministry, not only in parishes but in administrative posts and college teaching. Two of our group became college presidents. Our record of longevity has been fairly good. Of the forty-seven men who graduated in June of 1936, thirty-three were still living at the time of our Fiftieth Reunion in New Haven, May 29-31, 1986.

The irony is that I was not able to attend. On the week of that great event I came down with the flu, was in bed in Minneapolis, and could not make the journey east. Twenty-two were present, including wives, and had a rich experience of renewal. They phoned me, and sent many notes of affection.

5

Thoughts of a Seminarian

THE TRANSFER TO YALE DIVINITY SCHOOL in September 1933 marked the third stage in my philosophic and religious development. The Hand Always Above My Shoulder was leading me toward my major life stance and career. Through Plato I had come to recognize a noumenal world of the Unseen, fashioned by God. Through the Hindu classics I learned to appreciate the unity one can enjoy with both the created world and the unseen Spirit. Now I was to integrate these insights from the East with our precious Judeo-Christian heritage.

Though I had not recognized the rich dimensions of Christianity before entering seminary, there was a sense, of course, in which I had always been a Christian. Most of us who are born in the United States accept Americanism and Christianity as part of our background. My family were regular church attendants, and much of our life revolved around the fellowship of the congregation. Most of the Congregational ministers in the first third of the twentieth century were liberals who might be characterized as theistic humanists. They believed in God, but their concerns were with the problems of daily living, and for these they lifted up the human Jesus as their teacher and guide. After I had been converted at college by Platonism, I wondered whether our parish ministers were speaking out of a truly cosmic perspective. The first sermon I ever preached was in our Fresno church during a vacation period. Its theme was the assurance of immortality as proven by the arguments which Plato set forth in the *Phaedo*. Like the vast majority of churchgoers, I was a nominal Christian but with only the vaguest notion as to its essential beliefs.

I thus entered seminary with an openness to new insights. I was not even familiar with, let alone committed to, any dogma or theology that usually motivated seminarians.

And I was thrilled at what I found. The Bible was like the Platonic Dialogues and the Upanishads, offering a fresh witness to the excitement of life. I read it not as authority handed down by God, but as testimony of the spiritual insights of a sensitive people, insights that were constantly broadening as their experience developed. There are thought patterns and terminology that differ from Greek to Hindu to Hebrew to Christian; but underlying all are the same basic speculations as to who we are, where we come from, and where we are going.

During our first year in seminary, we had courses in both the Old Testament and the New. We studied the Scripture verse by verse, chapter by chapter, book by book. All members of the faculty accepted the scholarship of the previous two centuries, which developed the historical approach and form criticism. They recognized the Bible as a collection of sixty-six books, each written at a different time and assigned a place in the canon at a much later date. They taught us to ask of each verse: By whom was this written? When was it written? For what purpose was it written? How does it relate to other passages of Scripture? Such questions do not detract from the value of Scripture but help to bring into focus its wondrous insights.

The Old Testament was especially fascinating to me because it contains a rich collection of stories about people in various situations. Some are legendary characters who emerged from folklore before the time of written records. Others are heroes whose deeds gave pride and purpose to an early society. All of them carry a significance that contributed to the self-understanding of the Hebrews.

Because I had read the books of Herodotus, I recognized how the earliest historians employed stories and anecdotes to convey the significance of world events. Familiarity with this Greek "father of history" is a helpful introduction to Bible study, for it places one in the era out of which the Scriptures come. The Book of Genesis is of momentous import when approached in this perspective. Long before the time of recorded writings, the Hebrews were speculating about the same questions that arose in all ancient civilizations: How was the world created? From whence comes suffering and pain? Would God destroy the world and start over again? Why do women suffer in childbirth? Are we responsible for one another? Why are there so many languages?

Primitive societies did not write heavy treatises to explore these questions. Instead, their artists and poets told stories that dramatize these issues. Such stories were transmitted from generation to generation by word of mouth, formalized and handed down by repetition until later recorded in written word. The narratives of the Old Testament show evidence of a blending and meshing of several strands of tradition into the matchless stories that we treasure today.

I soon recognized, however, that though the Old Testament writers used dramatic stories to give their message, there is a marked difference between them and the Greeks. The latter developed a mythology to portray the divine activity. Their stories were more about imaginative characters than about flesh-and-blood mortals. They pictured Mt. Olympus as the home of the gods, each of whom represented one of the forces that influence human life. Zeus was the mighty God, but along with him were a myriad of lesser deities. Poseidon was lord of the sea; Artemis goddess of the moon; Aphrodite goddess of beauty. These might influence human destiny, as when Artemis withheld the wind needed for the Greek fleet to sail from Aulis toward Troy until Agamemnon sacrificed his daughter Iphegenia. The stories in the Greek epics of Homer and the Tragedians belonged to a dream-world of fantasy that might have lessons for mortals but was distinct from reality.

The Hebrews, on the other hand, assumed that God moves through history. Theirs was a monistic faith, with no fantasies of lesser deities. The sovereign Lord of the universe is the one Creator God who moved on the face of the waters to bring light out of darkness, and who in successive steps brought forth the earth and then created man in the divine image. This same God is concerned with the world, and acts through historic events that his will may be done on earth as it is in heaven. Christianity, which evolved out of Judaism, carries this same strong realism. The righteousness of God is not confined to abstract ideals or some celestial realm, but is to be obeyed here in earthly society. God uses peoples and nations to fulfill divine ends.

How literally or figuratively this movement of God in history as told in the Bible is to be taken became an issue with which I have been concerned throughout my ministry. It is sufficient to say that I was thrilled by the true-to-life stories we read in seminary because these seemed to me illustrative of the living out in daily experience of the philosophic insights I had learned through the Great Tradition in that discipline.

In the early years, when I taught at summer camps and conferences for young people, my favorite course was the Hebrew prophets. Their writings constitute about a third of the Old Testament. They were preachers who saw the universe governed by strict principles of moral order, and they called the people to return to the decency ordained of God rather than to rely on ceremonial observances to cleanse them from their wicked dealings. "Let justice roll down as waters, and righteousness as an ever-flowing stream" (Amos 5:25). "And what doth the Lord require of thee, but to do justly, to love mercy, and to walk humbly with your God" (Micah 6:8). I saw these preachments as universal in their impact. Though they were delivered by prophets at specific and datable moments in the history of Israel and Judah, their relevance is for all times.

It was in this spirit that the Old Testament thrilled me. Here were a people who in their personal and national life understood that the eternal principles of the universe—God's will—were creative factors in their decisions. It never occurred to me that the Divine Promises were given to Israel to be theirs alone. We were taught that these promises are universal to any peoples or individual who enter into a covenant relationship to live according to cosmic principles.

I found the New Testament equally exciting. We were taught the historical approach. The four gospels present Jesus, but they are not accurate biographies in any modern sense. Each was written from a special perspective to present Jesus to the early church, and to persuade readers of his divinity. The earliest of these, the Gospel of Mark, is dated around 70 A.D., which is a whole generation after the crucifixion; and the last, the Gospel of John, comes after nearly a century had passed. These cannot be considered as eyewitness accounts, but as collections of incidents and sayings of Jesus which had been cherished by his followers.

The focus of our New Testament studies was on the problem of the historical Jesus. How can we get behind the presentations to know what Jesus was actually like, what he did and what he said? How can we evaluate the reliability of various passages?

The Jesus to whom I was exposed at divinity school was consistent with the Jesus of whom I had heard through the preachings of the Congregational ministers of the Northern California Conference. He was not a divine being but a human figure in the succession of the Hebrew prophets of the Old Testament. He was a spokesman for God. He is the highest revelation because both by his teachings and his sacrificial life he gives the world the clearest picture of what God is like. Through him we see that God is love, not because God sent his only begotten Son to save the world, but because Jesus so loved his disciples and all humankind that he was willing to be crucified by a jealous professional clergy in order to demonstrate that the nature of the universe is such that ultimately love will prevail.

I found the Sermon on the Mount to be an exciting statement of the most profound ethical and moral insights. This is the heart of Christianity as taught by Jesus, though orthodox Christian faith has emphasized something quite other. I was not as fully aware of this distinction until some years later, so I shall not elaborate on it at this juncture.

In the third month of my first year at seminary—in November 1933—I wrote a paper for our New Testament course entitled, "The Adequacy of the Ethics Contained in the Sermon on the Mount." Without referring to Professor Henry Waldgrave Stuart by name, I interpreted Chapters 5, 6 and 7 in Matthew as an expression of the principles which he had taught at Stanford. We must distinguish between moral codes that give us specific rules for action and an ethical system that deals not with specific rules but with the method or motivation for arriving at these codes. It is only as an ethical system that the Sermon on the Mount is adequate. It does not offer specifics of morality.

Instead, it gives a method, that we should do unto others what we would have them do to us. This is ambiguous as a rule of conduct because it does not specify how we want to be treated. Jesus is suggesting sympathetic relationships between people as a means of learning from one another what is a worthy type of action.

This contrasts with the then current types of ethics taught by Stoics, Epicureans, Plato and Aristotle. All of these were rationalistic, using the intellect to determine the good. These will always bind us to the conventional because reason always argues from what is known and familiar.

The Sermon on the Mount challenges us to adventure into unknown territory in pursuit of continually expanding horizons. Jesus calls us to the kingdom of God—a relationship certainly unknown to reason and to the prevailing standards of society. The Beatitudes extol qualities which hardly seem reasonable: meekness, purity, suffering, peace-making, submissiveness to persecution. We are told not to judge, not to strike back, to go the second mile with someone who orders us to go, to give a second garment to the oppressor who asks for one, to forgive those who trespass against us. All of these sayings deal with motivation. They are foolish by the standard of reason, but if practiced they will lead us into relationships with our neighbors that will open new understandings of what life can be.

Many of the parables that Jesus taught go against the reasonableness of conventional thought. The love of the father for the prodigal son goes against the expectations of the elder brother. The king who invites his friends to the marriage feast of his son finally turns to the rabble to be his guests. The farmer who hires workmen pays the same wages to those who labored two hours as to those who toiled all day. These and many of the parables must have puzzled—even disturbed—those who first heard them. Perhaps they were passed on from person to person precisely because they were so disturbing.

Jesus proclaimed the coming of the Kingdom of God, but he never defined it. Instead, he disturbed those of his hearers who wanted rationalistic codes by suggesting that blessedness is something quite other, something which turns traditional values upside down, but which can be embraced only by a sympathetic identification with one's fellow beings. If you seek first the kingdom, all particulars will be added to you.

While these Biblical studies were opening a new field of interest for me that was to remain throughout my ministry, nevertheless my major focus at Yale continued to be the philosophical interpretation of life's meaning. I have preserved all the term papers I wrote during those three seminary years. In addition to the one I have just discussed on the Sermon on the Mount, I want to mention three others. I think it significant to do so for two reasons. One is that they indicate how solidly my life-long perspective was being developed, even in those early years. The other is that they illustrate how differently ministerial training was conceived fifty years ago than it is in most seminaries today.

The 1930s were the last days of the truly liberal period, whose dominant issue had been the Fundamentalist-Modernist controversy. At the major university seminaries the Modernists prevailed. Biblical scholarship accepted form criticism and rejected the notion of the inerrancy of Scripture. Karl Barth's continental theology of Neo-Orthodoxy was only a faint glimmer on the American horizon. Kierkegaard had not been translated into English by the time we graduated. The hard discipline and heroic sacrifice of Dietrich Bonhoeffer were yet to come. The Great Depression in our country and the rise of Nazism in Germany were to shatter the complacent optimism of the liberal era, but this did not occur until the opening of the Second World War.

In our student days of 1933-36, the atmosphere at Yale Divinity School could be characterized by a favorite phrase of Professor Henry Hallam Tweedy as one of "boundless, courageous goodwill." We were allowed wide choices in the courses we took. There was no such subject as Biblical Theology. After taking the basic courses in Old and New Testament, I was allowed to focus my attention on philosophy, comparative religions, and the arts.

In the class on comparative religions, I wrote a paper on "Mysticism and Rabindranath Tagore," which shows the profound influence that the eastern view had upon my thinking. I began by writing that there are two paths to the single gate of Justification. One is the Road of Estrangement, along which the pilgrim feels that he is journeying in an alien world, seeking to come into relation with a sovereign God by somehow bridging the gulf which separates him from his creator. Orthodox Christian doctrine offers this means through the assurance that God sent his Son Jesus the Christ to pay the supreme price for our estrangement and reconcile us with the Heavenly Father.

The other path is the Road of Ecstasy. The traveler here is not seeking Deity as a distant goal, but is walking in fellowship with a divinity that pervades the journey. Both in nature and in himself, man has mystic communion with a godhead that is not distinct and separate, but who is the very life and being of the whole universe.

Tagore—the cultured, philosophic Hindu—followed the Road of Ecstasy. In his life from 1861 to 1941, he was a prolific writer, the greatest Indian poet since Kalidasa. It is said that his poetry and drama alone came to one hundred thousand lines as compared with eighteen thousand for Milton! He founded a school at Santinikaten in Bengal, from which he wrote verse that best expressed mysticism to the western world. In 1913 he was awarded the Nobel Prize in Literature, the first time that honor had gone out of the orbit of Western culture.

In my paper I outlined seven elements on Tagore's Road of Ecstasy. First, the goal we are striving to seek is unity with the universe. We are distracted by pursuit of the fragmentary, and we seek the whole. Second, we come to view the world of nature in terms of spirit and personality. Third, we find that God is everywhere. Fourth, this means that God is in our own hearts. Fifth, we must seek to attune our lives with the power of the universe. Our destiny is one with the ever-flowing rhythmic dance of creation. Sixth, such harmony brings strength and renewal. "I feel that my life is made glorious by the life of the ages dancing in my blood this very moment." Finally, the life of mystic communion is one of joy and ecstasy. It is only as singers that we come into the presence of the divine.

Clearly in my seminary days I was opting for the path of mysticism rather than that of orthodox Christianity. Professor John Clark Archer commented that I may have exaggerated the contrast, but he gave an A plus to the paper.

Another significant paper was done for the class in theology of Professor Douglas Clyde Macintosh. It is entitled "Culture and Religion." Though written more than fifty years ago, I could not do better today. It has many references to poets and philosophers that I have forgotten. The theme is that religion and culture each need the other.

Too frequently the germ of Puritanism has made religious folk suspicious of "strange matters" in the outside world that may corrupt orthodox faith. The Church has often looked with suspicion upon every new theory and every scientific advance as potentially undermining the existing system of faith. In Biblical times, Paul warned the Corinthians not to be yoked with unbelievers. Yet to withdraw from the cultural appreciation of art, literature, music and science is to fail to meet the challenges and fresh insights for our exploring minds. Bigotry and exclusivism follow. While it is true that broadening cultural contacts may lessen the intensity of religious faith, this broadening may develop a faith that gains in real significance what it may lose in external expression. A deep faith must relate to the cultural environment in which it lives.

The unfortunate result is that many persons who are liberated from dogmatism may think that they have outgrown religion altogether. This is to take from life its basic foundations. It is to keep the "cultured gentleman" excited by the many attractions of the moment, but to leave him uneasily untethered from the meaningful whole in which existence abides. T.S. Eliot, Gilbert Chesterton, and Eugene O'Neill were cited as writers highly critical of organized religion, but in those works there was expressed the need for a faith that unites us with the wholeness of existence. It may be difficult to state what the "more" is that religion adds to culture, but without faith there is an ultimate void.

The third paper of my seminary days I mention not to summarize as much as to indicate how unique was my training for ministry. During the three quarters of my third and final year at Yale Divinity School, I was allowed to take only three courses rather than four, and to devote one-fourth of my time to the writing of a thesis setting forth my own religious philosophy. The result was a 189-page tome entitled "Philosophical Idealism and Its Religious Aspects: The Outline of a Personal Philosophy." It begins with a quotation from Chekhov's *Three Sisters*: "Either you must know why you live, or everything else is trivial, not worth a straw."

What turned me to philosophy at Stanford and to the ministry at Harvard was the conviction that the meaning of life is the greatest problem every person faces. Throughout fifty years of ministry I have addressed myself to this problem, and in my sermons have tried to bring insights that will give guidance, strength and hope to men and women. My approach, however, has not been through the Bible nor traditional Christian theology. In fact, I reject orthodox Christianity as being an artificial and contrived world view as contrasted with the Great Tradition in Philosophy from Plato onward.

In this senior thesis I developed a system of metaphysics. It involves belief in the universe as meaning, the world as expression of purpose, the reality of values, the presence of cosmic mind, and the unity of the finite with the infinite. I concluded, "To take such a metaphysics seriously means to be religious."

Though there were few Biblical references in this tome, and no traditional theological positions, I was given another A plus and graduated to be a Christian minister! That simply would not happen in any seminary today.

More revealing of my outlook than these seminary papers, perhaps, is my first published article in a national journal. I have been writing all my life, and while in divinity school began sending to religious publications. The first effort to be accepted was written during my senior year at Yale and was published in the official magazine of the Universalists, and opened a friendship with its editor, Dr. John VanSchaik of Cobbleskill, New York. That article was entitled "Is Religion Larger than Jesus?" and expressed the thought that has characterized my ministry through more than fifty years. Important as Jesus may be, he is only one embodiment of the more universal religious sensitivity of the human spirit. In a recent sermon in 1988, I said that it is not as essential to be a Christian as it is to be warmly related to the Unseen Spirit at the heart of creation.

Yale Divinity School added an understanding of the Judeo-Christian tradition to my religious orientation. It blended that understanding with my Platonism and my mysticism, but it did not replace them.

Clark and I showed my article to his father, Dr. Dan Poling, who said to me, "You will outgrow this."

Fortunately, I never have!

6

My First Job

AS MY FIRST YEAR AT SEMINARY drew to a close, I told the field work department that I would like a church position when we returned in the fall. Dr. Paul H. Vieth was professor of Religious Education and director of Field Work. Most of the students had weekend jobs, as pastors of small-town churches or as youth workers in city churches. It was by this means that they supported themselves and paid for their education. Dr. Vieth told me that he could not give me one of these opportunities because I had family resources with which to finance my education, and I would be taking a job from a student who needed it for livelihood. I replied that I had come to Yale to be trained for the parish ministry, and that experience in a church was part of that training. He reiterated that the school was obligated to provide paying positions for students in need. I told him that I would return before opening of the fall quarter in order to seek a church experience.

So I did. I had a Model A Ford coupe with a rumble seat. My father was dying from Parkinson's disease at our home in Fresno, but my mother insisted that both my sister and I continue our education because our lives were ahead of us. I left, knowing that I would not again see my father in this world, and drove my little car across the country to New Haven. Dr. Vieth made the same response that he had given in the spring. I could understand his decision, for we were in the midst of the Great Depression, and most of the

59

student body had critical needs. I was determined, however, to have a job, and confident that the Hand Always Above My Shoulder would provide an opportunity.

The second morning back Dr. Vieth called me to his office and said that a chance opening had arisen for which he could in good conscience recommend me. For several years the Union Memorial Church of Glenbrook had hired a Yale student to guide its youth program. This was one of the more lucrative jobs. My recollection is that the pay was $53 a month, which in those days was quite good. The minister had come to the campus the previous day. Several students had been introduced to him for interview, but he was not impressed by any of them. He had left, saying, "I think I will go down to Union Seminary in New York and see whom they may have to offer."

Dr. Vieth said he did not think I had had enough experience to be acceptable, but if I could get the job I would not be taking it from another Yale student. I eagerly got the minister's name, telephoned him, and made an appointment to be at his home at 2:30 that afternoon. It was a dark, rainy Saturday, but I drove my car with keen anticipation for this important interview. We talked for more than an hour, whereupon he sent me to the home of a young couple who had two children and had been active in sponsoring youth work. A few days later, word came to the school that the Glenbrook Church wanted me for its youth worker. Little did I realize then that the good people of that church would be the focus of my professional life for the next seven years.

For the next two years, I drove to Glenbrook each Friday afternoon. Sometimes we had a social that evening for high school youth. Saturday mornings I had junior high programs at the church. In the afternoons I called in homes. Sunday was a busy day, as I conducted worship for the senior high department and often assisted in the church service. In the evenings we had senior high youth group, which involved forty to sixty young people. When the meeting was over, I was weary and drove back to divinity school. Usually at Bridgeport I picked up another student, Donald Frazier, who was doing youth work at one of the churches there. While in Glenbrook I had a room and meals with a church family, Mr. and Mrs. Irving Branch. They were fine people and took me in as part of their family.

Glenbrook was a small residential community of modest homes from which many of the men commuted to professional and midlevel managerial positions in New York City. Others were with major companies headquartered in Stamford. It was a quiet, friendly, homogeneous community.

Part of its uniqueness lay in its relation to the family of Dr. Charles H. Phillips, who resided there, and whose Milk of Magnesia plant was on the outskirts. Dr. Phillips and his brother had passed away before my time, but Mrs. Phillips was still living. I later assisted at her funeral. They were kindly, generous people who made no demands on their neighbors, but whose paternalistic generosity made the community dependent on them. In earlier days they had sold lots to young couples whom they judged to be home-loving folk. They built the church, the fire department, the library and a large apartment house—all of which they gave to the church that it might continue this custodial care. The core area was several streets and blocks of attractive homes whose residents were like one large family of friendly people who exemplified the traditional values of American society.

The Union Memorial Church was organized in June 1896 with twenty-five charter members, several of whom still retained leadership roles forty years later. The minister was the Rev. Samuel J. Evers, a Yale Divinity student who had come down weekends during his senior year to conduct services in what was then a small chapel. Upon his graduation in 1896 the church was organized. Three years later he married Katherine White, the daughter of a family prominent in the little church. They were a gracious and charming couple through all the years, greatly beloved. Their son and their daughter also lived in Glenbrook. The Phillips family gave the Evers three large houses, and took them on trips to Europe.

Over the years the church plant was enlarged. The lovely sanctuary had nicely carved beams after an English country church. An excellent social and educational extension was added. Mr. Evers remained as pastor for five decades, and created a friendly, comfortable congregation.

Mr. Evers was a short, plump man with a kindly and expressive face, a gentleman through and through. He was sympathetic with people, and a good pastor. His supreme wish was for tranquility. He took no stand on issues, but wanted the life of the church to run smoothly. When they did his health was good, but if there was any dissension he was distressed. He was in his sixties when I first arrived, and from time to time he mentioned the possibility of retiring.

As my graduation approached, he and the church suggested that I come as his associate with the expectation that he would retire in the near future. Inasmuch as the church had developed naturally around him and had never called a minister, it was said that I as the youth worker for two years could likewise grow into the position and remain for my lifetime. I was fond of the people, Mr. Evers and I got along beautifully, and the situation had potentials seldom offered a young minister.

Mr. Evers offered me the opportunity to preach on alternate Sundays. This was a great boon, for it gave me the experience of regular preaching yet without the pressure of producing a sermon every week. There had never been an office in the church building, since Mr. Evers had a study in his home. The trustees agreed to provide an office and a part-time secretary for me. Nor had there been Sunday bulletins or a parish paper. I was interested in producing both. Since there was money available, Mr. Evers gave his blessing. He agreed to all my requests and never put any hindrance in my way. During the seven years I was at Union Memorial, I visited him regularly to talk over plans. He was always cordial, sympathetic and supportive. No young minister could have been treated with greater kindness.

However, we were quite different in temperament, and I did not wish to stay long in what was to me a nonproductive atmosphere of congeniality. I was ambitious, was writing articles published in religious journals, was being noticed by denominational leaders. I had ideas and innovations I wanted to try. Mr. Evers had none of this drive. For five years I attended board meetings with him and saw him as a silent observer. I cannot sit quietly by, but want to direct the discussion toward the objectives I have in mind. When I had new programs I wanted to try, I would lay them before Mr. Evers. He usually agreed, and encouraged me to present them to the trustees or deacons. Though we had discussed the matter thoroughly prior to the meeting, when we got there he scarcely ever said a word. He never undercut me, but simply left me to carry the issue with the appropriate board. This was good training for me, but it was not an environment in which I wished to remain long.

Union Memorial Church belonged to the Fairfield County Association of Congregational Christian Churches, one of the oldest associations dating back to the seventeenth century. I was ordained by this group on June 15, 1936. A number of the churches in this association were led by young ministers in their first or second parish. We enjoyed a rich fellowship within which I was nurtured by friendly colleagues, many of whom went on to distinguished ministries.

A focal point that contributed greatly to my development was a prayer group that met fortnightly in the spacious colonial parsonage of New Canaan. Merrill Fowler Clarke was the host pastor, an older man of wisdom. In gathering the group he was joined by Richard Elliott, minister of the Saugatuck Congregational Church in Westport. Dick Elliott had a rich interior life of prayer and meditation, and in a quiet way encouraged us to develop these capacities.

We met late in the afternoon, sat in a circle, and spent forty-five minutes to an hour in silent meditation. Over the decades I have belonged to several ministerial groups who have studied, prepared papers and engaged in discussions. All of these were productive, but none made the lasting impact of this fellowship of silent meditation.

It was during this Glenbrook period that I was married—probably driven in part by the frequently offered admonition that a young minister ought to be married. During a few of our growing-up years, Viola Mann from the Benicia church and I from the Fresno church had attended the annual summer conference for Congregational youth at the beautiful YWCA center on the beach at Asilomar. We had seen each other at a distance. In August of 1937 we were both on the faculty for the week. She was then a senior at the University of California and state president of the college group. At the conference we were together briefly, and then I left to return to Connecticut. Our courtship was mainly by correspondence. I visited her home during the Christmas vacation, we announced our engagement in the spring, and were married in her home church on June 26, 1938.

We really did not know each other. From the first it was not a good marriage. By temperament we were not well matched, but we stayed together for thirty-four years until we were divorced in 1972. Vi is an exceptionally fine person, and she made an excellent minister's wife. She loves people, has a keen mind, and has been a stalwart help throughout my ministry.

We are both grateful to our friends in Plymouth Church Minneapolis, who were stunned by the announcement of our impending divorce, but who took no sides and stood by both of us. The church officers talked with both of us to be sure that the situation was truly as we described it. They asked us to stay home the following Sunday, when the chairman of the deacons, Lynn G. Truesdell III, reported from the pulpit, saying, "Howard and Vi have supported us over the years; now it is our turn to support them." We have both remained active in Plymouth after this separation.

In 1941, after five years as associate minister at Glenbrook, Vi and I decided it was time to move on. Mr. Evers understood, and said that I was destined to minister in a much larger setting. I notified Dr. Charles C. Merrill at the Board of Pastoral Supply in Boston. Soon we were visited by a committee from the First Congregational Church of Great Barrington, Massachusetts, a beautiful town that is the commercial center for southern Berkshire County. The area minister for the state conference was the Rev. George Tuttle. He and his wife had a beautiful old stone house in Monterey, a few miles from Great Barrington. They were members of the church, had two teenage children at that time, and encouraged us to come. At the end of May in 1941, we left Glenbrook and moved to the first parish where we would be on our own.

7

Great Barrington Years

WE MOVED INTO THE MANSE on Main Street of Great Barrington, Massachusetts, the last week in May 1941. My first official act was to join the police chief in leading the Memorial Day parade up Main Street. We had arrived in town only a few days earlier, and the situation made me feel awkwardly uncomfortable. This was in part because I am not much for parades, but more particularly because in this introduction to the community I was dressed in clerical attire, an oxford grey suit with clerical collar. This was an innovation for me, and one in which I felt conspicuously self-conscious. Out of this episode came a vivid insight into my own nature.

During the five years in Glenbrook, I enjoyed a cordial relationship with a fine group of younger clergy who brought vitality to the Stamford Ministerial Association. The rector of St. John's Episcopal Church was a kindly and generous elderly priest with warm ecumenical instincts. Gerald Cunningham gave encouragement to us younger men. I have always remembered a phrase he used in a note to me because I have never encountered it elsewhere. He wrote, "I have an apartment house full of love for you." This is a unique phrase to suggest abundance. His assistant was a younger man named Stanley Hemsley, who was elected by the parish to succeed him. Stanley was more formal than Gerald. Most of the time he wore the traditional clerical collar and vest. He was friendly and well accepted among our younger clergy, but he somehow gave the impression that as an Episcopal priest, he was in the true apostolic succession and thus a bit more authentic than the rest of us. As a nonconformist, I resented such a supposition and believed that I had as much right as Stanley to dress in the conventional attire of a clergyman.

When I realized that I would be moving to a new church in which the parishioners would have no knowledge of my custom, I decided to make my initial appearance in clerical collar and vest. These I would wear on Sundays and at weddings and funerals. I went to an ecclesiastical tailor in New York and had such a suit made. It was this that I donned in Great Barrington for my initial appearance in that Memorial Day parade.

But I felt very foolish. This was not the real me. It was an artificial pose. Clerical vestments were not a part of my nature. Wearing them was a gesture made in response to an assertion by someone else for whom such an act was genuine. I wore this suit for a few Sundays, and probably it would have been accepted by the congregation as proper attire for a minister. Yet each time I realized that this was an act in which I was responding to an outside norm, and that such behavior undercut my integrity. I am who I am. My proper role as a pastor and teacher is to be myself, and to witness through word and deed those insights which the Holy Spirit has given me. Other clergy may have traditions and insights to which they are entitled, but I destroy my own validity if I imitate or follow them.

After a few Sundays I retired my clergy suit to a closet and have never worn it since!

The First Congregational Church of Great Barrington is a lovely situation, and fortunate is the young minister who makes his start there. Few remain very long before they are called to important posts. Two of my living predecessors became moderators of the General Council of Congregational Churches in the years before the merger. Oscar E. Maurer, beloved pastor of Center Church New Haven, was in Great Barrington from 1907 to 1909, and Vere V. Loper served from 1919 to 1921 before going to Plymouth Church Denver and then First Church Berkeley, California. Both were held in great esteem as elder statesmen in Congregationalism.

The church was gathered in 1743 by the Reverend Samuel Hopkins, a pivotal figure in New England theology. It took more than a century for the early settlers to make their way westward from Cape Cod and Massachusetts Bay. The topography of New England has three major valleys or rivers running north and south. First to be reached was the Connecticut River on which are Springfield and Hartford. Beyond rise the beautiful Berkshire Hills, through which cuts the Housatonic and its towns of Danbury, Great Barrington, Pittsfield and Williamstown. Beyond the river the hills rise again to descend into the Hudson River Valley of New York State, which was settled earlier by Peter Stuyvesant and the Dutch.

Samuel Hopkins was a brilliant but cantankerous soul around whom controversy readily swarmed. During his twenty-year tenure in Great Barrington, there were many quarrels within the congregation. A meeting would be called in which the members voted to dismiss him, but within a short period a rival faction called another meeting in which his supporters prevailed. These struggles are marvelously preserved in the church record books, written in longhand. After twenty years he was called to Newport, Rhode Island, where he wrote his monumental volume on theology which became the classical version of Calvinism in America. His teachings, known as "Hopkinsianism," were the rallying point for orthodoxy for more than a century. He held that one must submit unconditionally to the will of God and be willing to be damned if the will of God requires it.

The Hopkins family has a long association with the Berkshires. The distinguished educator, Mark Hopkins, was the grandson of a younger brother of Rev. Samuel Hopkins. His tenure as president of Williams College merited the aphorism that higher education was Mark Hopkins on one end of a log with the student at the other. He had a cousin of the same name who married his own first cousin, Mary Frances Sherwood, whose aunts ran a select school in Great Barrington and later in New York. This Mark Hopkins was a great-grandson of the founding minister, though there is no indication that he ever lived in Great Barrington. He went west to California after the discovery of gold. He made a fortune, and joined with Leland Stanford in building the Union Pacific Railroad, which became the transcontinental link between east and west. He died in 1878, but is remembered because of the fashionable hotel on Nob Hill in San Francisco which bears his name.

On Saturday evening, March 4, 1882, the wood-frame meeting-house of the Congregational Church was demolished by fire. The congregation began immediately to plan for a new stone edifice. Mrs. Mark Hopkins and her brother-in-law Moses Hopkins, each from San Francisco, sent five thousand dollars for the project.

As the new Romanesque edifice was being built in 1882, Mrs. Hopkins bought an adjacent house on the corner, had it moved across the street, and financed a magnificent stone parsonage to connect through cloisters with the chapel and sanctuary. It is said to have cost $115,000 in 1885, and was regarded as the finest ecclesiastical residence in Massachusetts. The house was finished in marbles and woods imported from Europe, with six bedrooms upstairs, five fireplaces, a living room, library, large entry hall and huge dining room. The kitchen was spacious, with ample area for living. Originally the parsonage was furnished, but by the time of our pastorate only a few items remained. The whole complex was more than the townspeople could have afforded, but they were proud of the gifts of Mrs. Hopkins.

Timothy Hopkins, an adopted son of Mark and Mary Frances Hopkins and a life-trustee of Stanford University, underwrote the installation of a magnificent tracker Roosevelt organ in the rear balcony. This organ is the only original Roosevelt left in the United States, and is still regarded as one of the great organs of the country. Through this gift the Congregational church has maintained a strong musical program ever since. When we went there in 1941, the staff consisted of the minister, a full-time organist-choirmaster, and a sexton. There were multiple choirs, from juniors, seniors and adults. Worship was centered in the most handsome pulpit I have ever seen—large, three-sided, but fairly plain in rich mahogany, centered on a deep platform before a recessed Romanesque arch. Painted in this recess was an inscription taken from Isaiah 33:17: "Thine eyes shall see the king in his beauty; they shall behold the land that is very far off."

This quotation seemed to me a strange focus for worship, as it makes the goal of religious living some state in the distant future. With the help of three dedicated women—Florence Logan, Marjorie Evans and Marjorie Sweet—we had the recessed area painted to remove the inscription. In its place we hung a dossal cloth of crimson damask, with a brass cross suspended before it.

In Great Barrington we found a vibrant congregation of interesting people who deeply loved their church. They had gone through some difficult experiences. My predecessor was a controversial figure whose life-style aroused such questions as finally forced him to leave. The minister before him was elderly, an exemplary gentleman, but with whom nothing very exciting had happened. The people were ready for leadership, and they welcomed Vi and me with real warmth. We enjoyed probably the three happiest years of our married life in that parish. The four hundred members knew each other well, had been long-time neighbors, and showed none of the factionalism which can characterize smaller communities. We were accepted into their lives and soon felt at home among friends, many of whose friendships continued to be close after we left in three short years. I was nearing my thirtieth birthday when we arrived, and eager for a pastorate on my own.

An amusing incident of introduction has brought many chuckles to us. Like many New England towns, Great Barrington in this century had received so many immigrants from Europe that the Roman Catholic population far exceeded that of the Yankee descendants who traced their Congregational lineage. St. Peter's Roman Catholic Church was a large granite structure two blocks north whose communicants far outnumbered the Congregationalists, the Episcopalians and the Methodists. The public school system was strongly influenced by this fact, as many of the young women of the town went away to Catholic training colleges and returned to be teachers in the local schools. The superintendent, however, was an active member of our church and superintendent of our Sunday school. On our first Sunday he welcomed me and presented me to the boys and girls, concluding, "I want you to meet our new pastor, Revener Conn." Whenever I am introduced by whatever title, I am reminded of the strangest one of all, when I was called "Revener!"

Summer is a pleasant time to begin a pastorate in the Berkshires, for there are many seasonal visitors and the surrounding hills are lovely. The spacious lawns behind the church and manse provide appropriate setting for receptions and afternoon vespers. The Summer Bazaar of the Women's Guild is an annual attraction that is a social event as well as a financial source for the ladies' work. The summer home of the Boston Symphony at Tanglewood in nearby Lenox was getting started in those days, and Ted Shawn was developing his dance theater at Jacob's Pillow. Vi and I were regular attendants on Friday afternoons for many years at the latter, where we received a broadening education in the three phases of dance: classic, ballet, and ethnic.

In our first seven months we received nineteen new members. The church had an average attendance of 211, with local expenses in 1941 being $7,862, and benevolence gifts of $1,009. In our second year we received fifty-three new members and nearly doubled benevolence giving. The church was clearly moving forward, and the people were enthusiastic.

The atmosphere of our ministry was shaped by World War II, because our tenure was during the dark hours of that conflict. I recall vividly that we heard the news of the bombing of Pearl Harbor over our car radio on Sunday afternoon, December 7, 1941, as Vi and I were driving to Northfield, Massachusetts, where I was to be preacher at the evening service at the Northfield School for Girls. Several of our families sent their high school daughters to this excellent boarding school, which had been founded by Dwight L. Moody. Many missionary families in far countries sent their children home to the Northfield schools, so word of this broadening of the war brought some uneasiness to students whose parents might be in possible danger zones.

By the end of 1942, we had fifty-seven members of the parish away in military service. A weekly service of intercession was held on Thursday afternoon. We tried to keep an accurate mailing list and to send frequent reports.

A dramatic coincidence occurred on V-E Day. The Committee for War Victims and Services of our Congregational Church Council had brought to this country for speaking engagements the Rev. Leslie Cooke, whose church building at Coventry, England, had been completely destroyed by the German blitzkrieg over that city. Because I was chairman of the western Massachusetts committee to raise funds for this relief, Dr. Cooke was assigned to spend two days with us. I had made appointments for him to speak to the ministers in Pittsfield, forty miles north. It was while we were on our way to that assignment that word of the Normandy Invasion came. Such news of course made a strong emotional impact on this Englishman, who had experienced his country threatened and damaged by the Nazi. This was the long-awaited turning point in the struggle of the free world.

Back in Great Barrington, all the school children were taken to their respective churches for impromptu prayers for victory and for peace. Leslie Cooke and I had gone to Pittsfield, but the Congregational church was opened up as were the others. It was Vi who led the service that morning. She was eminently qualified to do so, and made a significant contribution on a historic occasion.

The war years brought marked changes in patterns of living for those of us who remained at home. Goods and gasoline were scarce. Rationing was instituted. It was costly and unwise to winter-heat a house as large as the manse, so we kept the thermostat low in most areas and moved into the kitchen for daily living. It was a large kitchen with a center space ample for a crib and three comfortable chairs. We installed a kerosene stove for warmth.

Blackouts were a part of the civil defense program. A center at Boston was in direct communication with defense centers around the state that were manned by civilians. I was on duty at the center above the fire department for four hours every Friday morning. I was also a warden for our neighborhood, under the direction of Leo Wells, a fine Catholic layman who operated a camera shop. A wall telephone in the manse was in a center stair hall in which there were no outside windows. Thus I could use a light in that area while calling neighbors to inform them of a night-time blackout when no light was to be visible from any window. There never was any air raid on American cities, but civil defense was wise in developing a system to cope with such an eventuality.

Every misfortune carries with it a compensating value, so that we learn as well as suffer from any disaster. Horrible as the Second World War was to civilization, I think that the atmosphere of solidarity and patriotism it engendered brought forth some noble responses in the American people. As I look back on those Great Barrington years, I think we cultivated a spirit of caring and generosity that brought strength to our church. Our denomination established a national Committee for War Victims and Services, which focused on the dislocations and sufferings of people caught in this world tragedy. Through my studies in world religions, I had early developed a universal perspective and a concern for global issues. As the pastor of a major church in the Berkshires, I was named chairman of this humanitarian effort for western Massachusetts.

At the end of my first seven months in Great Barrington I concluded my "Report of the Minister" to the annual meeting with this paragraph:

> All of us must now face the fact that our Church life for the period immediately ahead will be set in the midst of a world at war. We can be thankful for the Eternal Word that has been committed to us, and we must pledge ourselves that the Ministry of that Word be continued undimmed by the darkness of the hour to which it comes. As members of the Church of Jesus Christ we have a vision that lifts us above the discouragements of the hour. Ours is also a gospel of reconciliation. Only as we remain true to that vision and that gospel shall we have an eternal hope to bring to the confusion of men. On the level of politics and strategy we may have differences of opinion among our membership. In the spirit of goodwill we shall seek to understand and allow for these differences. But on the higher level of the spirit we shall be united in the Church of Jesus Christ to give ourselves to the glory of God and the brotherhood of all mankind.

I instituted a World Service Fellowship of those who would come together for a monthly "Hunger Supper," hear a speaker on missions or human needs, and contribute a dollar a month for the CWVS work. The response was excellent. We had between forty and fifty persons at each meeting. The suppers were potluck and proved to be far more bountiful that the name "hunger" implied. The first year we raised $872 for the CWVS, which was the fifteenth largest contribution among the four hundred churches in the Massachusetts Congregational Conference. In addition, this attention to human needs also doubled in one year the amount contributed to benevolence causes.

Far more important than the money was the spirit which this World Service Fellowship stimulated in the congregation. People were brought closer together because they were sharing in an extra-mile responsibility. They became more caring and more loving. Despite the fact that we were addressing human suffering, those supper evenings together were not solemn or sad occasions. They exuberated love and happiness at being a part of a committed group within a larger congregation. Those three years of my ministry at Great Barrington were remarkably creative in accomplishments. I think the secret lay in this World Service Fellowship, for here some wonderful people were brought together in a relationship of voluntary caring.

The experience of this fellowship underscored my understanding of love, that it is the one gift that is not diminished but increased through giving. If I give you a dollar, I am a dollar poorer and you are a dollar richer. A shift in our relative standing has taken place. But if I care enough about you to perform some act of loving service, both of us are enriched. Love is never diminished by giving, but is instead enlarged. We often compete for the goodwill and affection of others, and become jealous of those upon whom praise is lavished. In actuality, those who love others will be more inclined to love us also, because caring support is not given from a diminishing supply but from loving hearts who become more caring as they reach out to one another. This is a lesson many people—including ministers— need to learn.

One of the challenges in any church is to get younger people involved. The Great Barrington Congregational Church had not had a high school youth group, so we set about to form one. That first summer we had only a month to recruit for summer conference, but took three youths with us to the Connecticut Congregational discussions on the college campus at Storrs. I was on the faculty to teach a course on the Old Testament prophets. From this beginning we got a Pilgrim Fellowship youth group organized for Sunday evening meetings, and the second summer took twelve youths to the Massachusetts Conference at Williston Academy in Southampton. Both Vi and I were on the faculty, I serving as chaplain.

Another segment important to a church is younger families. In this parish a Married People's Club had been in existence for many years whose forty members represented a fair portion of the church's leadership. Even though these were war years, there were yet many younger families in the community. I was thirty and Vi was twenty-four, so we felt an affinity with this age group. In the fall of 1941 we invited several young couples to an evening in the manse, at which we presented the possibility of forming a group. The response was good, and soon we had an excellent fellowship established. The husbands were young businessmen in this town, which is the shopping center for the south Berkshire area. During our three years in which we received nearly two hundred new members into the church, these younger families constituted a large portion of our growth, and many of them remained to become leaders. In its second year, Vi directed this group in a beautiful and moving rendition of the third act of *Family Portrait*, a dramatization of the family of Jesus. This was well received by the community during the Easter season.

As I look back, I delight in the memory of how formative that period was in my own development. I learned a great deal from a congregation that was kind and receptive to leadership, and I gained confidence in developing a ministry that was expressive of my inner vision of what a church should be. We were busy because we were situated in a moment when significant things were happening. Again, the Hand Always Above My Shoulder must have guided us to be at this unique church at this particular time. I could not have had better preparation for the major ministry awaiting me than the Great Barrington experience.

Two major events took place. One was the church's bicentennial. This came in the middle of my brief pastorate, and enabled us to bring into focus the story of those two hundred years since Samuel Hopkins had gathered what he characterized as "a peculiar people" into a Congregational church. He became a prominent figure in New England theology, so the church had an illustrious origin. The annals of those two hundred years were preserved in the record books of the parish clerks. These were written in longhand, and until recent times contained rather full accounts of controversies and decisions. It is sad that in my lifetime church records have become terse legal reports that reveal none of the drama and human elements of parish life, so future historians will have scant access to the tough processes and emotions which congregations undergo in various crises.

I had access to all the record books going back to the days of Samuel Hopkins. In the town library I read through the weekly editions of the *Berkshire Courier*, in which journalism flavored factual reporting with personal comments. It was a delightful experience.

The church encouraged me to write a historical book for the bicentennial, and I entered into this project with enthusiasm. The research as well as the writing brought many hours of delight.

The Congregational church had artistically designed Sunday bulletins printed by the *Berkshire Courier* printing company, whose office was down a block on Main Street. I thus had ready access to the print shop, and was always concerned with details of layout and typography. I was greatly helped by the foreman, Mr. James S. Sinclair, a member of the church and active in the Married People's Club, who was an artist. As a native to the Berkshires, he was also interested in history. I thus had a printer with whom I could go over every detail and who was as anxious as I that we produce a creditable volume. He researched the early records of the first meetinghouse, and for the end papers drew a handsome sketch of the seating and interior arrangements.

In the summer of 1943 we produced a hard-cover book of 178 pages that traced the seventeen pastorates from Samuel Hopkins onward. The paper stock, the design, the type, and the binding were of high quality. I hope the content makes as good reading as the appearance! I am proud of this accomplishment. It is the first of four major books that I have authored.

The second major event was the redecoration of the sanctuary. The 1882 architect had designed a Romanesque sanctuary something like *Appolonarus en Classe* outside of Ravenna, Italy. The two outer sections are one story high, about twenty feet wide, then rise the length of the nave to a clerestory supported by columns. A peaked roof rests on this, the walls bound together by wooden trusses. It is a handsome sanctuary, quite large and expensive to maintain. In the years prior to my time, repairs had been neglected because of costs. In 1942 the "parish house," as it was called, was repainted and reroofed. This included the classrooms, dining room, fellowship hall and kitchen, which comprise a one-story section attached to the sanctuary. This was a significant undertaking, and preceded the major 1943 project of repairing the slate roof and repainting the sanctuary.

The original decorations were colorful stencils in arabic designs. Greens, oranges, yellows and light blues were blended tastefully. It was impossible in modern times to reproduce these. In Great

Barrington there was a talented Italian painter named Eugene Caligari. He was excellent with colors and with painting battered doors to resemble wood grain. To him was given the task of redecorating the sanctuary with soft colors selected by the committee, but without the stencil details. The first part of the assignment was the erection of scaffolding from which to reach the higher walls. During the summer of 1943 we watched the progress through a forest of scaffolding as the painters worked on the high ceiling and clerestory, while we worshipped in the adjoining parish room that had been redone the year before. It was an exciting Sunday when we returned to the sanctuary to celebrate two hundred years of faith and service of that historic congregation.

In October of that year, our newly redecorated sanctuary was the setting for a significant wedding, which in a way we did not realize at the time was to be a link between our Great Barrington ministry and what lay ahead in Minneapolis. The Hand Always Above My Shoulder was weaving a pattern out of seemingly isolated strands. The manager of the local textile mill was a devoted churchman and energetic businessman who illustrates what a caring layman can do to develop a minister. We see many instances of a clergyman shaping and building a congregation, but we do not always realize that a layperson may also be instrumental in developing a young minister.

Byron Allen and his wife Clara Louise loved the church deeply and were involved in every aspect of its life. They were a couple in their mid-forties when we came. They had a spacious home and three fine young children in their teens, two boys and a girl. Though many of the families offered us a close friendship through the fellowship of this loving congregation, the Allens were especially warm. Their home was open to us as though we were part of the family. They gave good counsel and suggestions. With them we could talk freely.

Byron Allen soon became convinced that I was destined to be a major religious figure, and he told the congregation that they would not long have this young minister as their pastor. His vision was that someday I would be chosen to succeed Dr. Ralph W. Sockman of New York as the preacher on the weekly broadcasts of the National Radio Pulpit. The forties were before the days of television, when evangelists would usurp religious programming by buying broadcast time. Up to then the networks donated time as a public service, with arrangements made through an interdenominational council.

The most popular of the programs was the weekly sermon of Dr. Sockman, minister of Christ Methodist Church in New York City, a preacher of extraordinary talent who related Biblical truths to human situations with courage and insight. Byron Allen's prediction for me did not come true, but neither was it entirely off the mark. In 1954 I was chosen by the Congregationalists, when it was their turn, to be the summer replacement for Dr. Sockman, and my sermons were broadcast across the country for thirteen Sundays.

Byron had a heart attack before I left Great Barrington and retired from active supervision of the mill. He was able to pursue many interests with vigor, and during my early years in Minneapolis wrote me many longhand letters of encouragement and appreciation. He had a lasting influence on my life because he believed in me and nurtured confidence and ambition.

The Allen's daughter Jane was a vivacious and beautiful young girl who attended the Barrington School for Girls, which was one of the prestigious finishing schools for young women. Her older brother Bob attended Princeton, where he developed a friendship with Leonard Vaughn Dayton of a prominent Minneapolis family. Two brothers, George and Draper Dayton, who were devout Presbyterian laymen, had established a department store at the turn of the century that flourished. Draper died at a relatively young age, leaving several children, of whom Leonard was the youngest. George Nelson Dayton took over the store. His five sons later merged it with Hudson's of Detroit and made Dayton-Hudson Corporation one of the merchandising giants of the country. All the Daytons have been people of integrity, vision, civic responsibility and Christian stewardship.

Bob Allen introduced Leonard Dayton to his sister Jane, and soon Len was coming to Great Barrington over weekends. Because Vi and I were young and were close to the family, we developed a friendship a minister seldom has with a young couple before their marriage. On October 9, 1943, our newly decorated sanctuary was filled for their wedding. Many members of the Dayton family came from Minneapolis for the event, after which Jane and Len went to

Evanston, where he joined the investment firm of an older brother.

Our ties to Great Barrington extended beyond the years of our pastorate through two events in our family. Though our marriage had not gone well from the first, Vi and I felt as do many troubled couples that perhaps having children would bring us closer together. Our first daughter Judith was born on February 15, 1943, a Valentine baby who has been a joy to both of us ever since. Our doctor was a fine young man who had come out of central Europe prior to the war, and had come to Great Barrington as a bachelor. Dr. Arthur L. Cassel came to the Congregational church where we welcomed him and regarded him highly as a friend as well as a physician. He married a talented nurse and soon established a fine practice. Judy was delivered by Caesarean section. Katrina Lord, one of the active women of the parish, sat with me in the father's waiting room while the delivery was taking place. After that I was not permitted to visit in the hospital because I came down with mumps! Judy was the first child born to a manse family since the days of Vere Loper twenty years earlier, and the congregation was delighted. When Vi was carrying our second child in 1946, she returned early to the Berkshires that she might have Dr. Cassel again. Janet was born amidst a tornado on June 11, 1946. Both girls are proud to this day to recall that they are Great Barrington children.

The other tie was through a wonderful old 1750 Berkshire farmhouse that we owned for fifteen years, and around which all four of us have happy memories. We came into this possession by circumstances strange and auspicious. My father had died in 1934 while I was still at seminary in New Haven, and I had come into a small inheritance. In 1937, during my first year at work, I had bought an acre lot in a new development off Middlesex Road in Darien. It was a lovely spot with a small brook running through it. The year of our marriage, a contractor in our congregation whose work was slow arranged to build us a house on this property. We built a two-story colonial with hardwood floors, nice paneling, spacious rooms and a large library over a two-car garage. It was one of the nicest houses we ever lived in. We had occupied it about two years when the call to Great Barrington came. This was to be my first job on my own. I wanted to concentrate on ministry and not be distracted by rental property. We put it on the market, and it quickly sold for $17,500.

With the coming of World War II a few months later, it soon became worth several times that. With today's inflation it is a valuable residence in Connecticut's Fairfield County.

This gave us a nest egg when we moved to the palatial manse of the Great Barrington church. I have always suspected that one of the features about us that attracted the pulpit committee was that we had handsome furniture to fit nicely into the large house which they provided their minister!

We thought it would be pleasant to transfer our investment to a country place we might enjoy regardless of our location. One day in August I spoke to Frank Lord, one of our active members who was a partner in Wheeler & Taylor, the largest real estate firm in south Berkshire. He said he knew just the place and took us to the house, which we knew at first glimpse would be a dream-come-true. It is a two-story white colonial high on a ridge exactly eleven miles from our church. It is now in the town of Monterey, but was built in 1750 as the manse for the church in Tyringham. It sits in the midst of two hundred acres, on which are remains of the old cemetery and through which the ancient Hartford-Albany Post Road passed. The floors and the paneling are original, beautiful wide pine and maple boards. It is built around a central dry-wall chimney, arched in the cellar for strength, off of which are five fireplaces. There is a large meadow below the house and another behind, but the rest of the property is heavily wooded. Old paths reveal spots where the sap from sugar maples was boiled in earlier days.

The property had been farmed until the turn of the century, and was known as the old Carrington place. It was abandoned about that date and vacant until restored in the early twenties by a Yale professor of mining, B. Britton Gottsburger and his wife. They had enjoyed it for twenty years as a summer place. She had died the year before, and he was too old to manage it alone. He was attracted to Vi and me. He could see that we had a feel for history and that we loved beautiful things. He thought that as minister of the nearby Great Barrington church we would preserve and love it as had he and his wife. In September of 1941 he sold it to us for $7,500, which he said was "just peanuts" to him and not as important as the appreciation for this lovely old place which he was passing on to us.

We did indeed love it. Mr. Gottsburger had restored the manse to structural soundness and had developed beautiful stone-walled gardens and terraces that sloped down to the lower meadow. He had done almost nothing in interior decoration, which gave both of us opportunity to express our interest in color and artistry. We began buying early American furniture, cranberry glass and Staffordshire plates. I developed skill in wallpapering which I have continued to practice in all the houses in which we have lived. The Second World War commenced within a few months after our purchase, and so for the three years we were in Great Barrington we could not go on extensive travels. But from May to September we were able to spend a lot of time in the country, just eleven miles from door to door. Being in the same telephone exchange, we were in contact with our parishioners, many of whom lived a similar distance in outlying villages. We entertained groups there, and over ensuing summers for eleven years we returned to what we called "The Farm." It was the scene of many picnics and potluck Sunday dinners for large numbers of our Great Barrington friends.

Both Judy and Janet came to love the place as we did, but as they got into their teens they naturally wanted to be with children their own age. They no longer enjoyed spending the summer in the midst of two hundred acres! I realized that it was no longer feasible to make the long drive eastward each summer, and that the family would be better served by a lakeside cabin in northern Minnesota. It was with real reluctance that we decided to sell, and it took three summers before a buyer came forth. Two young men who were antique dealers in New York bought it from us in 1958 for $16,000. I have been buying and selling real estate throughout my life, and have been involved in some twenty-seven transactions. This is the only property I truly regret selling. To see it again would break my heart, but the memory of happy times remains.

When the second of the two 1958 buyers died nearly thirty years later in 1988, he left the property to a public trust, that it might be enjoyed as a historic landmark. At that time the county assessor's valuation was $385,000! I would have had difficulty paying the real estate taxes on such a summer home!

8

From the Berkshires to Minneapolis

IF ANY SINGLE EVENT DEMONSTRATES the wonder of the the Hand Always Above My Shoulder, it is my call to the pulpit of Plymouth Congregational Church of Minneapolis, Minnesota. Through an amazing mesh of circumstances, a young minister of thirty-three in a small New England town was catapulted to one of the most prestigious parishes in the nation. None of the usual channels of ecclesiastical advancement were involved, for no regional or national denominational official had any knowledge that this move was taking place until the call was publicly announced. In a surprising way the usual procedures were bypassed, and the selection made spontaneously, quickly, and directly. So many strands in my own life interests and the history of Plymouth Church were brought together in a way that surely suggests the artifice of some Divine Architect. The beauty of it far exceeds any planning I could have made.

Perhaps the circumstances can be traced in their beginnings to an event that occurred in the fall of 1941. I was appointed to be chaplain for the 132nd annual meeting of the American Board of Commissioners for Foreign Missions, which is the oldest foreign missions board in the United States, having been formed out of the famous Haystack Meetings at Williams College in 1804. This is the overseas work of American Congregationalism. To have been chosen chaplain when I was only thirty years of age was an honor. Through my backyard newspaper of boyhood days and my high school paper, I had begun early to write, a discipline I have continued throughout my life. While in seminary at Yale, I had written religious articles that were published in the Universalist journal, *The Christian Leader*, in the Congregational magazine, *Advance*, and in the Quaker paper, *The Friend*. These had brought me to the attention of some of the elder statesmen of our denomination. I had been called to a Berkshire parish that was near the setting of this American Board meeting, Springfield, Massachusetts. Also, Dr. Hugh Vernon White, who as minister of a California Congregational church had known me as a boy and had preached my ordination sermon, was now theologian on the staff of the American Board. Probably these were factors that led to the invitation to be chaplain.

One of the giants of Congregationalism during the first half of this century was Rockwell Harmon Potter. He was a short, rotund man with a deep voice that could fill any sanctuary or auditorium. He was a raconteur par excellence who could embellish any incident to make it into a choice story. At national gatherings he would sit in a hotel lobby or lawn chair and soon be surrounded by a group eager to hear his stories. This gift for recognizing what is of interest to people made him a popular preacher in great demand. He had a keen mind and perceptive judgment to give substance to the charm he exuded.

Dr. Potter was truly a giant of his time. At an early age, he had been called in 1900 to the pastorate of Center Church Hartford, which gave him a strategic position in the geographical heartland of Congregationalism. He understood our heritage. He always referred to the building not as "the church" but as "the meetinghouse." After a twenty-five year pastorate, he was made dean of Hartford Theological Seminary, one of our best.

Another of his interests was foreign missions, and for several terms he had been president of the American Board. By 1941 he was retired both from the seminary and the board, but was present at the Springfield meeting. On that occasion he heard me for the first time and took an interest in me. It was an easy two-hour drive from Hartford to Great Barrington, and several times over the next three years he would telephone on a spring or fall morning to ask if he might drive up for lunch with Vi and me. In his extravagant language, he described our residence as "The Parsonage Palatial and the Manse Magnificent." We became good friends, and he seemed to regard me as one of his students, for he always signed himself "The Old Dean."

Dr. Potter was a favorite at Plymouth Minneapolis, and was guest preacher for two summer months of 1941. He became the link between me and my future congregation.

Plymouth at that moment was having difficulties, and was in a slump from the high point to which it had been accustomed for many decades. The church had been gathered in 1857, when many New Englanders had come to find their fortunes in the west. It grew rapidly and attracted many of the business and professional leaders. In its membership were Pillsburys, Boveys and Crosbys, representing families that had become giants in milling, lumbering and mining. Two of its earlier ministers became presidents of universities. Though this parish was on the western fringe of the denomination, it was recognized for its strength, and hosted several national meetings of denominational boards.

Between 1907 and 1909, Plymouth moved from its downtown location at Eighth and Nicollet to a corner at Nineteenth and Nicollet, which was nearer to the fashionable residences of some of the city's elite. A beautiful Tudor-Gothic structure was built by an astute committee that had a taste for things cultural and European.

At the same time the congregation brought from Portsmouth, New Hampshire, a Boston Brahmin who was to have the longest and most distinguished pastorate to that time. He was Dr. Harry P. Dewey, a minister of intellect, refinement and culture. His sermons were skillfully crafted, and articulated the best scholarship of the day. In the Modernist-Fundamentalist controversy of the twenties, Dr. Dewey was an able exponent of the liberal view. He was dearly beloved by his parishioners. It is said that when the maids in the homes of the wealthy canned fruits and vegetables over the summer, there were always jars set aside to be given to the Dewey family when they returned from their summer holiday in New England.

It was a fairly aristocratic congregation. At one time there were said to be twenty-eight millionaires in the membership. With a salary of twelve-thousand dollars, Dr. Dewey was rumored to be the highest paid minister in the denomination. He had lost some of his investments in the stock market crash of 1928, and he remained in his post until 1935 when he was in his seventies. By that time many of the younger generation of the old families had lost interest, and the church had declined somewhat from its earlier strength when Dr. Dewey was at his peak.

To succeed him the church called Dr. David Nelson Beach, whose father had been pastor in the nineties before he went to head Bangor Theological Seminary. As is often the case, in calling Dr. Beach the church was selecting someone quite different from his predecessor. Dr. Beach was a warm, hearty individual whose spontaneity and informality contrasted with the formality of the previous decades. He formed a group for younger couples that called itself "The First Name Club," in keeping with the new spirit. A significant achievement was the merger that brought the Park Avenue Congregational Church back to Plymouth, which had been its sponsor when it was formed. Some fine families were in this daughter congregation, but they too saw some decline ahead and decided that while they were yet strong they would return. Their decision infused new blood into Plymouth at a time when it was needed, and the harmonious blending of the two congregations was a fortunate move.

After a long and beloved pastorate, the next minister frequently has a difficult time and in many instances must make "a sacrifice bunt." This was the case at Plymouth. The old-timers were cool to Dr. Beach's outgoing approach, and after seven years he accepted a call to the historic Center Church on the New Haven Green. He left Minneapolis in the summer of 1943. The assistant minister, Rev. Arthur J. Snow, was to carry on until a successor could be called. Arthur and his wife Alice were a talented team, both ordained ministers. She guided the church school programs.

The church governing board appointed a strong committee of nine members to select a new minister. Harold G. Cant, a partner in one of the city's major law firms, was named chairman. He was a gentle, kindly man of wise judgment. Others were: Gideon Seymour, executive editor of the *Minneapolis Star and Tribune*, one of the finest Christian laymen I have ever known, the son of a minister with liberal instincts, a strong, influential leader of the community; Felton Colwell, one of the older families with civic consciousness who had built a printing empire; Wadsworth Williams, a conservative but wise investment financier; Mrs. Frank O. Koehler, wife of the general secretary of the YMCA, who died during the year; Edgar F. Zelle, a magnificently gracious, sensitive business and cultural leader who had built a prosperous transportation system; Terrance Hanold, a year younger than I, who then was lawyer for the newspaper but whose genius raised him to legal counsel, treasurer and finally president of the Pillsbury Company; Will Heintz, a businessman who had been a trustee at Park Avenue; and Lenore Potter, a young woman who had been chosen from the youth but soon left the area.

This able group set out to restore the past glory of Plymouth, and to choose the finest Congregational minister in the country. They felt they previously had had this distinction, and that it should be theirs again. How they went about their negotiations I do not know, of course, but was told that they inquired of Boston and New York headquarters to obtain a list of those regarded as ten outstanding ministers. From these ten they hoped to select a winner.

They began their deliberations in the summer of 1943. Various members of the committee went to meet and hear the men on their super list. Gradually one by one these prospects were eliminated as not coming up to the desired standard. By the end of spring in 1944, they had found only one man as suitable, the Rev. Dr. Wallace Anderson, minister of the State Street Church in Portland, Maine. He was a New Englander from the same area from which Dr. Dewey had come, and was a person of culture and ability.

The biennial meeting of the General Council of Congregational Christian Churches met in Grand Rapids toward the end of June in 1944. Every two years, this gathering brought together some eleven hundred ministers and lay leaders to review the general work of our denomination. It was an occasion to make friends and to develop contacts. The Plymouth committee invited Dr. Anderson and his wife to come on to Minneapolis after the Grand Rapids convention, to preach and to meet some of the people. They did so and made a favorable impression. At the conclusion of the weekend, the committee voted to extend the call to Wallace Anderson. He asked for two weeks in which to consider the matter, and returned with his wife to Maine. Sometime later he responded with appreciation for the honor of the invitation, but he declined, saying that he had never lived west of the Hudson River and could not picture himself ministering in the west. He was a New Englander by instinct and training.

This declination placed the committee in a predicament. They had been at their task a year. They had exhausted their list of possibilities. The congregation was becoming restless without acknowledged leadership. Some members were drifting to Westminster Presbyterian Church, a sister downtown church of Plymouth, to hear the powerful preaching of Dr. Arnold Hilmer Lowe. People were asking why the committee was taking so long. The church had secured Dr. Potter for a two-month period, and he was rejuvenating the situation. But his time was to be brief. What was to be done?

At this point Harold Cant invited Dr. Potter to lunch at the Minneapolis Club and explained to him their predicament. Dr. Potter responded with his usual enthusiasm. "Your committee is making a big mistake. You are trying to get the finest minister in the country. But such a person is already a prima donna, set in his ways. He might not fit well into Plymouth. What you ought to do is to find a young minister of promise who is on his way up. You can help train him in the way you want a minister to develop. Together the congregation and the young minister both could grow, and you might have a happy marriage to last for years."

"That sounds like a good idea, but we never thought of that," Mr. Cant responded. Then he asked the crucial question, "But where do you find such a person?"

Dr. Potter was never hesitant with counsel, and he said, "I know just the young minister who could grow to be a credit to you. He is in Great Barrington, Massachusetts." He gave his impressions of me, and concluded by saying, "He is not one of my boys, but Luther Weigle's. Why don't you write to him and get his opinion?"

Luther A. Weigle had been dean of Carleton College before becoming dean of Yale Divinity School. Harold Cant, his wife and many Plymouth members were Carleton graduates, so the name of Dean Weigle meant something to them. A short time later Mr. Cant phoned Dr. Potter to say, "Dean Weigle thinks even more highly of this young man than you do!" "I know he does," was the reply. "That is why I encouraged you to write!"

As a result of these recommendations I received a letter from the chairman of the pulpit committee, one of the strangest and in some ways one of the most pathetic I ever received. It said that Plymouth Church of Minneapolis was looking for a minister and that my name had been presented. This brief one-page letter then asked if I had any suggestion as to procedure. This came as a total surprise. I had never heard of this particular church, and had no thought of ministering in the midwest. I felt at home with New England Congregationalism. However, by referring to the denominational yearbook I recognized that this was a strong church.

By letter I replied that the normal procedure is for the committee to send representatives to the place of the prospect, to become acquainted with him and his ministry, and to get some impression of his standing in the community. I then said that I would not consider a church without visiting it. If the committee wished to shorten the process, I would be willing to come to Minneapolis to be interviewed there.

Within a few days I received a telegram inviting me to come the third weekend in August, to conduct morning worship and to preach in a neighborhood Congregational church. To this invitation I quickly assented.

Of course I immediately told my leading layman, Byron Allen, who had encouraged me to prepare for an important ministry and who had told the congregation that they would not keep me long in Great Barrington. The excitement was enhanced by the fact that the Allen daughter Jane had been married the year before to Leonard Dayton of a prominent Minneapolis family. All the Daytons were Presbyterians in Westminster. They would have no direct relations with Plymouth, but would have many friends in the social and business network represented by the congregations of the major parishes. Len and Jane at that time were living in Winnetka while Len was working in the brokerage office of an older brother.

We contacted them, and they were excited about the prospect. We had become good friends through the months of their courtship, and we were close to the Allen family. I would stay overnight with them en route. They phoned Glenn and Esther Wyer, who were staunch Plymouthites and whose home on Lake Minnetonka was next door to Leonard's family home. The Wyers then invited me to dinner on the Saturday evening before my Sunday appointment with the pulpit committee.

I can get ahead of the story by saying that when I did reach Winnetka on Friday, Jane was about to be delivered of their first child, and when I returned on Monday she was in the hospital with Lindsay. Within two years Leonard and Jane moved to Minneapolis to become associated with Smith Barney & Company. They took over the Minnetonka home, and because of our background friendship they joined Plymouth, where they quickly became active. They were one of the four largest families in our church school.

Nineteen forty-four was prior to the days of air travel, so I made the trip by train. When I arrived on Saturday, I was met at the depot by Mr. Cant and taken to the Minneapolis Club, where a room had been reserved. We were joined by Mr. William Heintz of the committee. After lunch these two gentlemen drove me to see Plymouth Church for the first time. It is a noble building, impressive from the outside, with its yellowish-orange and gray stones, its leaded windows in the parish house portion. Once inside, the sanctuary is inspiring, with its warm trusses and beams, its detailed oak carving across the front, and its glorious stained glass windows. I was happy to note that it had a central pulpit, in true Congregational spirit, as had both Glenbrook and Great Barrington. I liked what I saw and I liked the two men who had met me. They took me back to the Minneapolis Club, and that evening I had a delightful time with the Wyer family on Minnetonka.

Fortunately, that Sunday was a bright, sunny Minnesota day. I was taken to the Forest Heights Congregational Church on the north side, a small church with a declining membership. Besides the pulpit committee and spouses, there were a number of other Plymouthites who had been especially invited. Since I had met only Mr. Cant, Mr. Heintz and the Wyers, I had no way of differentiating between the visitors and the local members. I conducted the service by myself, as the resident minister was away on vacation. There were no printed programs, so I had to announce and direct. I announced that there would be a call to worship, a prayer of invocation, after which we would all sing the Gloria. The opening hymn went all right, but when we reached the point of the Gloria the high school girl at the organ said in a loud stage-whisper, "I can't play that!" I wondered what the people would think of such an error, but proceeded with the worship.

I preached from the words of Jesus to his disciples in Luke 10:23,24: "Blessed are the eyes which see the things that you see; for I tell you that many prophets and kings have desired to see those things which you see, and have not seen them; and to hear those things which you hear, and have not heard them." All generations have had religious intimations and have longed for better understandings. Through the generations there have been developments and gains. We have a potential to go far beyond primitive people, and to grow into a spiritual life that can indeed be a blessing. It is for us to respond and to grow.

After the morning service, the committee members, their spouses and a few invited guests went to the beautiful home of Edgar and Lillian Zelle on Lake of the Isles. There we had refreshments and an opportunity to meet one another and to visit. From the Zelles we went to the Minikahda Club for lunch. These were largely social events, with no formal questioning or discussions.

After the luncheon, I was told that the committee would gather at the Minneapolis Club for lunch on Monday, and that I was to be at Mr. Cant's office at eleven that morning. The afternoon program was a drive around the city conducted by Felton Colwell and Mr. Frank Bean. I presume that after our departure the committee may have convened to make a decision about the candidate. Perhaps it was that evening. I do not know. It was all very casual, without any occasion on which the members grilled me as to beliefs, attitudes or interests.

That afternoon ride, however, was possibly the testing period. Frank Bean was a unique and remarkable man, one of the finest and most interesting with whom I have ever been associated. We became quite close until his untimely death in 1955. His was one of the finest lineages in the Twin Cities, a man of absolute integrity, with a keen mind and great intellectual curiosity. He instilled these qualities in his family. A dictionary and an encyclopedia were in the dining room, so that any moot point in conversation could be immediately checked. His father before him had early failed in the milling business and been forced into bankruptcy. He started again, was successful, and when well established he invited all former creditors to a dinner at which he paid them in full. Such unswerving integrity was in his son, not a man fluent in speech but who meant every syllable of what he said.

He was president of the International Milling Company, whose Robin Hood flour was a household staple along with Pillsbury's Best and General Mills products. He held the Silver Beaver insignia, the highest award of the Boy Scouts of America. He was a loyal friend and supporter of Dr. Donald J. Cowling, president of Carleton College. His philanthropies were many but always given privately and without publicity.

Mr. Bean had not been impressed with Dr. Beach, and the committee regarded it as important that he should approve of the next minister. Within the year he had been made chairman of the trustees, a position he took with some reluctance on the death of E.C. Gale. The custom had been for a person to retain this post for some time, but Mr. Bean did not intend to follow this practice. He was willing to help where he could make a difference, then relinquish the post.

We had quite a conversation that afternoon. I was put in the front seat next to Mr. Bean, with Felton Colwell in the back seat. I was concerned about the future of downtown churches with the trend toward the suburbs, and I was aware that Plymouth was facing some particular problems. Early in the drive I asked Mr. Bean what he thought the future at Plymouth might be. He responded that he did not know if Plymouth had any future! This was a characteristic comment, for he was precise, blunt, often provocative, sometimes insulting. For him this was a form of humor as well as a method of testing. How would the other person respond?

On hearing this blunt comment, Felton Colwell practically leapt over the seat, leaning forward to give a positive answer to my question. He began to enumerate positive things about the church, as if in fear that I might be turned off with the conclusion that this was a no-future situation. We covered a wide field of concerns that afternoon, and it may be that unawares I was being given the grilling which normally would come from a committee.

The next morning I packed my bag for an afternoon departure, and went to Mr. Cant's office as requested. Casey was always quiet and deliberate in his manner. He told me that the committee had decided to call me to be their minister. When this action was taken I do not know. The terms would be the use of the parsonage, which was two blocks from the church, a six-week vacation in the summer, and a salary of five thousand dollars. My circumstances have been such that I have made it a point never to argue with anyone about money. I have never suffered from it, but have been treated generously all through my career. However, I remembered that Dr. Dewey had been paid twelve thousand dollars, and I thought Dr. Beach had received nine thousand. I was getting thirty-six hundred in Great Barrington, so this would be an advance, and I realized that the committee was taking a gamble in calling one so young. So I agreed without any comment.

"However," I said, "I am accustomed to having my summers free. We have a summer place in the Berkshires to which we will presumably go, and I would want a vacation period from Children's Day in June until Labor Day at the first of September." Casey demurred at this, saying that Plymouth gives six weeks whereas most churches grant only a month vacation. He did not think my request would be possible. I stood firm and said that I would not come except with this provision.

We adjourned to the Minneapolis Club, where other members were waiting. Casey explained to them that he had conveyed their decision and told me the terms. I had agreed to accept with the exception of the item about vacation, and that I insisted on being given the entire summer period. I explained to the group that New England was a distance by car, that we had this summer home, that I was accustomed to reading and study in preparation for the year's work. I was not willing to give that up. There was a long silence. Nobody seemed to know quite what to make of the situation. Finally, after what seemed like a long moment, Gideon Seymour spoke. "How many of us attend services during the summer?" Not a single hand went up. "Well," he said, "if we are not going to be there ourselves, and if we have a young minister who wants to spend the summer bettering himself and preparing for his work, I think we should agree to his request." Everyone acquiesced. As I look back, I think that was the best bargain I ever made!

From this hastily arranged weekend that began with a suggestion from Dr. Potter, I went back to the Berkshires with a call from one of the greatest churches in Congregationalism, with a door opened to a future that was to be exciting and rewarding through thirty-two years of active ministry, the longest pastorate in the century and a quarter of Plymouth's history.

Another unusual sidelight to this episode is that the members of the congregation never met me. The traditional procedure of having the committee's choice preach before the people and then be voted upon by them was bypassed. A congregational meeting was called, the committee's report was presented, it was accepted, and a formal vote taken to extend the call. At that point the members voted in faith, but had not actually seen or heard me.

One further incident bears mentioning, not because it was a factor in the call but because it illustrates the amazing interweaving of circumstances that led to the conclusion that a Hand Always Above My Shoulder must have been guiding this entire episode.

I have often commented that I am half a businessman and half a mystic. I am deeply concerned with the inner life and the kinship between the human soul and the divine universe. I have belonged to prayer groups and have studied the devotional classics of Christendom. In this pursuit, I became aware of Glenn Clark, a professor at Macalester College in St. Paul. In August 1924, the *Atlantic Monthly* published an article by him on "The Soul's Sincere Desire," and he began to develop programs for prayer and meditation. He formed a movement called Camps Farthest Out, popularly known as CFO. These were periods at summer camps which were not basically Bible study sessions, but experiments in expression through music, painting, and drama of the latent talents of the human spirit. Glenn Clark wrote several books on the inner life which I read with appreciation.

In the fall of each year, the Massachusetts Congregational Conference held a Pastor's Conference in Springfield as an inspirational gathering for the several hundred of our ministers serving in that state. I was on the Program Committee for the 1944 fall meetings. I urged that Glenn Clark be invited as one of the program speakers. Enough others had heard of him and went along with the suggestion. In the late winter I was authorized to write to invite him. In so doing, I extended a secondary invitation that he come a day early and preach to my people at the Great Barrington church on the Sunday morning preceding the conference. He accepted both invitations.

Only later did I discover that for several years, Glenn Clark had taught a Sunday morning class at Plymouth Church, and that a number of our members were participants in the CFO movement. At the time the invitation was issued, there was no connection whatever between me and Plymouth Church, but when in late September he came to the Berkshires I could tell him to his surprise that I was to be the new minister at the church where on Sunday morning he gathered listeners from many parishes!

We act in seeming independence, only to discover later that our lives are intertwined with others in patterns we never imagined. Surely we are part of a destiny inscrutable, but in which a Hand Always Above Our Shoulder leads to blessings unforeseen.

Thus at age thirty-three, a young minister happy in the Berkshires was called to a great challenge in the midwest.

9

A New Era: A Time of Testing

IN MID-OCTOBER OF 1944, Vi, our twenty-month-old Judy and I left Great Barrington to drive west. When a minister moves from one parish to another, there is often sadness at parting from friends who have become close and meaningful. In our case the separation was tempered by the realization that it was not a final farewell. Because of our 1750 farmhouse eleven miles away in the town of Monterey, we would be returning with the summer.

When we reached Minneapolis, we were guests for a week in the home of Mr. and Mrs. Harry L. Robinson, very gracious seniors who had a spacious home on Blaisdell within a few blocks of Plymouth. Mr. Robinson had made his fortune through the Gamble-Robinson Company, wholesalers of fruits and vegetables from the Pacific coast to the midwest. The Robinsons had been influential members of Park Avenue Church and had facilitated the return of that congregation to Plymouth in 1937. He was on the board of trustees.

The morning *Tribune* sent a reporter to interview us and a photographer who took an excellent picture of Vi and me feeding Judy. This gave some publicity to our arrival.

When the van came with our furniture we moved into the parsonage at the corner of Pillsbury and Franklin. We did not care especially for the house, and were concerned for the safety of a child in that location. Franklin is the equivalent of Twentieth Street, and is an

east-west thoroughfare that runs from the Mississippi River to Lake
of the Isles in the fashionable Kenwood district. Edgar Zelle thought
we would be comfortable there in a location just two blocks from the
church, but he assured me that if all went well after two years we
could have any house we wanted.

This was truly the beginning of a new era for Plymouth Church,
and the people seemed to sense a change of atmosphere. There had
been a transitional ministry after the glory years of Dr. Dewey. A
sense of drift was accentuated by the long search for a new leader.
Perhaps more than they realized, the members were looking for a
fresh start that would make vibrant their parish life. Expectation was
thus the first ingredient of the new era ushered in by my coming.

This element of anticipation is apparent in the notice that was
printed in the Sunday morning bulletin of September 10, 1944,
telling of the business meeting at which a call was extended to me.

> The calling of the Rev. Howard J. Conn to the pastorate of
> Plymouth Church, voted at the meeting of the Church and Society
> last Thursday evening, is reason for all of us to rejoice at our good
> fortune and to extend our thanks to the committee who chose him.
> They have spent long hours in consultation. They have read the
> records on scores of men. They have travelled thousands of miles.
>
> Mr. Conn is a graduate of Leland Stanford University and Yale
> Divinity School, and has done graduate work at Harvard
> University. His academic record throughout has been brilliant. His
> sermons are frequently printed in the *Christian Century Pulpit*. Thus
> we congratulate ourselves on securing for the leadership of
> Plymouth Church this young man from Great Barrington,
> Massachusetts, who comes with every promise of a great future for
> himself and for the Church which he will serve.

Most of the people had never seen me, and my exact age was not
mentioned, but they were stimulated to high expectations.

A second ingredient in the initial response was the honesty of
my opening sermon. I have always been candid in acknowledging
my fears, my doubts, my hesitancies. My experience is that people
will respond to a minister who expresses his true feelings and
thoughts. Their own humanity can relate to his. They will forgive
mistakes and overlook weaknesses, but they resent pretentiousness
and cover-ups.

My sermon was entitled "Two must Face a Third." I have adapted it for my introduction to all four of the interim ministries I have enjoyed in retirement years, for it is expressive of my basic philosophy. The text is from the Old Testament story in II Chronicles, which tells of Asa inheriting the kingdom of Judah. A prophet says to him, "The Lord is with you, while you are with him; and if you seek him, he will be found of you; but if you forsake him, he will forsake you." Asa heeded this warning. He and the people entered into a covenant to seek the Lord God of their fathers with all their hearts and with all their souls.

My opening paragraph was this:

> It is with a very real sense of humility that I stand in this pulpit for the first time to undertake the privileges and responsibilities which you have entrusted to me as your new pastor. The task of the ministry in a great parish such as this would be impossible for any man were it not that the relationship into which we are entering is one of partnership—in which you and I together must work, must pray and must grow. I think of myself as a pilgrim with you in this thrilling adventure of living, and only as we mutually help one another can any of us hope to enter into the Kingdom. But so lofty are the aspirations that bring us together this morning that even you and I together would fail were it not that the partnership which we are launching is more even than a partnership. It is deepened to the level of a fellowship because we covenant not only between ourselves but with Almighty God, to become fellow-workers with Him, to seek and to do his Holy will. As I look into your faces and you look into mine, we not only face each other. The two of us must face a third.

I went on to say that I was somewhat frightened by the challenge, that there were more people in the sanctuary that morning than at any three Easters combined in my New England parishes!

> I hope that this will be a new era—an era of growth, an era of courage, an era of joy, an era of continually deepening fellowship and satisfaction in Plymouth Church. Certainly this is a great congregation here this morning. If every person will decide to come regularly, to pray faithfully and to work generously, then the potentialities of this new era are limitless. I tell you quite frankly that I am not a wonder-man nor a miracle-worker, but I want to be

your true friend and pastor that together we may do the things which none of us could do alone. And so hand in hand we shall build a new era for this distinguished church.

A third ingredient was our love for people. Both Vi and I enjoy friendships and delight in being close to people. The parish was already organized into a Colony system with thirteen colonies and twenty-nine neighborhood groups. Under the auspices of the Colony Council, people were urged to attend one of twenty-nine neighborhood gatherings held in homes to give them an opportunity to become better acquainted with Mr. and Mrs. Conn. During the winter we attended all of these, and thus were brought into closer contact with the membership.

A comment I have cherished came from Mrs. Hamlin Hunt, one of the beloved ladies from the Dewey era whose husband Hamlin Hunt had been the church organist from 1900 until his retirement in 1939. When asked if she had been to one of these informal gatherings to meet the new minister, Mrs. Hunt replied, "No. I think he is wonderful, and I don't want to be disillusioned!" Such a comment showed great wisdom!

The accomplishments of those early years were aided by the support of able persons on the staff that I inherited. Foremost was Miss Hazel Fraker, who had come as Dr. Dewey's secretary in 1921. She was exceedingly well-organized and efficient, a person not given to idle words but one who came right to the point. She was no casual employee, for her loyalty and affection were for Plymouth Church. Over the years she had become Financial Secretary who kept all records. I trusted her advice and came to discuss every new idea with her before launching into action. She continued in office for half of my ministry.

Martha Lobeck was the minister's secretary, a highly intelligent and attractive young woman of Norwegian ancestry. She had an excellent mind for retaining information and handling my filing system. She wanted more out of life than a secretarial career. In August 1951 she left to take an overseas secretarial assignment with the State Department. She was assigned to Vienna with a fine bachelor diplomat, Findley Burns, Jr. After a year they were married. He rose rapidly in the diplomatic service, and became our American ambassador to Jordan. They have had a fine marriage. Martha was a charming hostess in various embassy situations. They are now living in retirement in North Carolina and continue to travel extensively.

Mrs. Matthew (Adele) Anderson had been parish visitor for nearly a quarter century. Dr. Potter described her as "Christian grace personified." She guided me in my pastoral calling, suggesting the families that particularly needed attention and briefing me as to their background. She was beloved by all. I had her assistance for only a year, for in the fall of 1945 as we were starting our second round of Colony meetings, she did not show up at one of these evening gatherings. We got no answer on the phone. Dr. Claude C. Kennedy, who was present, and I drove to her home and found that she had died peacefully of a heart attack.

Also to be mentioned is Clinton Sjosten, who had joined the three-man custodial staff a year before my arrival. He began calling me "Howard" from the first day, and was ever ready to help. Clint stayed through all my thirty-two years, and after retirement is to this day a part-time helper. He knows everybody, remembers all their family connections, and can locate where any item has been stored in the building. He loves to assist at weddings and funerals. His whole life is Plymouth Church, and he is held in affection by all.

The organist and choirmaster was Arthur Bates Jennings, one of the great musicians of his day who over the years contributed greatly to my ministry. Since its gathering in 1857, Plymouth has had a strong music program that attracts community involvement. The earliest choir was invited to sing at many public events.

In 1900 Hamlin Hunt became organist and served until 1939. He was Dean of the MacPhail School of Music, and gave Sunday afternoon recitals that were well attended. Both he and Mrs. Hunt were beautiful embodiments of the old Plymouth during the early years of my ministry. When Mr. Hunt retired, Arthur Jennings had been University of Minnesota organist for a year. He was selected as our music leader in 1939 and served through 1966, when he was made Organist Emeritus.

Mr. Jennings was the son of a well-known New York architect. He was always modest and said that he had to practice continually to maintain his skill. The Jennings had no children but were fond of young people. Among friends they were known as "Herr" and

"Frau." They collaborated on anthems that gained national recognition among choir circles. Among their numbers are "Springs in the Desert" and "Mary to the Temple Went." Herr had a real sense of worship and knew how to make the music flow with the liturgy. This was important, as I regard the mood of worship to be as important as the preaching. Whenever he was in Minneapolis, Dr. Potter quipped that there were many elderly people in the congregation because they were not eager to trade Mr. Jennings's music for the angelic choir!

To get ahead of my story, yet to pay tribute to Plymouth music, I am mentioning at this point later developments. After Mr. Jennings's retirement we had temporary organists for three years, Mary Ann Willow and Marlene Baver, with Charles Schwartz as choirmaster for one year. In 1969 we brought Philip Brunelle to Plymouth. I had seen him as a boy of twelve coming to take lessons from Mr. Jennings. Philip is a music genius, a person of unflagging energy, remarkable with many talents. In addition to his work as organist and choirmaster, he asked to start a Plymouth Music Series that would be independently financed and governed by a board chosen by him. Over two decades this has offered premier concerts that attract crowds, and Philip has gone on to become an acclaimed conductor in England and Scandinavia.

The vitality of worship at Plymouth can be attributed in part to the enthusiasm, skill and dedication of Philip Brunelle. Plymouth must be unique in having had only three organist-choirmasters during the nine decades of the twentieth century, each a musician of national reputation.

To return in my story to the 1940s, it is clear that in coming to Plymouth I was entering a fine tradition and an excellent company of professionals.

One who was keenly concerned was Frank A. Bean, who had tested me first on that automobile ride in August. At the annual meeting in January of 1944, he had been elected to the trustees to replace the long-time chairman, E.C. Gale, who had died in September at age eighty-three. At that same meeting, Terrance Hanold was elected church clerk to replace Stanley Gillam, who had served for many years. Mr. Bean took seriously every responsibility entrusted to him. He was not one to accept a position for the honor it might represent, but assumed that he was chosen in order to accomplish something. It was a learning experience for me to work closely with him until his untimely death ten years later. Without him my ministry could not have been so effectively launched. Though a layman, he understood the principle of Congregational independence in its basic meaning. I often contrasted his simple, clear integrity with the sophistry with which many clergy on the national level tried to justify their complicated interrelationships.

At my arrival Mr. Bean said to me: "We have chosen you to be our minister, and I look upon you as the chief executive officer of Plymouth. You are to use your judgment. If you need a new type-writer, don't ask me about it, but go ahead and get one in the same way I would as chief officer of my company. There is one important difference between you and me, however, that you need to keep in mind. I am the principal stockholder of my company, and you are not the owner of Plymouth Church. Power rests with the congregation. Any time we do not like the way you are operating we can fire you, and there is no power on earth that can save you or guarantee you another job."

That is the simple, straightforward mode of operation in a Congregational church, and I have proceeded on that premise throughout my ministry.

At the first meeting of the trustees that I attended, Mr. Bean put the challenge to me. "This past summer you asked what I thought was the future of Plymouth, and I replied that I do not know whether we have any future. Now we have hired you to lead us into that future. I would like you to come to our next meeting with the program you suggest." I did write an outline which I presented a month later, but Mr. Bean was blunt. "I don't think that is very good. Try again, and see if you cannot come up with something better." This kind of report and rejection went on for several meetings. Out of a sincere desire to get the church moving, and also from his particular sense of humor, he took this form of goading. I often say he tried to make my life miserable that first year, but somehow I realized that it was for my own development. He was testing me and stimulating me. I did not get angry, but tried to respond to all his requests. I was helped by Miss Fraker's support. She confided in me that Mr. Bean would ask her, "How do you think our young man is doing?" When she replied, "Quite well!" he said, "I think so too, but don't tell him!"

My first initiative took place on Christmas Sunday, when I asked the congregation for a special offering of one thousand dollars to finance a parish paper. I have always been interested in writing, and I believe that a weekly or bi-weekly paper mailed to the homes is the best way for a minister to communicate parish programs and needs. People will respond if they feel that the pastor is taking them into his confidence, sharing with them, and reporting the results. They need to be informed and challenged. That morning they contributed $688, and by year-end the full amount was subscribed. Thus the *Chronicle* was originated, with its first issue dated January 15, 1945. I wrote most of it myself, and continued to do so throughout my years.

It is important at the beginning to make a request that may seem too ambitious, and then carry it through. The first success is the foundation for others to come. It encourages a congregation to think that they can do more than they had realized.

My first reception of members was on January 15, 1945, when thirty-eight new friends joined. That morning I preached on an ancient New England phrase, "Bound Together in the Bundle of Life." This was another expression of my basic philosophy that a church is a fellowship of people who are seeking meaning for their lives and bind themselves together in mutual support.

At the beginning of 1945, Plymouth had 1,497 persons on its rolls. By the end of 1945, we had taken in 137 new members. I had officiated at thirty-three funerals, nineteen weddings and fifty-two baptisms. The average attendance was 693. The 1944 budget was $47,005; 1945, $52,250; 1946, $67,560. The endowment at my coming was $65,000.

In those early years I did a lot of calling in homes. Weekday afternoons I visited hospitals and members. On Saturday and Sunday afternoons I called on newcomers and prospects whose names I had obtained. In the 1940s and 1950s, people were not as busy outside their homes, and they were generally flattered that a minister would seek them out. Over the years this changed. People became more jealous of their privacy, and random calling became increasingly difficult. I look back with pleasure on the contacts I made with people when I could visit with them spontaneously and informally. I was not embarrassed by whatever they might be doing and tried to put them at ease so that they were not embarrassed. I would go to the basement, the backyard, or the garage, wherever the husband might be working.

Young couples have always been one of the foci of my ministry. It never disturbs me that college students stay away from churches, for they are in the freedom, innovative years. They are exploring new possibilities. Later when they marry and have children, they often return to religion. Thus the ages of twenty-five to forty are the critical period for formulating beliefs, values, and lifestyles. If a minister can bring an intellectual as well as emotional appeal, if he can show warmth and friendliness, if he can introduce them to a fellowship of kindred persons, he may have a lasting influence for good upon these young families.

As I made these calls that first winter, I made note of couples that I thought would be congenial. Though there were 240 Plymouth men and women who served in World War II, there were still a substantial number of young families in town. Vi and I invited sixteen couples to our parsonage on Franklin Avenue one evening. We had some mixers to acquaint them with one another, and then I suggested the formation of a couples' group. I told of our experience with such in Great Barrington, said that we hoped to be at Plymouth for a long time to come, and that by relating to one another we could grow old together. They responded favorably. Several declared that they would not want a larger group because this number could meet in homes. It was Terrance Hanold who suggested that we call ourselves "Local Number One," and that if I wanted to gather more people I could start other groups. This was a wise suggestion and led to my practice of retaining gatherings to that size. Over the years I started fifteen different clubs, most of which were groups selected and invited by me on the basis of those whom I thought would be congenial friends. Several of these original groups still meet regularly and have kept active over these thirty and forty years. This formula for smaller, more intimate gatherings was basic in the growth of Plymouth Church. Once a group was started I attended as often as I could, but left to each the development of its own programs. My lasting friendships through the years and into retirement have been meaningful, especially through the first two clubs, Local Number One and the Forty-Six Club, named for the year in which it was gathered. There have been additions along the way as men returned from military service, some have died, and new people have joined. Here are friends, centered in the church, who have indeed grown together through the successive stages of life. I treasure each one of these people.

An Ecclesiastical Council of the Twin Cities West Association was held on February 1, 1945, to install me officially as the twelfth minister of Plymouth Church. In the afternoon I read a paper on "My Christian Experience and Faith." It began with the usual sketch of family background, education and experience. I summarized with three attitudes basic to my ministry: gratitude for all the blessings of my life; stewardship, to use our treasures for God's purposes; and joy in seeking to bring enrichment to others through ministry.

The section on my religious beliefs is interesting because it sets forth concerns that I have followed through more than forty years, yet also indicates some shifts in theological emphasis. I said that the Christian faith fulfills four demands of the human soul. First is a philosophic need for an understanding of the meaning of life. I affirmed that this meaning is wider than the Christian religion, and is glimpsed in the insights of world religions as well as in philosophy itself. Second is the demand for a theological expression of this philosophical insight. Here I said that I believed that the doctrines of Christ's Divinity, the Trinity, the Incarnation, the Atonement, the Resurrection, and the Redemption distilled the universal message. I soon abandoned that acceptance of orthodoxy, and even then went on to commend the Kansas City Affirmation of Faith as covering the essentials while safeguarding the right of the individual to freedom of interpretation.

A third demand of the human soul is for fellowship. This is the keynote of the gospels, as Jesus said repeatedly, "You are my friends." Jesus gathered disciples into the fellowship of the Church. I expressed faith in the Universal Church as a mystic union. The fourth demand is for righteousness, as taught by the Old Testament prophets. "I feel that we as Christian men and women have a sacred obligation to lead our churches into straight and hard thinking regarding the problems of world order, of economic justice, and of interracial brotherhood."

The paper seemed well received. That evening we had a dinner in the church dining hall for dignitaries and friends. My mother had come for the occasion, and the two dignitaries from the east who participated were Dr. Rockwell Harmon Potter, who gave the charge to the congregation, and Dr. Douglas Horton, titular head of the denomination as Executive Secretary of the General Council, who preached the sermon. It was an exciting and happy evening which formalized a relationship that was to continue for thirty-two wonderful years.

My emphasis on fellowship goes beyond binding people together in the local congregation and extends to the concern that we have for the human family everywhere. I have been a strong supporter of missions, not in the sense of sending evangelists to convert people of other faiths, but to reach out to help improve the conditions of life where standards are low. I saw that Christmas and Easter are the two festival occasions of the Christian Church. These should be made opportunities to stretch our giving, to reach out in helpfulness to people whom we have never seen.

Encouraged by the results of my first Christmas offering to raise funds for the *Chronicle*, I persuaded the Prudential Committee to adopt a $2,500 goal for Easter morning. This would be sent for relief and rehabilitation in the war-torn areas of Europe and Asia. There was some skepticism that such a sum could be contributed in one morning. However, by appeals in the *Chronicle* and the Sunday bulletins the people came forward with $3,137.93! This was the second visible sign that an advance plan with a challenge would be effective, and was another step in making my first season the promise of a new day dawning.

Two events of that first season are worthy of mention. For many years, four mainline Protestant churches of downtown Minneapolis had held a union service on Good Friday evening. There was a good spirit among them, and as the other clergy commented in welcoming me, each was probably more like the others than any one was to the sister churches of its denomination. Each was served by a minister of distinction. Dr. Charles F. Deems was dean of the Cathedral Church of St. Mark, a gentle and gracious man. Dr. Arnold Hilmer Lowe was at Westminster Presbyterian, the most powerful preacher

I ever heard. The longest in service was Dr. Richard C. Raines, who had been at Hennepin Avenue Methodist Church for nearly fifteen years, and two years later was elected a Methodist bishop. He was an eloquent speaker and a beloved person.

Soon after my arrival, a few people warned me that the real test would come at the Good Friday service when I would be compared with the other three colleagues! The ministers met early in Lent, selected a general theme, and then divided it into four subtopics, one for each man. The service that year was held in Hennepin Avenue Methodist. I was the only one of the group who had not received an honorary doctorate, so the large painted bulletin outside the church announced the event, listing the other three with their titles and me as the Reverend Howard Conn. That afternoon I took a snapshot of the sign, and hung it in my study with its title, "Howard Among the Doctors."

For the last two years of his ministry, Dr. Beach had as his assistant the Reverend Arthur J. Snow, whose wife Alice was also an ordained minister. She had been education director. They had served ably during the long year without a leader, but with my coming looked for a new opportunity. In March they went to the Congregational church in Stoneham, Massachusetts. That left me free to build my own staff.

The other event which reveals something of the spirit of the church is connected with the sudden death of President Franklin D. Roosevelt. I had invited Dr. George P. "Perry" Conger to speak the Thursday of April 12 at our monthly Church-Night Supper. Perry was a professor in the philosophy department at the University of Minnesota, a clear thinker with a beautiful spirit. I was with him for several years in a clergy group known as the Saturday Evening Dinner Club, which met regularly during the church season. I learned a great deal from him. On his death, Paul Holmer of Yale Divinity School and I conducted his memorial service.

April 12 was the day of Roosevelt's death. Perry put aside his prepared topic and spoke extemporaneously and movingly of what FDR had really meant to the country. It was fitting and appropriate.

The war in Europe was drawing to an end, and people were shifting their thoughts toward what peace could mean. The Federal Council of Churches had a committee headed by John Foster Dulles to study a "just and lasting peace."

The next Sunday we too shifted our plans, and I spoke on "The Last Best Hope of Earth," taking Lincoln's description of the Federal Union and applying it to the world union which might come out of the forthcoming conference in San Francisco that was to form the United Nations. I had attended a study session at the university with John H. Ravlin of our congregation. Quite a few Plymouthites were among the civic leaders who were concerned for the peace. We drew up a resolution to be sent to Governor Harold Stassen, who was a delegate from the United States to the San Francisco Conference. It read as follows:

> We, the undersigned worshippers at Plymouth Congregational Church, Minneapolis, Minnesota, meeting this morning in public worship, do mourn the loss of our President, Franklin Delano Roosevelt, and express the hope that the San Francisco Conference may achieve the advancement for peace for which he planned. We record herewith our common dream that the sacrifices of this war may result in the establishment of a just and cooperative world order based on law. To this end we urge the delegates to the San Francisco Conference to bear in mind the hope of the people; and we pledge ourselves to support our nation in such forward steps as may be taken to create an international organization for the better ordering of the interdependent life of nations.

At the conclusion of my sermon, I invited the people to do something about the issue. We had twenty-two copies of this memorial spread on tables at the front of the sanctuary, and monitors appointed to help people come forward to sign. In twelve minutes 804 people did so. We had a prayer dedicating the signatures, and joined in singing "America." It was an impressive service related to the problems of the time.

When in June Vi, Judy and I got in our car to drive east to the 1750 farmhouse, we felt that it had been an exciting year with the promise of many more to come. We were leaving a host of new friends to go back to the Berkshires to spend our first vacation summer with beloved friends there.

10

Gathering Momentum

WHILE WE WERE IN THE BERKSHIRES for the summer of 1945, an event occurred in Minneapolis that became a catalyst for new growth at Plymouth. Jerome Jackman died. It seems crass to suggest that a Cosmic Power would arrange the death of one individual to foster the career of another. Yet after a year of testing and new beginnings, the death of Mr. Jackman did introduce an element that precipitated a forward step that might not otherwise have come as soon. The fortuitous sequence of events again gave me the sense of a Hand Always Above My Shoulder.

Jerome Jackman was an inconspicuous member of Plymouth Church. He was a bachelor who had served in the First World War and still wore his army-issue winter coat. He was a lawyer with very few clients. District Judge Harold N. Rogers, a prominent member of the church, had given him desk space in his office. Harold commented that when taking the offering in the balcony on Sunday mornings, he hesitated to pass the plate past Jerome. Mr. Jackman had lived for many years in the downtown YMCA, but two years earlier the "Y" had enacted a rule that men over sixty could no longer have permanent residence. This irked Mr. Jackman, but he moved to a room near the University of Minnesota. He was a student of the Bible, a man of intelligence. Vi and I met him during our first year at the Colony meeting in his area, and remembered him as a pleasant individual.

While on the bench one morning that summer, Judge Rogers was passed a note saying that Jerome Jackman had been found in his room dead from a heart attack. His first thought was that he would have to pass the hat among a few legal associates to raise money for funeral and burial expenses. However, when he got back to his chambers at noon, Judge Rogers was told that money and bank passbooks had been found in Jerome's room under cushions and in boxes. Inventory revealed nearly two hundred thousand dollars.

His will directed his friend Stanley Gillam, for many years the clerk of Plymouth Church, to handle his estate. After a few bequests to relatives, the residue was to be divided equally between Plymouth and First Baptist Church. The original will had made Plymouth and the YMCA the residual legatees, but when the "Y" ousted him from residency Jackman replaced that organization with the Baptists. First Baptist is a staunch Fundamentalist church, and its long-time pastor in the twenties, Dr. W.B. Riley, often clashed with Dr. Harry P. Dewey of Plymouth as spokespersons for contrasting views. First Baptist was only two blocks from the YMCA building, and probably Jerome Jackman went there from time to time for evening services. As a Bible reader, he no doubt was more of a literalist than most Plymouthites. At any rate, he must be credited with playing safe with his inheritance, for in whatever heaven there may be either the Congregationalists or the Baptists must be right!

Plymouth's share of the estate came to eighty thousand dollars, and though probate took some time, this was new money that had not been anticipated. It was an incentive for action.

Clearly the church was growing. New young families were coming. In my first year we had received 137 new members, and I had officiated at thirty-three funerals, nineteen weddings and fifty-two baptisms.

We had a new staff in place. Over the summer of 1945, two friends whom I had known in Massachusetts came. Miss Ruth E. Bailey, a Mt. Holyoke graduate from a fine Boston family, became director of Religious Education. She is a charming person who inspired teachers and was beloved by all the congregation. At a Colony gathering out in the Minnetonka area one evening, John S. Pillsbury, who was a lifelong member of Plymouth but seldom attended, said that if he did come in on a Sunday he thought he would rather go to one of Miss Bailey's classes than listen to me preach! Ruth was with us for thirteen years before going to a similar post at Central Union Church in Honolulu. Her ability and charm were significant in our ministry.

The Rev. David J. Julius came to be associate from Central Congregational Church in Middleboro, Massachusetts. He was seven years older than I, but we had served together on conference committees. David is a Christian gentleman, quite reserved but with a real sparkle in his eyes. His wife Dorothy was equally fine, and their three children an asset. They were with us three years before they were called to the Congregational Church in Pullman, Washington. From there they went to Tacoma.

During our first year, Vi and I had attended thirty neighborhood or Colony meetings, which meant a heavy schedule of that many evening gatherings in the homes of members. Though such a pace was strenuous, it is an ideal way to become acquainted in an informal setting. As we returned in September of 1945, we faced a similar schedule of thirty evenings. We now had Ruth Bailey, David and Dorothy Julius to go with us as we carried through another cordial round of informal visitation.

In any church, a task of the fall is the stewardship campaign to underwrite the budget for the coming fiscal year. The enthusiasm of our first season gained momentum. The trustees had appointed Glenn Wyer to chair the canvass, with Lawrence Woodard and David Lee Sutherland as vice-chairmen. They decided to shift from personal solicitation to a mail effort based on informing the members of all the facts and details. David Gale Jones assisted them in preparing an elaborate booklet illustrated by Oz Black, the *Minneapolis Star* cartoonist. They built upon the theme of partnership that I had emphasized throughout my first year: "Because you are a partner. . . ." The 1944 budget had been $47,005; and the proposed 1946 figure, $67,560.

In the brochure they wrote: "1946—the first year of peace—is important, for it gives us the chance to make a fresh start. We can develop a new individual devotion, a new church life, and a new society. We are therefore partners in a new dedication, a new church, and a new world."

The people responded well, and a thirty percent increase in the budget was accomplished without a single personal solicitation. This established a pattern that succeeding campaigns followed for many years. In my "Epistle to Plymouthites" in the December issue of the *Chronicle*, I wrote:

> We have succeeded because together we have caught and shared a vision, so that the budget means not merely dollars but fuller program and ampler service. The achievement of our goal indicates what partners together can accomplish, and is a tribute to the enthusiasm and willing spirit of every member. I salute you again as on previous occasions.

With this 1946 budget we also developed a ratio of three to one for local expenses and benevolences. I am a firm believer in a unified budget rather than asking donors to allocate between two. A subscriber has no way of knowing what preferences others are expressing nor what the pressing needs in either direction may be. Stewardship encourages the individual to consider a percentage of personal income as a responsible gift to Christian service in the work of the local church. That gathered community through its boards will allocate in wiser judgment than the individual can do. A unified budget means fewer appeals, with the total needs covered in one significant pledge.

At Plymouth we introduced from the beginning of my ministry substantial Christmas and Easter offerings as the only other appeals outside the fall financial canvass. On these two Festival Sundays of the Christian year, I asked that families try to make gifts between ten and one hundred dollars. On my second Easter I persuaded the Prudential Committee to set a goal of five thousand dollars. Through boxed paragraphs in each Sunday bulletin of Lent, I wrote what was intended to be an intelligent yet moving appeal. That morning the total came to $5,690.80. This success set five thousand dollars as a goal figure for the years ahead. With the Christmas and Easter offerings added to the budgeted benevolences, they brought gifts for others appreciably above the twenty-five percent level.

The Jackman bequest stimulated the trustees to thoughts about a long-range future. The leadership of its chairman, F.A. Bean, was to play a major role. During my first year he had been cautious to test what skills I had and to watch the response among the congregation.

When we returned for our second season he became a staunch supporter and creative leader. He told the trustees he was convinced
that Plymouth now had a young minister who could lead the church
in substantial growth, and that it was the responsibility of the
trustees to provide him with the plant and equipment with which to
do the task. He himself was ready to make a substantial financial
contribution, and he hoped the others would do likewise.

At the annual meeting in January 1946, Mr. Bean presented a
proposal for four projects. First, the rebuilding of the sanctuary
organ; second, modernizing and repairing the present building;
third, erecting an additional wing to our parish house; and fourth,
securing a suitable parsonage. Dale R. McEnary, a member of
Plymouth and of the architectural firm of McEnary & Krafft, was
engaged to make preliminary drafts and sketches. A year later these
were shown at Colony meetings and given full discussion. I want to
write an account of our several building projects in a separate chapter, and am content here merely to show how the initiation of this
1946 program contributed to the gathering momentum of my first
five years.

Prior to Pearl Harbor, Mr. and Mrs. Edgar F. Zelle had contributed twenty-five thousand dollars for the rebuilding of the
Aeolian-Skinner organ, under specifications prepared by Mr.
Jennings. A contract for the work had been signed, but during the
war nothing of this nature could be done. The Zelles were among
the most gracious, generous and beloved members of Plymouth.
Edgar had grown up in New Ulm, had attended the University of
Minnesota, and had worked his way as secretary to one of the officers. He married Lillian Nippert, the attractive and cultured daughter of a northside physician, and together they had one of the most
beautiful family lives I have ever known. Lillian was an outstanding
violinist whose talents both Mr. Hunt and Mr. Jennings utilized on
festival occasions. They were active members of the board of the
Minnesota Symphony Orchestra almost from its beginning. Mr.
Zelle bought a small bus company and built it into the highly successful Jefferson Transportation Company. They were both ardent
music lovers and devoted members of Plymouth. They were a couple from whom I learned a great deal and whom I dearly loved.
Edgar's quiet manner, his modesty, his gracious way of treating

every person as an equal made him a model and a leader for the financial, social and cultural communities of the Twin Cities.

All the parts for the new organ were made in Boston. Representatives of the Aeolian-Skinner Company began their work in Minneapolis on August 4, 1947, and completed installation by the end of December. The original organ built by them in 1909 had 2,455 pipes. The new renovation brought the number to 3,918 pipes, and made it one of the finest instruments in the Upper Midwest. Mr. Jennings played an inaugural recital on Friday evening, January 30, 1948.

Another of Mr. Bean's four projects was the securing of a suitable parsonage. On our arrival, we moved into the parsonage where Dr. and Mrs. Beach had lived, and which had been purchased at his request. The house had been the home of Mr. and Mrs. J.A. Ross, one of three adjoining homes on Franklin Avenue occupied by members of the Bovey family, one of the pioneering families that had been part of the nucleus out of which came General Mills. Ann Bovey Ross and her husband lived on the corner; then came the house of Mr. and Mrs. William H. Bovey, and beyond, that of Miss Caroline Bovey. Mr. Ross was treasurer of Plymouth Church for several decades. At Dr. Beach's request he had given the house to Plymouth for five thousand dollars, and in 1946 the trustees sold it for fifteen thousand. We lived there two years, and though it was comfortable and within two blocks of the church, it was on a heavily trafficked thoroughfare. By spring of 1946 our first daughter Judy was three years old, and in June our second daughter Janet was born. We wanted a quieter and safer neighborhood.

The trustees gave us liberty to look for any house we wanted. The dominant feature of Minneapolis is its many lakes and parks, and we hoped to be near water. On Xerxes Avenue, just south of Lake Calhoun, we found for sale a two-story brick house in somewhat colonial style. Strangely, though, its interior was Spanish in atmosphere. We thought it to be a good location and a suitable residence. The trustees inspected it and decreed that it was not good enough for the minister of Plymouth Church. They described it as being "schizophrenic" in style.

In the meantime, Mr. Bean learned that the president of the Minnesota & St. Louis Railway, Lucien C. Sprague, wished to sell his beautiful home in Kenwood. He inspected it, decided that it would be an excellent parsonage, and took Vi and me to see it. We were overwhelmed initially. The house sat on a large pointed lot where Newton and Oliver Avenues meet in the peninsula of Lake of the Isles. It had been built in the days of horse carriages, with a porte-cochere and a driveway going around the house and yard from one street to the other. The living room and dining room on either side of a large entrance hall were each thirty-five feet long. A sun porch and a den were off the living room. On the second floor were five bedrooms and a sun room. There were also a finished basement and third floor. It was situated in an ideal neighborhood where children and grandchildren often buy their family homes. The area is convenient to downtown Minneapolis, a short walk to Lake of the Isles and its winter skating rink, and there is no through traffic. This house at 2320 Newton Avenue South was one of the first built in that subdivision, so the insulation was not modern. The storm windows and screens required a lot of maintenance. But it was ideal for entertaining. We enjoyed its spaciousness, and lived in it as a parsonage for eighteen years until our younger daughter graduated from high school.

The purchase price was $25,000, with Mr. Sprague making a contribution of one thousand dollars a year for five years. Mr. Bean and Mr. Zelle provided the money so that no church funds were used for the acquisition. When we moved out in 1964, the trustees sold the house for $40,000.

In these early years we developed many strategies to make the members of the congregation feel important. We continued the annual series of Colony meetings as already mentioned. We tried to develop a special theme for each round. In 1947 we combined some of the groups and scheduled all to meet at our house over twenty evenings between September and December, so that people had opportunity to visit in the new parsonage. When I offered this plan to the Prudential Committee, Luther Ford commented, "Howard knows how to lead with Mrs. Conn's chin!" Vi was an excellent hostess and had always had a genuine love for people. The following year during Lent, we planned for simultaneous meetings in twenty-seven homes, with a trained lay leader to discuss Elton Trueblood's book, *Alternative to Futility*. Three hundred copies were sold in a reading project.

Another innovation was to have a New Members Dinner for those who had joined during the year. A committee from each group planned its own program, with the emphasis on closer acquaintanceship and a lighter vein of humor. The first was especially delightful because of the wit among the crowd. On December 3, 1945, William P. Steven, the newly arrived associate editor of the *Minneapolis Tribune* was toastmaster for the 137 who had united during my first year. The Steven family arrived in Minneapolis at the same time as did the Conns, and we often quipped of an agreement whereby they would join Plymouth if we would subscribe to the morning paper! Also in that first-year group were Dr. and Mrs. Donald J. Cowling, recently retired after thirty-seven years as president of Carleton College. He regaled the guests with a fluid flow of humorous stories that sent everyone home in a laughing mood.

The next year Roy W. Larsen, president and founder of Twin City Federal Savings and Loan, was toastmaster for the 147 friends who joined in 1946. He too had a fund of good stories. Three years elapsed before the next dinner, when on January 27, 1950, realtor James Emerson chaired the gathering for 248 who had joined in 1948 and 1949. These parties helped to bring together people of all ages and neighborhoods and contributed to the warmth of fellowship.

Several other innovations contributed to the spirit of openness and partnership. Each year we had thirty-five to fifty young people away at colleges, and we invited them to a breakfast while they were home during the holidays. This provided an opportunity for them to see one another and to share stories of happenings on their various campuses. On the Sunday between Christmas and New Year's, I invited a corps of the young men to replace the deacons in taking the morning offering.

For those at the far end of the age spectrum, I began the practice at each annual meeting of reading the names of those who had been members of Plymouth for fifty years or more. At first there were some sixty in this group, but in the latter part of my ministry the number was always more than a hundred. We honored these faithful, and stressed loyalty. In church school and baptisms we noted the continuity of three and four generations within our fellowship. In later years the parish visitor, the deaconesses and the Plymouth

Women's Organization held a tea for shut-ins near my birthday in June, at which drivers were sent to bring to the church the elderly who could not readily get about. This became a time of happy reminiscence.

A year after the death of Adele Anderson, we were fortunate to find another wonderful woman to be parish visitor. Miss Ruth J. Easterday had been director of Religious Education for twenty-three years at Westminster Presbyterian Church in Lincoln, Nebraska. She was a dynamic person with a deep spiritual life, one who had an extensive collection of inspirational poems, who was well-organized with an ability to make firm decisions. She was ideally suited for welcoming visitors, for integrating new members into women's groups, and for tending to the needs of those in nursing homes who could no longer shop for personal items.

When Ruth came, one of our tasks was to find housing for her. An equally able single woman in the congregation was Miss Lois Zickafoose, a highly regarded elementary school teacher. She and her mother lived in a large apartment, but that spring her mother had died. We persuaded Lois to accept Ruth Easterday until the latter could find a suitable place of her own. This proved to be the beginning of a beautiful friendship, for these two women shared apartments and vacationed together on the North Shore until Ruth entered the Jones-Harrison Retirement Home. Ruth was a valuable member of our staff. She looked after the shut-ins, held the confidences of many elderly. I trusted her judgment completely. Whenever she said that one of our flock was hurting or near the end and would appreciate a visit from me, I went immediately. Of course I called on all who were hospitalized, making these rounds in late afternoons several days a week; but I left regular visitation of shut-ins to Ruth until she alerted me of a need. I enjoyed calling on the sick and the dying because it brought a special relationship. One comes to appreciate the real character of a person when he or she is removed even temporarily from the fast pace of modern life and comes to reflect on the basic values. Many, many times I have come away from hospital rooms feeling that I had received from the patient more than I had been able to give.

Always I tried to enter a sickroom in a calm and friendly manner so as not to alarm the patient. What a minister says is not as

important as his presence, for he symbolizes the faith and the experience of the member. What a person has put into religion comes
back at a time of crisis, and when the relationship has been warm
the pastor's presence at the bedside calls up deep assurances.
Usually I offer a brief prayer at the end of a short visit, but not
always. A pastor develops a "feel" for what is welcome. If not with a
prayer, I always bring the visit around to the expression of a spiritual affirmation. My favorite scriptural passage for such a situation
is from Isaiah 30:15:

> In returning and rest shall be your health;
> In quietness and confidence shall be your strength.

After Ruth Easterday retired, we were fortunate to find a member of the congregation to assume the duties of parish visitor. Miss
Hazel Christensen had served in rehabilitation work in Europe after
World War II and was sensitive to people's needs. She had compul-
sion for work and was tireless in her service to others. She also
attended to the details of weddings and Sunday flower distribution.
She too was a real help in pastoral work, and continued on another
five years after my retirement.

We were receptive to opportunities to expose the congregation
to the wider reaches of religion and society through inviting outside
dignitaries to speak. Two favorites were Walter Judd and Larry
Gould. Dr. Judd represented Minneapolis in Congress, and was a
part of Plymouth Church. He had been a medical missionary in
China under the Congregational American Board of Commissioners
for Foreign Missions. He gained national attention in the thirties,
when he came home to warn Americans that in his hospital he was
taking from patients shrapnel made from American steel sold to
Japan and used by that country in its war with China. A group of
Minneapolis people led by Gideon Seymour, executive editor of the
Star–Tribune, urged him to run for Congress from our district. On
that basis he was elected in 1942 and served for twenty years,
becoming chairman of the House Foreign Relations Committee. He
retained his membership in the small Nebraska church in which he
had been commissioned a missionary, but his active participation
was at Plymouth. He and his wife Miriam are staunch Congrega-

tionalists and have continued with the National Association since the merger controversy.

Another distinguished Minnesotan who became a good friend and frequent guest was Dr. Lawrence McKinley Gould. In October of 1945, he was inaugurated as president of Carleton College at Northfield, Minnesota. He was a popular professor of geology at the college who had been with Admiral Byrd on his trip to Antarctica. He is a friendly, dynamic person who gained many new supporters to Carleton. Though he and his wife Peg were themselves Episcopalians, he recognized the part the Minnesota Conference of Congregational Churches had played in the founding of the college, and he was always generous and cordial in his relations with Plymouth. In 1948 he had me elected a trustee of Carleton. I served on the board for twenty-four years and have been an emeritus trustee since 1972.

Dr. Gould was an engaging speaker and often appeared at Plymouth. His manner was informal, which drew listeners close to him. He often spoke from a stack of three-by-five cards, and quipped that Peg said he never knew in advance how he was going to shuffle them!

A milestone event in these first six years was the dedication of Jackman Hall in our new building project. Though I have told of the impetus for a building program gained from the bequest of Mr. Jackman, I am leaving the details of that story for a chapter devoted to the several building projects during my thirty-two-year tenure. By the spring of 1949, new construction was sufficiently completed to allow for a memorable evening on April 28, 1949, the second Thursday after Easter. Seven hundred sixty-five persons crowded the dining room for a housewarming dinner, after which they went into the sanctuary where a play, *Our Church*, was presented. Written by Mrs. Myron H. (Theresa) Powell, this drama depicted the spirit of Plymouth Church in its past years. Through swiftly moving scenes, the humor, the aspirations and the struggles of ninety-two years were depicted. It was a moving and delightful production involving more than twoscore costumed participants. At the conclusion Dr. Cowling spoke on his vision for the future.

During these early years we were experiencing rapid growth. By the end of 1951, we had received 833 new members. For each group on the Sunday evening preceding reception, I held what I called a "Refresher Evening," in which over two hours I attempted to give a survey of the Congregational concept of the Church, a sketch of Christian Church history, the belief of Congregationalists, the story of our congregation, the responsibilities and privileges of membership. I considered these evenings important, for many attendants commented that though they had joined churches in previous communities they had not been given such a sketch of the essentials. These groups were generally quite sizable, the largest comprised of seventy new friends who joined on Maundy Thursday of 1946. Throughout my ministry, I have trained myself to learn names so that I could go down the line and call the name of each person to whom I was extending the right hand of fellowship. This takes discipline, but is a help in making newcomers feel accepted.

Many of those joining were younger couples, and we had many infants presented for baptism. On Children's Day—June 8, 1947—we had twenty-eight couples lined two deep across the front of the sanctuary for the baptism of infants. I almost never held a child in baptism, though many ministers are skilled in holding aloft the infant to the delight of the congregation.

By the fall of 1951, the church school enrollment had more than doubled from its 1944 figure, up 216 percent. There were 544 youngsters enrolled, not counting the Crib Room. This was a tribute to the expert guidance given by Ruth Bailey, and the loving care shown by the scores of teachers whom she trained.

The growth of Plymouth is attributable not only to these family-oriented activities, but also I hope to the presentation of a distinctive message. I think of myself as a teacher as much as a preacher, trying to bring a universal perspective rather than a dogmatic answer to life's problems. Though I treasure the Bible, I do not use it as an authoritative rule book but as the record of the experiences of flesh-and-blood human beings who faced situations akin to ours. Though I used more conventional terminology in my early ministry than in later years, it was always evident that I was presenting a view wider than the traditional Christian message of sin and salvation so popularly packaged by many clergymen. In Minneapolis the upbringing of the majority of people is either Roman Catholic or Lutheran. I often commented that to be trained a Lutheran is an excellent preparation for becoming a Congregationalist, because Lutherans are brought up to take religion seriously! Yet in forming new families they often say, "We want our children to have religious training, but we do not want them confined to the rigidities in which we were raised." They look for new affiliations, and they find appealing the combination of spiritual devotion and intellectual freedom of a liberal congregation.

In my preaching I try to speak directly to questions that are in the minds of the congregation. Some of my early topics at Plymouth were: "What Shall We Say to This War's Wounded and Bereaved?"; "Is There a Purpose in the Universe?"; "Can Your Conscience Be Your Guide?"; "Does Conversion Have Any Meaning Today?"; "Beginning Again in Religion"; "How Shall We Pray?"; "God Has a Plan for You"; "The Tiny Importances of Life"; "The Historical and Mystic Elements in Religion"; "Bright Colors in a Dark Universe"; "The Value of Nonconformity."

The Bible has been very important to me ever since seminary days, when I was exposed to it as a fresh record of spiritual pilgrimage. I love to teach courses in various portions of the Scripture, and regret that liberals so often leave Biblical classes to leaders who take the evangelical rather than historical approach. Throughout my ministry we continuously offered Bible study courses. These were held on weeknights during the fall, and on Wednesday mornings during Lent. In series over the years, we covered every portion of the Bible. In addition I gave series on: Poetry and Religious Faith, the Devotional Classics, Plato, and Asian Religions. In the fall of 1947 I introduced my course on Robert Browning's *The Ring and the Book*, which I have given six times through the years, the most frequently offered of my many courses. I myself had been introduced to this through William Lyon Phelps at Yale, and regard it as the greatest delineation of Christian character in English literature. Browning took a sordid tale of murder in the fifteenth century and made of it a fascinating masterpiece.

During these early years, quite a number of invitations came to expand my witness into a wider area beyond Plymouth. One that was to be the most far-reaching was a phone call in the fall of 1947 from Mrs. Judson (Mary) Fiebiger, who represented the Nominating Committee of the Congregational Board of Home Missions, offering me a place on its Executive Committee. This was one of the five national agencies of Congregationalism, and a powerful one because its endowment assets exceeded that of any of the others. The following year I was elected to the first of two four-year terms on the BHM Executive Committee, a body of twenty-four persons who met quarterly to make decisions. During those eight years I was also made a member of the five-person Policy and Planning Committee, whose approval had to be secured before items could be brought before the larger board. For the second four years—1952 through 1956—I was chairman of this strategic committee. This opportunity put me into the central arena of denominational politics during one of its most turbulent periods—that of discussion, negotiation and decision regarding the proposed union of the Congregational Christian Churches and the Evangelical and Reformed Church to create the United Church of Christ. Because of what I observed in these close contacts, I became opposed to the merger and was the only person in this inner circle who stood out against the leaders with whom I was in intimate association. Because this controversy became one of the major emphases of my career, I shall devote a separate chapter to it.

In October of 1947 I was made chaplain of the Midwest Regional Meeting, in conjunction with which the Board of Home Missions held its annual meeting. I conducted three worship services at the four-day meeting in Colorado Springs, and spoke on "Living Out of the Abundance of the Omnipotent Father." This has been a central theme of my ministry, that we are vessels through whom flow strength, beauty and purpose from the heart of the universe.

In the spring of that year we observed the Ninetieth Anniversary of Plymouth Church, at which time I preached on "Forward in Unbroken Line," a title taken from Frederick Hosmer's hymn which we sing to the tune of "Onward Christian Soldiers."

As a liberal I have always believed in cooperation among all Christian groups. We Congregationalists never claim to be "the true church" because we cherish the freedom by which all persons may shape their own beliefs and affiliations. When I came to Minnesota, I discovered that the Minnesota Council of Churches was an active group under the leadership of the Rev. Dr. Hayden L. Stright, an American Baptist minister who for nearly forty years was the executive secretary. I was put on the board of directors, and we became good friends until his death. He had the dream of building a Protestant Center to house the staffs of the major denominations, a dream which over the fifties was to be realized. Before that could be accomplished it was necessary to find a location central to the Twin Cities area and to make small beginnings. I found the work of the council stimulating and challenging because it was guided by laypeople from several denominations who shared the view that what we could do together was as important as our separate programs. These were laypeople—business executives, doctors, social workers, teachers, housewives—who were true ecumenists, people with loving hearts that reached out beyond barriers. They were a grassroots group that seemed to me to have a truer vision of ecumenicity than the professional denominational clergy who were shaping world councils on a more legalistic plane.

Across the street from the parsonage to which we initially moved at the corner of Franklin and Pillsbury was a grand old mansion that was the home of Mrs. Horace Ropes. Though not a member of Plymouth, she was kind to our family and had many friends in our congregation. She passed away in 1947. I conducted funeral services in her home. When her house was put on the market, the estate made it possible for the Minnesota Council of Churches to purchase the property as a headquarters building. Several groups moved into the main house, while the spacious garage in the rear was remodeled for the Presbyterian and Congregational conferences.

In 1952-54 I was president of the Minnesota Council, and ten years later was vice-chairman of the building committee that designed the new six-story Protestant Center that was built on the same site after demolition of the older structures.

On January 22, 1950, Plymouth Church was selected by the Columbia Church of the Air to have its morning worship broadcast over national network. My sermon title was "On the Edge of the Spiritual," and the choir sang Mr. Jennings's well-known anthem, "Springs in the Desert."

The expectation of my encouraging layman in Great Barrington, Byron Allen, that I might succeed Dr. Ralph W. Sockman of New York as preacher over the National Radio Pulpit was partially fulfilled when I was chosen to be summer replacement for nine weeks in 1955. My general theme was "New Wine of the Spirit." I was coached in manner of radio speaking by the Rev. Everett W. Parker, director of communications for our denomination. I went to New York to record these services at sessions which prepared tapes for three Sundays at a time. This was a stimulating experience, and we received many letters from listeners.

My honorary Doctor of Divinity degree came from Yankton, a liberal arts college in South Dakota founded in pioneer days by a Congregational missionary, Rev. Joseph Ward. A number of Plymouth members were Yankton graduates, and one of them, Reinhard Nordness, was a trustee. I think it was he who recommended me for this honor. I preached the baccalaureate sermon on June 7, 1948. My sermon for that occasion expressed a basic theme of the combination of earnestness and modesty. It was based on a passage from the Platonic Dialogue, *Phaedo*. At the conclusion of the myth concerning the future life, Socrates speaks these words:

> A man of sense ought not to insist that everything is exactly as I have described it; but he may venture to think that this or something like it is the truth about our souls and their habitation. That, I think, is a venture fitting and worthwhile. Wherefore, let a man be of good cheer, . . . and be ready to go forward on his journey.

These words of Socrates represent an attitude toward life which all of us may profitably adopt. We live from day to day on certain basic assumptions which we may not be able to prove but which nevertheless prompt us to trust. There is no such thing as final knowledge or absolute certainty in religious matters, for the spiritual life belongs to the realm of mystery in which we follow surmises. This is a venture fitting and worthwhile. Dogmatism and bigotry are out of place in the exciting adventure of the human soul.

Five years after our arrival at Plymouth came the only offer of a career change that was in any way tempting. In the spring of 1947, Dean Weigle offered me an appointment as a full professor at Yale Divinity School in the chair of homiletics. Professor John Schroeder was leaving the seminary to take a full-time post in Yale College, and our beloved and esteemed Halford E. Luccock had only a year remaining before retirement. The latter wrote me a beautiful letter, saying in a paraphrase of John 3:30, "You must increase, but I must decrease." From all the faculty members who had been my teachers fifteen years earlier I received notes of encouragement and welcome.

My three years in New Haven were happy ones, and I have always had a deep affection for the Divinity School. As permanent secretary of our class, the ties have been kept through the years. To become a member of the faculty was a tempting honor. However, quiet reflection made clear to me that the Hand Always Above My Shoulder was not truly pointing in this direction.

This would have been the last appointment Luther Weigle made during his deanship, and I was grateful for the honor and for the support he had given me ever since my student days. However, I declined, and have never regretted this decision. Two years later when Yale did honor Dean Weigle upon his retirement, I was one of six speakers invited to an evening of commemoration at the Divinity School on April 27, 1949. We covered six areas of his influence, and I was called to speak of his preaching and pastoral ministry. Thus my associations with this Christian statesman were close from my student days to his death.

Another significant recognition which came early was the opportunity to give one of three theological lectures on the Trinity at the biennial meeting of the General Council of Congregational Christian Churches at Cleveland in June of 1950. Because of my philosophical bent, I was assigned the First Person, and spoke on "The Paradoxes of God." I mentioned three: Immanence and Transcendence, Universalism and Particularism, Mercy and Judgment. At that point I was only thirty-nine years old, and yet given national recognition as a thoughtful minister. In this address I foreshadowed my growing differences with Truman Douglass and the "Christus Victor" movement, which stressed the uniqueness of Christianity over its harmony with a universal spirit.

As a young minister with strong convictions, I of course appreciated these several opportunities to come in contact with national leaders of Congregationalism and to gain recognition as a significant minister. However, these contacts, which might have ensconced me in the heart of the establishment, actually served to alienate me from national trends. I recognized the difference between my thinking and that of denominational executives.

One significant change I instituted at Plymouth was to yield long-range benefits, which was accomplished with full agreement within the congregation. When I arrived in 1944, I discovered that Plymouth was operating on the old New England system of a division between the *society* and the *church*. This arrangement provided two organizations. One is the *church*, composed of all the baptized and covenanted members. They elect the minister, the deacons and committees which operate the spiritual and social activities of the parish. The minister is the presiding officer at all meetings and functions. Alongside the church is a parallel organization, known as the *society*, which holds title to the property, adopts the annual budgets and controls the financial arrangements. Its officers are a president, a clerk, a treasurer and a board of trustees. A dichotomy exists between the business and the ecclesiastical functions of the congregation.

This appears to be a logical division. No harm comes from it if the two groups are identical in membership and work together in harmony. Historically that did not always happen. In New England it sometimes developed that the society became a smaller group than the congregation, and that posts within it, such as treasurer, became somewhat hereditary, with a son who seldom attended worship succeeding a father. This put the purse strings and the determination of the minister's salary in the hands of persons who might not even be members of the church. Such a division invites conflict.

Fortunately at Plymouth there was no tension, but this dual system had been adopted probably because many of the early settlers had come from New Hampshire and Vermont, where they had been familiar with it. As my ministry became settled and we began to expand, I suggested that we abolish the society and have a unified church structure. My principal reason for such a change of course is that it unites the members into one responsible body, but beyond that is a second feature that is also significant. It symbolizes this shift by creating the office of moderator, in which a layperson becomes the visible head of the congregation. He or she, rather than the minister, presides at all meetings and stands beside the pastor at all ceremonial occasions. An effective minister should not seek control by the visible act of authority in presiding at decision-making meetings. He or she is actually strengthened if the rank and file of the membership see a prominent and respected layperson identifying with the ministry by publicly standing as spokesperson. A lay moderator adds dignity to the church and symbolizes the lay-centered power of the congregation. I was eager to have this transition made because Plymouth was blessed with such an outstanding array of lay leaders, whose support made possible the congregational partnership to which I was dedicated.

This brings the story back to that remarkable man, Frank A. Bean, to whose support I owe so much. He had become chairman of the trustees just prior to my arrival, and he considered this office to be a responsibility to the congregation rather than a personal honor to be coveted. I have already recorded how in his unique manner he tested me during my first year, but after which he made clear his concept that it was up to the officers to provide the materials and support for a new era in Plymouth's life. He told me that he had no desire to perpetuate himself in office, but only to set in motion the factors for Plymouth's growth. He saw the merits of my proposal to restructure our organization, and by my second year a committee was formed to study the proposal for a single corporation. Six top Plymouth leaders and myself constituted the group: Mr. Bean as chairman; Lloyd Hale, president of the Tennant Company, manufacturers of floor-polishing equipment; Richard L. Kozelka, dean of the School of Business Administration at the University of Minnesota; Ellwood H. Newhart, trust officer at the Norwest Bank; Judge Harold N. Rogers of the District Court; Glenn Wyer, head of a large insurance agency.

After eighteen months of study we were ready. Judge Rogers had prepared the legal papers for new articles of incorporation and new bylaws. These called for a single organization with a moderator, a clerk, a treasurer, an auditor, nine trustees, twenty-one deacons and twenty-one stewards. Three governing bodies were established: one for finances, one for spiritual life, and one for parish activities.

A meeting for business was called for December 4, 1947, to act upon the proposal. That evening brought a severe snowstorm, and only twenty-six parishioners braved the elements to come for an eventful change. Harvard S. Rockwell, chairman of the society, presided over a favorable and unanimous vote. The first meeting of the new organization was held at the time of the usual annual meeting, January 15, 1948.

This inaugurated a program that every two years elected a distinguished member to be moderator. We were most fortunate that the first person to hold this post was Dr. Donald J. Cowling, the retired president of Carleton College who from 1912 had been a leading figure in shaping the national policies of our denomination. In accepting he said that his sole motive was to help Mr. Conn, whose ministry he warmly praised as outstanding for its clear thinking and strong support of right ideas. "I know of no church anywhere that has a greater opportunity or brighter future than Plymouth Church." Years later at my twentieth anniversary he wrote, "Perhaps the simplest statement that I could make showing my deep appreciation of Dr. Conn's ministry would be to say that I hope he will spend at Plymouth Church the remaining years of his active ministry."

We were fortunate to have created this office of moderator. Gideon Seymour, executive editor of the *Star–Tribune*, was the second incumbent. Over the years the roster has included important leaders of the business and cultural community. I am happy to say that by the time of my retirement we had elected our first woman trustee-chairperson, Mrs. Voight O. (Catherine) Lenmark, and our first woman moderator, Mrs. Lester (Millie) Bolstad.

This consolidation of the society and church into a single organization had one interesting parallel effect that was not a factor in motivating it. Several active parishioners who had not been church members automatically became such because of the provision that all persons who had belonged to either group were now fully part of the church. Mr. Bean himself was one of these, along with several other prominent individuals who were of the older generation of industrial builders of the Twin Cities. These were men well educated and cultured, highly successful in the business world, deeply committed to community welfare and moral decency. Frank Bean and the lawyer John Crosby come readily to mind. I regret that I did not question them as to why they had not united with the church earlier, but from knowing them I can surmise that two factors may have been involved. Their intellectual keenness may have questioned the ancient creeds of Christendom and made them reluctant to assent to a public statement of faith. They supported the church as a worthy foundation of society, without agreeing with all that was said or done. A second factor may have been a reticence toward public display. They probably would have been reluctant to stand before the congregation and pledge formal allegiance to the institution that they were already serving with a high degree of loyalty.

While I think that for most people there is something symbolically valuable in the act of uniting with a congregation and accepting the right hand of fellowship in a loving community of faith, nevertheless there are others for whom this formality is not necessary. In the case of these particular men, I felt that the membership requirements of our new structure were fully met by their character and involvement.

F.A. Bean was a remarkable man whose support at the beginning of my ministry was a decisive factor in the new life coming to Plymouth. He was a generous benefactor with his gifts, which were always made anonymously so as to attract no attention to himself. More importantly, he became involved with details and procedures in giving oversight and wise counsel. It was through his initiative that our first building project was started, that the organizational structure was consolidated, and that the first parking lot was purchased. Later, when he became aware of some of the practices of our national boards, he studied minutes and procedures of these agencies, familiarized himself with details, and started a national movement for reforms. He was intensely concerned with what was going on in those institutions he supported, but he had no desire for personal recognition or control. He was elected to the board of trustees in 1944, the year that I came, and was made chairman. He gave active leadership for the purpose of launching Plymouth into a new era, but he had no interest in perpetuating himself in office. He declined to be reelected to the board after serving a three-year term. However, he kept an active interest until his death in August 1955. I was close to him through these first eleven years of my ministry. We were in frequent contact by phone, and I was often in his office as he was in mine. I learned a great deal from his insights, and many expressions of his character make fascinating anecdotes.

Previously mentioned was the grueling examination through which he put me during my first year. He often took delight in making a person feel uncomfortable, but the purpose was always to test how the individual responds and what his real character is. When he got involved in the controversy with the Council for Social Action in its practice of taking stands on social and economic issues, the defenders of that policy criticized him as being anticlerical. This was a hasty criticism that did not understand the broader perspective from which Mr. Bean approached such matters. He was not opposed to ministers, to Boy Scout executives or professionals of any organization. He expected them to look after the interests of their institutions with the same partisanship that the head of a business enterprise looks after his company. We all have the bias of our particular concerns. The function of a layperson or a board member is to hear the proposals of the executive and then to evaluate them in the broader perspective of persons not so immediately involved. Thus to criticize a minister or denominational official is not to accuse that person of dishonesty or intrigue, but to curb the excessive enthusiasm of that professional leader for a proposal that may not coincide with the values of the larger constituency. I consider this to be a sane and wholesome interpretation of the role of laypersons, particularly within the polity of Congregationalism, which posits the laity as having the final word of authority.

Frank Bean was scrupulous about honesty. Once I was talking with him over the phone about a church matter upon which I wanted his opinion, and commented that he had said that he was to be out of town the next week. He corrected me. "I did not say I was going out of town, only that I would not be available next week." He was going to the hospital for cataract surgery, did not want to call attention to his problem, but had wanted me to know that for an interval he could not be reached.

My favorite story about Frank Bean involves a conversation in his office prior to the annual meeting of 1947 or 1948. He had asked me to bring recommendations for the salaries of staff members for the coming year. I gave him my thoughts, which involved modest increases for each person. When I finished he said, "What about yourself? You haven't told me what you think you should have."

"That is not for me to say," I replied. "That is a matter for the trustees to determine."

"You must have some idea as to what is appropriate."

"I never argue with anyone about money. I am willing to leave it to the trustees."

In his engaging way Mr. Bean kept pressing me, knowing all along that he was playing a game in which he delighted. "Every person has some notion of his worth, some expectation of what he or she should receive. I want you to tell me what you think your salary ought to be."

After some further bantering back and forth, I finally ventured the suggestion of eight thousand dollars. Immediately I mentioned a figure I was caught in the trap which Frank had skillfully devised.

"You mean to tell me that you think you are worth eight thousand dollars to Plymouth!"

"I don't know whether I am, but you asked me to set a figure and so that is what I am doing."

He wanted to play for at least one more minute, so he said, "You are telling me that that is what you think you are worth, and that if we do not grant you this figure you will think you are not being adequately compensated, and will therefore be unhappy."

I remonstrated that I would not be unhappy with the trustees' decision, but was only responding to his persistent request for a figure.

"Very well, then," he said, "if we agree to the eight thousand figure, you will be satisfied?"

When I replied that I would be he ended the game with the pronouncement, "You have just talked yourself out of two thousand dollars because I think you are worth ten!"

I did not really lose anything, because the trustees agreed to Frank's recommendation that my salary be set at ten thousand dollars. No doubt he got two thousand worth of pleasure out of our interchange!

A visible sign of the new spirit in Plymouth was the decision to do away with the requirement that the deacons on Sunday wear morning coats or cutaways. It was they who came down the aisles to pass the collection plates each week, and for many years by their formal attire they had made a statement about the dignity and affluence of Plymouth. Within three years of my arrival there were some rumblings against this practice, but an early vote went against any change. As many new families were brought into membership and newer men were selected for the boards, resistance increased to such a formalized custom. When Sam Campbell and Phillip Sherman were asked to serve as deacons, they spoke strongly against the continued use of cutaways as required attire. In the fall of 1951, a ballot of the congregation was taken, this time with the request of the deacons that business suits be favored. This was the fourth try, and it passed by a vote of 450 to 239. We were the last church in Minneapolis to discontinue the wearing of cutaways. In order to preserve dignity, it was agreed that the proper attire should be dark navy blue suits, black shoes, white shirts and a uniform necktie. An agreement was made with a Minneapolis clothier to stock striped gray ties that could be purchased by new deacons not fortunate to secure a hand-me-down from a retiring incumbent!

In the winter of 1950 to 1951, Dr. Donald Cowling brought his experience as the long-time president of Carleton to the trustees with his suggestion that a minister should have the privilege of a sabbatical as do college professors. The trustees readily agreed. Gideon Seymour wrote to thirty-five of the more affluent Plymouthites, asking each to give one hundred dollars for our travels. Mrs. Frank Sprague, a dowager from the Dewey era who had taken us under wing, said that before we toured Europe we should visit the Middle East, from which so much of western civilization had arisen. We considered this sound advice and outlined a trip that began with Egypt and the Holy Land.

Vi arranged to have our older daughter Judy stay with the Spencers, who lived across the street and whose daughter was a Kenwood School classmate. A young couple from Wisconsin doing graduate work at the university and sponsoring Plymouth's high school program took Janet into their home. Vi and I left immediately after Easter. From the Middle East we went through Italy and France until mid-June, when Vi flew home at school's end to take the girls to our Berkshire farm for the summer. I went on to England, where Dr. Sidney Berry, head of the Congregational Union of England and Wales, had arranged preaching appointments for six Sundays. I had told him that I was not concerned about large churches, but rather those in interesting areas. He made some excellent appointments not only for Sunday preaching, but for hospitality in homes of church members. Out of this experience I made two lasting friendships. In Surrey I stayed with Mr. and Mrs. Reginald Hobbs, whose two children were close to the age of ours. Reg was a teacher of math in a private school who later retired early from active teaching and became an examiner in academic testing. Over the years I visited them a number of times, as we shared common interests in travel and education.

Out in lovely Devon Dr. Berry had contacted Mr. and Mrs. James S. Bruce, whose beautiful home, "Leat," was on the edge of the Dart moors. It was a short walk from their estate to Haytor, one of the landmarks of this beautiful area. The Bruces owned the local grain mill in Bovey Tracey, and were active members of the Congregational church at Newton Abbott. Through many visits over the years, "Leat" became my home in Britain, and on several occasions I was invited to preach at the Newton Abbott church. In 1955 Gwen and Jimmy came to the United States. I entertained them first in Minneapolis and introduced them to the Phillip Shermans, where Phil was legal counsel and secretary of the Pillsbury Company. Then Mrs. Frank Sprague joined us as we drove to the Berkshire farmhouse, where Vi and the girls had preceded us. We then made a motor excursion through the New England states.

The following summer of 1956, Vi, the girls and myself made a nine-week summer trip to the British Isles. The Bruces provided the equivalent of an American station wagon for our extensive tour, joining us for the first three weeks circling Ireland. When they went back to Devon, we continued for three weeks in Scotland and a bit less time in England. We were delighted with this marvelous exposure to the charms of Britain.

Thus ended our first period at Plymouth, with the church steadily gaining momentum as it moved forward through thirty-two years of a happy ministry.

11

The First Building Program

A CHURCH IS NOT A BUILDING, though it is often identified by its physical edifice. A church at its best is not even an institution, but more basically a fellowship of caring people who are bound together by ties of commitment and love. Years ago at Plymouth's Centennial I defined a church in terms of three basic elements: "a fellowship of people committed to live in relation to great ideas through the power that comes from God."

Nevertheless, the visible structure is a vital element in the life of any congregation. People identify with it, pointing to it saying, "This is my church." They often select the parish they choose to join on the basis of location, beauty and style of architecture. Though it is perhaps a sad commentary, one may say that no aspect of churchmanship excites a congregation as much as plant expansion and beautification.

Plymouth Congregational Church of Minneapolis has been fortunate in its buildings, and today toward the close of the twentieth century has one of the loveliest and most functional edifices in the country. Throughout the thirty-two years of my ministry we were almost continually in plant enrichment. We were involved in four major building programs, but between these were less dramatic improvements. By my retirement in 1976, we had expanded to cover almost an entire city block on the edge of downtown Minneapolis. These accomplishments were possible because the Hand Always

Above My Shoulder placed me at the end of World War II with a people who were ready for growth, and at strategic moments provided me with three men of wealth who caught the vision of what Plymouth could be. They recognized that there must be physical facilities to attract the people, who may then hear the message around which to organize their lives.

Since its gathering in 1857, Plymouth has interesting stories associated with its plants. Eighteen charter members organized the parish when Minneapolis was a tiny western village of forty-two hundred persons. Because they came from New England, they built a white colonial meetinghouse at Fourth and Nicollet. Three years later this building was destroyed by fire. Legend has it that this was the work of arsonists representing the liquor interests. The second minister, the Rev. Henry M. Nichols, preached a powerful temperance sermon on Sunday evening, March 31, 1860, in which he urged the women of the congregation to visit saloonkeepers, asking them to close. On Wednesday next near midnight the church was burned to the ground, as the clerk's minutes record, "by the hand of some fiend in human shape."

A second church was built on the same site. Under the third minister, Dr. Charles C. Salter, there was a large influx of new members as the town began to grow. In 1866 galleries were added to seat another two hundred and fifty.

The Twin Cities rapidly became an important commercial and agricultural center, and the residential area expanded. In another decade the Westminster Presbyterian Church, which had been our neighbor on Fourth Street, moved three blocks south to Seventh and Nicollet, where the Dayton's Department Store now stands. The Congregationalists recognized the need for more imposing quarters, and in 1874 bought the corner of Eighth and Nicollet, where now stands the Midwest Federal Building. The minister was Dr. Henry A. Stimson, who was to become prominent in the denomination. He had come five years earlier as a young Yale Divinity graduate of twenty-seven. He proved to be a good businessman as well as an excellent minister. During a period of economic depression, he had paid off the debt on the old edifice and raised funds for the new large stone building. A cherished remembrance of our history is Dedication Sunday, October 10, 1875, when Dr. Stimson said to the worshippers, "We cannot dedicate what is not ours." He turned the morning worship into a subscription service until $23,000 had been pledged, and postponed the dedication until evening.

That dramatic event, more than a hundred years ago, set the financial tone for the congregation. Since that Sunday in 1875, Plymouth has never had a debt. During my ministry we invested nearly two million dollars in building projects, but each time we raised the funds before we undertook the work.

As Minneapolis continued to expand, many of the affluent business and professional families moved further south, building mansions on Mount Curve, in Kenwood, Ridgewood, and Park. The Pillsburys, the Crosbys, the Kingmans, the Boveys, the Egglestons, the Woodworths, the Gales, and the David P. Joneses were among Plymouth members to build in the area not far from Nicollet and Groveland, which is the equivalent of Nineteenth Street. It was here that in 1907 the trustees bought land to erect the fourth and final home of Plymouth. The last service in the Eighth and Nicollet building was in 1907, when the property was sold for $234,000, nearly enough to pay for the new edifice. Dr. Harry P. Dewey was called from the east to begin his distinguished pastorate. During construction the congregation met for two years in the YMCA. Dedication was in March 1909.

Plymouth is fortunate in the building committee of 1907. They were seven men not only of financial substance, but of education, culture and good taste. They had traveled in Europe and were familiar with the lasting traditions of Christian art. They engaged the distinguished Boston architectural firm of Shepley, Rutan and Coolidge, who used as a model a beautiful Congregational church in Newton Centre, Massachusetts. The style may be called Tudor-Gothic, often seen in English country churches, of greater width and less height than the pure Gothic cathedral type. Its exterior is constructed of seam-faced granite, which by exposure over the centuries has mellowed to yellowish-orange hues. Fortunately a quarry near St. Cloud, Minnesota, was found which had this stone. The building is set back from the street and surrounded by green lawns. The leaded windows of the parish house blend with the stone to make it a building set apart from the usual as a place to which men and women can come for strength and inspiration.

The sanctuary is an inspiring place of worship. The open timber roof of hammer-beam construction and the rich oak paneling give warmth and an intimacy of feeling. The pews seat 920 persons. There are no columns to obstruct the view, and no matter where a worshipper sits he feels near the pulpit and part of a compact group.

The arrangement at the front of the sanctuary—the chancel—is as nearly perfect as can be devised to interpret our Congregational traditions. The central pulpit on a large platform is historically correct, affirming that the heart of public worship is the proclamation of the gospel through the preaching ministry. Yet the wise builders of Plymouth avoided the frequent sin of sanctuaries with central pulpits, that of having the choir flanked behind the minister facing the congregation. Instead, they placed the choir behind a beautifully carved rail seated in chancel formation on either side of the organ console in the center behind the pulpit chairs. In our time we had a splendidly carved reredos constructed to hide the organ and choirmaster, with a shelf on which the weekly flowers can be arranged. The elaborate oak paneling goes around the sides and rear of the chancel beneath the large central stained glass window.

An amazing feature is that, while the building has side transepts to make a cruciform pattern for the sanctuary, there is no cross in all the carvings and embellishments. This is witness to the liberal, open-minded faith of Plymouth through all its history. We have been a God-centered congregation embracing a more universal outlook upon religion, rather than one confined to the exclusivism of Christian doctrine. This is congenial to my approach, though rare among churches. Again, I consider it a leading of the Hand Always Above My Shoulder that at age thirty-three I was called to spend the major years of my ministry in a sanctuary that artistically expressed my own faith.

I vividly recall in memory that Saturday afternoon in August of 1944 when I was taken by Harold G. Cant and William W. Heintz of the pulpit committee into the sanctuary for the first time. My spirit was lifted immediately. I had just arrived from Great Barrington, where we enjoyed an imposing Romanesque sanctuary. Here was the Lord ushering me to a new opportunity of artistic and spiritual delight! It was a blessing beyond measure!

Exquisite though every detail was, the building had limitations.

It reflected the complacency of a stable congregation in its own traditions. There was no land for expansion, there were inadequate facilities for religious education if young families were to be attracted, no parking area, and the neighborhood was deteriorating. Already many of the mansions had been vacated by death or removal of wealthy families to Lake Minnetonka. The affairs of the parish were oriented toward the past more than to a dynamic future. I was told that a few years earlier the Van Dusen home across LaSalle had been offered at a modest price, but the trustees turned it down. They recognized no need for more property. We were well located from Nicollet Avenue on the east to LaSalle Avenue on the west, but there was scant depth. Behind the buildings was a narrow strip, which we used as an alley, but we were confined to a third of the north-south distance between Groveland and Franklin, the arterial that is equivalent to Twentieth. Behind us on LaSalle was 150 feet of the Kidder family home and 150 feet of a vacated lot on which had once stood the mansion of a Harris family. On Nicollet directly behind was the 150-foot warehouse used by the Walgreen Drug Company, and beyond that a large Standard Oil gas station.

I thus came to a congregation whose plant was sound in its architecture and exquisite in its details, but which was confined to a limited area without visible signs of possible expansion. The years that were to follow provide a fascinating story of unexpected opportunities until the facilities of a growing Plymouth covered all but the far corner of that entire city block. Each time a challenge came, there were people to come forth with the finances to meet it.

This building expansion began with my second season. I have already mentioned that F.A. Bean, chairman of the trustees, put me through close scrutiny my first year, but that when we returned from vacation in September of 1945, he told the board that he was convinced they had a young minister who could lead the church forward, and that it was up to the board to provide him the facilities for his program. At the next annual meeting in January of 1936, Mr. Bean laid before the congregation a fourfold building program to improve the existing plant and to provide classroom space and construct a chapel. The Jackman legacy was to provide $55,000, and a few trustees and others had come forward with another $80,000 more. He estimated another $45,000 would be needed. The final costs came to twice the total, but now the challenge of expansion was openly set.

On April 18, 1946, two lovely carved chairs were dedicated in memory of the twenty-eight-year pastorate of Dr. Harry P. Dewey. The chancel from its inception had three handsome pulpit chairs, but when the ministers came down from the platform to serve communion, these new gifts at the ends of the table gave them a place to sit. Friends of Dr. Dewey had provided the funds two years earlier, and the chairs were designed by Dale R. McEnary.

Another minor improvement under way was the installation of an elevator off the Nicollet entrance. Like most churches built before the modern concern for accessibility, the main entrance to the sanctuary is approached from two tiers of steps, though a door at the other side is almost at street level. Miss Edna Crabtree provided funds for an elevator at the Nicollet end of the parish house, where the entrance was half way between the basement and first-floor levels. This was a real help to persons in wheelchairs or with heart ailments. Once inside, the main-floor offices, parlor and Guild Hall are on the same level as the sanctuary narthex.

Though parking lots were not among the four items Frank Bean proposed to the January 1946 annual meeting, he nevertheless recognized the future need for such. To appreciate the foresightedness of this remarkable man in his concern for Plymouth, one needs to recall that at that time not one of the downtown churches had any provision for off-street parking, and probably none of the suburban congregations had thought of such. Mr. Bean eyed the large vacant lot at the far end of our block, with 150 feet of frontage on LaSalle and 191 feet on the Franklin thoroughfare. He suggested purchase to the trustees, but they were lukewarm, feeling that people would not contribute money for a vacant lot. With this rejection by his colleagues, Mr. Bean went ahead and bought the property himself as a gift. The purchase price was $17,000, with an expenditure of $3000 to blacktop it for parking purposes. The value of this land in the eighties was over $200,000. This gift was further confirmation of his confidence in the future of the congregation. This recognition of the practical functioning of a church was a tremendous assistance to Plymouth. Before his death ten years later, he and Frank W. Griswold acquired more land for parking.

With well over a hundred persons a year joining Plymouth and with the rapid growth of the Sunday school, it was evident that we needed more space. In accordance with Mr. Bean's suggestions at the January 1946 annual meeting, the trustees authorized Dale McEnary, a long-time member of Plymouth and a partner in the prominent firm of McEnary & Krafft, to explore plans for a building addition.

At a congregational meeting in October of that year, an advisory building committee was authorized. Glenn Wyer, then president of the Plymouth Society, appointed fifteen persons for this task: Frank O. Koehler, chairman; Robert E. Ford, Philip H. Nason, Mrs. Stuart W. Rider, Mrs. Jay Summy, Mrs. Roland S. Vaile, Mrs. Glenn Wyer, Mrs. Harry L. Robinson, John H. Ravlin, W. Howard Bovey, and five of us from the staff.

Considerable exploration went on between the trustees, the advisory committee and the architect. Agreement was reached that we should purchase the 150-foot property between the church and the Franklin corner lot. This contained the spacious home and gardens of Mr. and Mrs. William Kidder. In discussions with them they were reluctant to sell, and in each discussion raised the price. Mr. Bean became provoked at this tactic and concluded that we should proceed with plans that involved only land we owned. By closing the alley behind us, extending to the south property line and going out to the LaSalle sidewalk on the west, we could have an addition forty feet deep and running nearly the whole block except for the Nicollet setback.

Three possibilities were considered, but technical problems of roof lines and excessive costs argued against them. Mr. McEnary and the building committee engaged as consultant Mr. E.M. Conover, a distinguished Boston architect who was then serving as head of the Interdenominational Bureau of Church Architecture. He came to Minneapolis, surveyed the situation, and expressed approval for what is the fourth plan that evolved through more than a year of discussions.

The trustees appointed a building committee of three to finalize the plan and supervise its implementation. F.A. Bean was chairman, associated with Willard A. Morse and John H. Ravlin. These men devoted untold hours in their concern for every detail, and the final results are witness to their dedication. During the construction period they were on hand nearly every day.

Two years after the original suggestion, the January 1948 annual meeting voted to proceed. An agreement was reached with Fred O. Watson Company to act as contractors. Ground-breaking ceremonies were held on Sunday morning, April 18, when after worship friends were invited to go to the site at the rear of the sanctuary. This was the first ground-breaking in forty years, since 1907 when dirt was turned for the start of the main edifice. Construction began the next week.

The total cost of the project by then was estimated to be $271,400, more than half of which had been raised by the Jackman legacy and special gifts. During the last two weeks of May 1946, a canvass was launched to raise $115,000 from the general membership. Luther Ford was chairman, joined by Roswell V. Curtiss, Voight O. Lenmark, Maurice K. Mark, Arthur W. McMillan, Glenn Sullivan, Lawrence Woodard, Hazel Fraker, and J.A. Ross. The committee had a group of visitation captains, each leading a group of ten callers: John W. Barber, Jr., Marth L. Bergquist, Robert C. Burton, Robert S. Carney, William C. Christopherson, George H. Dow, Floyd L. Dwight, J. Martin Erbele, Iver G. Hovland, Ellwood H. Newhart, Myron H. Powell, John A. Sivertsen, Robert J. Stallman, and Willard A. Stevenson.

While the canvass was successful, costs kept escalating. When the final costs were tabulated at the end of 1949 they came to $422,000, which was far more than the estimate of $271,000 made two years earlier. Various items were added along the way. In the fall of 1949, the committee said that $50,000 beyond pledges would be needed, and one member offered $25,000 if matched by other gifts. This was accomplished, and then a final $22,000 was needed, with one man giving $7,500 toward that. Throughout this two-year period of planning and construction excitement was high as we saw rising before us a skillfully planned structure that provided new space and actually enhances the old.

By November of 1948, the new structure was roofed over, and on April 28, 1949, we had an open house and dinner to mark completion of the educational and dining room additions. The chapel area was not roofed and enclosed until that month, and the furbishing of that interior ran to the early part of 1950.

What was gained was considerable space for educational and social programs. The large baronial hall of the original building was known as "the chapel," with a platform at the west end and a balcony at the east end. For many years this was used for Sunday school assemblies and for various meetings. In this first building expansion, the balcony was walled off to provide Sunday school rooms and the platform removed so that the area had an even floor and could be converted into what we now called "Guild Hall." It was a splendid area for receptions and after-service fellowship or coffee hours. The room had three large Gothic tracery windows to the back alley that provided daytime light, but with the new construction these no longer had outdoor exposure. Recessed electrical lighting was possible because of the thickness of the stone walls. A row of dormer or transom windows was cut into the high roof to provide illumination from the sun.

Immediately behind the windows or south wall of Guild Hall were built two restrooms and a storage space. Along these ran a corridor, and beyond that three rooms for toddlers, nursery and cribs. These went to the property line and looked out upon the Kidder house and garage. Further along this forty-foot width were robing rooms for clergy and choir, and at the end of the corridor was the narthex and chapel. At the second-floor level, further classrooms were built that connected with those in the original Nicollet end parish house. The second level behind the sanctuary was left open to give light to the large chancel window of the sanctuary, and then rose again to provide the upper space of the new chapel. In the basement, the significant gain was the removal of the base wall of the old building to provide an opening into a new dining area adjacent to the old, which we named "Jackman Hall" in honor of Jerome Jackman, whose unexpected legacy initiated the entire project. One of the problems was the securing of a forty-foot steel beam across the opening to support the structure. We designed the room with wainscoting and recessed lights in a curved dropped ceiling, so as to make this area attractive for smaller gatherings.

The central portion of the basement became a storage area, and the large room under the chapel was designated for the Boy Scout Troop. This room was later attractively paneled as a gift of Mr. and Mrs. Merlin L. Pugh.

The successful conclusion of this first major building project was a cause for great rejoicing, and gave us improved facilities for our expanding program. By April of 1949, our new Sunday school rooms were ready for use, and a year later the chapel was completed.

12

The Plymouth Chapel

FOR ME THE BUILDING OF PLYMOUTH CHAPEL from 1947 to 1950 was the fulfillment of a dream. Every minister hopes that someday he or she may have the opportunity to construct a sanctuary that will lift the spirits of worshippers to communion with the Eternal. Inasmuch as I had let pass an appointment to the Yale Divinity School faculty, I sensed that probably the years of my ministry would be spent at Plymouth Minneapolis, and that this would be my only chance to design a sanctuary.

Beyond that, we needed a chapel for our spiritual enrichment. What was called "the chapel" in the original 1909 building was basically a large meeting place for assemblies and informal gatherings. Though beautiful in ceiling trusses and wall paneling, it lacked intimacy and warmth for special occasions when families gather for weddings or funerals. The floor was covered with brown utility-grade linoleum, which was of no aesthetic value. In no way could this room be regarded as a worship center.

Early in my ministry I had become interested in stained glass, and loved the jewel-like effect when sunlight illumines great chunks of blues, reds and yellows. The windows of European cathedrals created an atmosphere of wondrous awe and mystery conducive to reverent meditation, and the figures depicted are like open books that remind beholders of the Biblical heroes of ancient days. While we were yet in our first pastorate at Great Barrington, I had conceived the notion of a series of windows depicting the "Seasons of the Christian Year." I knew of no church in which such a sequence had been attempted. Though I am liberal in theological interpretation, I am also liturgically oriented. I feel that the orderly progression of the Christian calendar, built especially around the ministry of Jesus, provides a rhythm and a balance to worship.

As plans for our first major building expansion at Plymouth developed, the inclusion of a truly worshipful chapel became as important as classroom space for the Sunday school. By utilizing the forty-foot alleyway and extending to the sidewalk on LaSalle, we had an adequate area and could provide for easy access from the street. McEnary & Krafft were expert craftsmen with high artistic sensibilities, and designed a lovely Gothic high-ceilinged chapel, with the chancel at the street end and a balcony at the rear over an inviting narthex.

The building committee of F.A. Bean, Willard A. Morse and John H. Ravlin deserves great credit for its accomplishments. There was no thought of scrimping on details or of making the chapel area merely a utility space for small gatherings. They realized that we were building the equivalent of a small church, and that the design and furnishings should be harmonious with the quality of our main sanctuary. They allowed me to work closely with the architects on details, so that the Plymouth Chapel is an expression of my thoughts as to pews, communion table, pulpit, floor and windows.

As a Congregationalist I believe firmly in the central pulpit as a symbol of the centrality of the preaching ministry, and am thankful that the three churches to which the Hand Always Above My Shoulder led me in the forty years of my major ministry do have central pulpits. However, in designing a chapel I realized that the chief function within it would not be preaching but worship. A chapel would become precious as a sanctuary for funerals, weddings and baptisms. People would come for meditation and reflection. For these purposes the eye is carried by the red carpet of the center aisle up the two steps of a stone chancel floor to a central communion table toward the back wall. A crimson drape framed by a handsome reredos carving, with a Celtic or Ionic cross against the crimson, leads the vision upward to the beautiful chancel window above. The carved inscription on the face of the communion table is not the traditional, "Do This In Remembrance of Me," because the serving of the sacrament is not the main function. Rather, we inscribed the assurance of Jesus, "My Peace I give unto you" (John 14:27).

Because the chancel area is small, and as low churchmen we wished to avoid walking from side to side, we omitted a lectern but projected from the right a handsomely carved pulpit. Around its three sides are inscribed the charter of freedom spoken by Jesus in John 8:32: "Ye shall know the truth, and the truth shall make you free." Freedom of the minister to speak the truth as God gives light is one of the cherished principles of our fellowship.

Pews on either side of a central aisle comfortably seat one hundred and sixty persons on the main floor, with pews in the balcony for another fifty. The design called for an organ console to be in the balcony, with the speaking pipes on the chancel walls. Professor Arthur B. Jennings, our beloved organist, did not approve of electronic instruments, so he secured an old-fashioned pump reed organ to place in the balcony. The geography of the plant was such that when the rear doors of the main sanctuary were open, the sounds of the sanctuary organ were sufficiently audible in the chapel to serve for the triumphant tones of wedding marches. This arrangement prevailed for nine years until in 1959 Frank Griswold gave $25,000 for the securing of a Moeller organ for the chapel.

The fund-raising projections for this 1946-1950 building project did not include any item for the chapel windows. We would be able to use the chapel with temporarily installed plain glass. However, in the fall of 1948 I suggested to the trustees and the building committee that the full beauty of the area could not be achieved until the windows were filled with stained glass. I laid before them my dream of a series of lancets depicting the "Seasons of the Christian Year." The situation in most church edifices is that the filling of open space is left to the random offer of parishioners to give a memorial to a loved one, with the result that windows are designed without any overall plan. Donors choose a subject that is pleasing to them, even though there may already be treatments of that theme. I pointed out that my dream was to have a uniform theme designed from the outset that would result in a meaningful sequence of incomparable value. Furthermore, I said that if the committee would agree to this proposal, I would undertake to raise the money outside the fund campaign then under way. Mr. Bean and the others listened sympathetically to my proposal and agreed that I might proceed to secure this crowning completion to the chapel.

Mr. Willard Whitcomb Morse, father of Willard A. Morse, who was one of the three members of the building committee, offered to pay my expenses to travel to various stained glass studios in the country to select the one I considered best able to achieve the desired results. I visited three: one in New York, one in Boston, and one in Philadelphia. My choice was the Willet Studio in Philadelphia.

This window project was one of the most exciting of my life, and through it I met two men whose friendship has ever since been precious to me.

The first is Henry Lee Willet, whose father and mother were pioneers in bringing the best of medieval glass tradition to the United States. They used pot-metal glass, as did the artists of the twelfth and thirteenth centuries, mastering the subtleties of color to achieve glory rather than to paint pictures. As Henry Adams wrote in his classic description of the Cathedral of Chartes: "No doubt the first command of the Queen of Heaven was for light, but the second, at least equally imperative, was for colour."

Henry Willet was at the height of his career when I visited him and his wife Muriel in Philadelphia in 1948. He had already done windows in some of the major churches across the country. He was excited by the prospect of our series, as he realized that no one had previously designed a sequence on the "Seasons of the Christian Year." We have sixteen lancet openings along the two sides of the chapel, with a large chancel window, a balcony rose window, a narthex screen of six panels, and three lancets in the narthex. We invited him to come to Minneapolis to discuss the project. Mr. Bean said to him, "I want you to give us a price for the finest work for the total series, so that whatever Dr. Conn and the committee ask you to put into the windows you will gladly do." On these terms a contract was signed.

With the window contract signed, we began selecting material for each of the Christian year seasons. I am not an artist in visual imagery, nor can I draw any recognizable figure. I am, however, an art lover and am interested in symbolism, mythology and iconography. The building committee was magnanimous in giving me a free hand to conceive this series. Mr. Bean had made clear that the Willet Studio was to create the finest work possible and to respond to every suggestion made at our end.

In the fall of 1948 I assembled an advisory committee to help select the days that were to be included in the sequence and to make a study of possible imagery connected with each. Members of this group were: Mrs. Atherton Bean, Mrs. Harrington Beard, Dr. Nelson L. Bossing, W. Howard Bovey, Mrs. Joseph C. Bruce, Mrs. Felton Colwell, Mrs. Stanley S. Gillam, Hamlin Hunt, Rowland R. McRoberts, Mrs. Ellwood H. Newhart, Miss Lois Powell, Harlow C. Richardson, Mrs. Stuart W. Rider, Mrs. Gideon Seymour, Mrs. Arthur P. Stacy, Miss Mary Truesdell, Ben S. Woodworth, Ruth E. Bailey, and Ruth J. Easterday.

The first question to be decided was the theme for the chancel window. Its three high lancets would be the largest of the chapel and as the focal point would determine the atmosphere. Should it be Christmas or Easter, the two principal festival days of the Christian Season? I opted for neither. Even though as a Christian church Plymouth celebrates these two high points, as a liberal congregation we do not adhere to either of the theological doctrines centered around them, neither the Divinity of Christ nor the Resurrection. We are more involved in the way of life that Jesus presents.

My choice was World-wide Communion Sunday, the most recent addition. It was first celebrated in 1939 at the suggestion of Dr. Jesse M. Bader, executive secretary of the Department of Evangelism of the Federal Council of Churches of Christ in America, and accepted by the World Council of Churches and the International Missionary Council. In an age of denominational differences that divide the Christian world into several hundred sects, this observance recalls all of us to the basic affirmations that unite us. We have differences in theology and patterns of liturgical worship. No attempt is made to judge among them, but we are invited to celebrate the eucharist according to our own customs in the remembrance of our spiritual unity in Jesus, whom all of us call Lord. In this designation we are not making metaphysical statements about his nature, but affirming our commitment to him as the supreme revealer of the nature of God and the ways of his kingdom.

We suggested a window with the central figure of Christ enclosed in an elongated nimbus or aureole. Bright rays emanate from this. In his right hand Jesus holds the communion chalice, and in his left the symbol of cross and orb, made by a Latin cross on a banded globe, denoting the triumph of the gospel over the world. At his feet is a communion table around which are gathered persons of different races.

At the top of the window is the daring affirmation from the second-century letter to Diognetus, "Christians Hold the World Together." At the bottom is the message of Paul in II Corinthians 5:19, "God was in Christ reconciling the world unto himself."

In the two side lancets are six scenes of ways in which Christians may hold the world together, each with a different national setting. Around the margins are small figures that illustrate scriptural instances of crossing over boundaries that separate.

Henry Willet took our suggestions as to theme and symbols and created a magnificent chancel window that establishes an atmosphere of love, tolerance and goodwill as worshippers move to the hope of peace on earth. I am particularly happy that our committee chose World-wide Communion to express the centrality of our ecumenical affirmations, because in the decades to follow, when I led the congregation in opposing the sacrifice of Congregationalism into an organic union of a political structure, we could always point to this window as evidence of our commitment to spiritual unity. Also, we selected for the rose window in the balcony the seal of the reorganized World Council of Churches after Amsterdam. We see the ship as a symbol of the Church, encircled with the Greek word *oikumene*, meaning "universal," pertaining to the habitable world. From my earliest ministry I have been a universalist, seeking to stimulate the spiritual life of all peoples. I am not a Christian exclusivist. The chapel windows attest to this ecumenical vision.

In 1949 Plymouth published my second book, *Symbolism in Stone and Glass*, with photographs and a full description of all the stained glass at Plymouth. I am therefore at this writing not giving an account of the chapel series. It is enough to record that the sequence of the seasons is Advent, Christmas, Epiphany, Ash Wednesday, Palm Sunday, Maundy Thursday, Good Friday, Easter,

Pentecost, Children's Day, Trinity, Reformation, All Soul's Day, and Thanksgiving. For each Henry Willet designed a brilliant creation.

During the more than two years in which these many lancets were being designed, my wife and I developed a close friendship with Henry that lasted until his death. He traveled extensively across the country to confer with church building committees, as he was recognized as probably the foremost artisan in his craft. On these travels he often stopped to stay overnight in our home, where he was welcomed as akin to a family member. Our daughters called him their "Uncle Henry" and looked forward to visits from this engaging redhead who recited lengthy passages from "Slovenly Peter."

Over the years Plymouth commissioned the Willet Studios to do further work. In the sanctuary by the balcony stairs, Henry did the third in the trilogy of "Faith, Hope and Love," the first two having been done earlier by Charles J. Connick of Boston. When Minor B. Gold, Jr., was killed in an auto accident, his parents provided funds for this memorial.

Through the influence of Quaker mystics I have been interested in the devotional classics, and we arranged to have three of these commemorated in corridor windows. Mr. Connick designed one for Bunyan's *The Pilgrim's Progress*, a gift of Mr. and Mrs. David Lee Sutherland in memory of two prominent businessmen who had been pillars of Plymouth in the early 1900s: David C. Bell and James B. Sutherland.

Henry Willet did two larger corridor windows in the series on the devotional classics. The first one commemorates the eighteenth-century New Jersey Quaker, given by the family of Attorney Charles C. Carlson. The other is a stunning modern design in brilliant colors depicting scenes from the life of William Law, who authored *A Serious Call to a Devout and Holy Life*. This is the gift of Mrs. Roland W. Chambers and Mrs. Carl L. Nordly in memory of their parents, Mr. and Mrs. Broder Johansen.

Henry was not only a gifted artist, but also an active Presbyterian layman. He served on national bodies of that denomination, and was particularly active in behalf of the rights of Japanese-Americans interned by our government during World War II. Vi and I visited the Willets in Philadelphia on several occasions and kept our friendship until the death of both of them.

With the selection of the window themes under way, I set about my second responsibility for the chapel, to obtain donors to underwrite the cost as memorials to their families. Due to the design of the chapel walls, the lancets came in pairs. We established as a price $1,200 for a single lancet and $2,000 for a pair. The resulting gifts would pay for the Willet contract. As one reflects forty years later, these were bargain prices, as the appraised value of the chapel glass has escalated more than twenty times. Most families subscribed for pairs. Only Good Friday, because of the exterior door, stands alone. We specified that there would be no names included in the glass, but the memorials with season designation would be carved on a beautifully designed wooden tablet in the narthex. I had no problem in securing willing donors, for when the magnitude of the project was explained, families generously responded. Thus we were able at the outset to complete the total series on the "Seasons of the Christian Year." In May of 1950 we dedicated a chapel of glorious beauty.

In the process of solicitation for these window memorials, I made the second significant friendship to come from the chapel project, that with my dear friend and "angel," Frank W. Griswold. From 1949 through my retirement in 1976, Frank was a benefactor of Plymouth in many ways. Not only was he a provider of funds for every need, but he took a personal interest in all details. He built a business empire through founding and selling companies to manufacture structural items, starting with the creation of electric signal lights for city streets and railroad systems. He is an astute developer of commercial real estate, buying older buildings, renovating them, and selling at good profit. Not only has he sound business judgment, but he is himself a mechanical genius. When some function goes wrong he can analyze the trouble and find the solution. He is a gentle, kindly man, never angry, who treats his employees with such integrity and respect that they willingly do their best for him. In his shops he was never unionized, but always paid above the going rate. He kept personal contact with every employee, always handing out the paychecks personally. He never fired anyone, but where trouble arose he discussed the situation with the person involved, and pointed out other possibilities until the employee decided to make a change.

We made Frank the Manager of Properties for Plymouth, and from 1949 until the 1980s, when he was no longer physically able to move with ease, he took responsibility for every item that needed to be done on the church plant. He was on the premises nearly every week, and in any emergency he would come to remedy the situation with a crew of dedicated and talented artisans from his staff.

Frank became one of my closest friends. Over the years we visited together on many matters, and after each of us was divorced, we dined together in restaurants several times a month. I have learned a great deal from him about getting along with people, and we laugh together over many human predicaments. Now in his nineties, Frank's mind is as sharp as ever, his memory excellent, but he no longer has the strength to move about freely.

Frank Griswold is a life-long Plymouthite. He was born in 1896, one of ten children of Mr. and Mrs. Franklin Griswold. The father was a lawyer and a deacon. Each Sunday the family of five boys and five girls was brought to church. More than one pew was needed to seat them! Frank formally joined in 1915. Soon after his marriage he dropped out of participation, as his first wife was a Christian Scientist who preferred her own church. By the time I came to Minneapolis the couple was divorced, and Frank had recently married a younger woman.

Our friendship began as I was making calls on long-time families to invite them to subscribe for chapel windows. Our financial administrator, Miss Hazel Fraker, told me of the Griswolds. At the moment no member of that family was in Plymouth, but Frank was known in the city as a wealthy and generous philanthropist. Miss Fraker mentioned that one of his sisters, Mrs. Harry Lauderdale, was active in a Congregational church in north Minneapolis. I made an appointment to call on her, and suggested that her brothers and sisters together might underwrite a window for their parents, who had been active in the early part of the century. She was cordial and said, "Why don't you talk to my brother Frank?"

I was somewhat hesitant to approach such a busy man who to me was a stranger, but I phoned his office and was given an appointment. I remember vividly that interview. I explained that I was the new minister at Plymouth Church, and that I had been told that he was raised there in a family whose parents had been devoted members. I apologized that on my first visit to him I should be asking for money, but told him of my plan to have windows in our new chapel dedicated to those who had loved Plymouth. Frank asked what sum was involved.

"Two thousand dollars for a pair," I said.

His instant reply startled me. "I will give that sum, whether or not my family contributes. You can do what you like as to talking with them."

I had not anticipated such an immediate favorable decision. In thanking him I said, "I very much appreciate your help, but in accepting your offer I would like to impose one condition. Your money is important, but beyond that I would like you to understand what we are doing. I invite you to come to the chapel to see where the windows are and what your gift will accomplish."

Frank replied that that was a fair request. We made an appointment for late afternoon a week hence. By this time the chapel had been roofed over with the trusses in place, but otherwise it was a bare room with nothing but cement and plaster visible. On the appointed afternoon Frank came with his wife. I showed them through the new Sunday school addition and into this barren room. They were polite and interested in my story. Then he said, "When you were in my office you apologized for coming on your errand the first time we had met. It was the first time you had seen me, but it was not the first time I had seen you. We have been coming to Plymouth several Sundays this fall. I like your sermons, I like what you are doing, and I want to help."

This was the way our friendship began. From that afternoon in 1949 until the present, Frank Griswold has been of inestimable help to Plymouth Church through active participation at many levels, and he has been one of my closest and dearest friends.

Our 1950 chapel dedication was a happy occasion for all of us. We had come through a long process of planning and fund raising from January 1946 when Mr. Bean had first proposed plant expansion. Along the way we had learned a great deal, had come to know and trust one another more fully, and now sensed the tremendous potential within this congregation. We had an exquisite chapel sanctuary to accommodate two hundred persons in which to celebrate high moments in the lives of our families. It quickly became the custom to hold memorial services for departed loved ones within this chapel, for weddings to be performed here, and for the church school youth to be taught the significance of the Christian holy days through study of the glorious windows.

13

Securing Room to Expand

By 1950 WE HAD ACHIEVED OUR FIRST significant plant expansion. We now had an attractive new dining room to accommodate one hundred fifty persons, new classrooms, and our beautiful Plymouth Chapel. Yet we were still confined to the property at the north end of a city block, the same area that had been purchased at the time of the original construction in 1907. In our first project we had utilized the forty-foot alley area behind the original building, but we had not gained any property enlargement.

On the LaSalle Avenue side the adjacent 150-foot lot to the south contained the house and gardens of Mr. and Mrs. William Kidder. In 1948 Mr. Bean had tried to negotiate a purchase for the church, but when Mrs. Kidder kept raising the price, he abandoned the idea and settled for building on our alley area.

On the Nicollet Avenue frontage there was also a 150-foot parcel, which housed the warehouse operation of the Walgreen Company drug stores. The only approach was from the street, so large trucks had to swing into traffic and then back through a drive entrance. Nicollet is one of the main north-south avenues, and it seemed to me that the day would come when the city would no longer permit such interference with the smooth flow of traffic.

In the fall of 1953 I suggested to the trustees that we communicate to the Walgreen Company in Chicago that whenever they considered moving their operations from this warehouse, Plymouth would appreciate an offer of first refusal to purchase. The trustees agreed, and to our surprise within a few months the Chicago executives did give us this opportunity. Frank Griswold was delegated to negotiate terms, and a price of $80,000 was agreed upon. He explained to the company that although the trustees had agreed to this purchase, no guarantee could be given. The affairs of a church move slowly because so many people are involved. According to Plymouth bylaws, no property can be bought or sold without a vote of the congregation. A special meeting must be called with advance notice of three weeks, the call being read from the pulpit on successive preceding Sundays. The Walgreen people accepted this condition and allowed the trustees sufficient time to get legal authorization. They later told Mr. Griswold that in the intervening period they had received a higher offer from an unnamed bidder, but they would not consider it while the Plymouth proposal was pending. This consideration corroborated my experience that there is real integrity among leaders in the business community.

This opportunity came at a moment when the church was already involved in outside real estate purchases. We were financing several lots in the block north of us on Nicollet to add some sorely needed parking spaces. But we also required more area for our rapidly growing church school. In the 1948 building project we increased classroom space by 52 percent, but Ruth Bailey, our education director, pointed out that enrollment had increased by 60 percent, so we were already more crowded than at that time. We were currently using 10,713 square feet for classes, including dining room space. Renovation of the warehouse would make available another 6,000 square feet.

Willard A. Morse and Robert E. Ford spoke to the specially called meeting to present the challenge as seen by the trustees. There was considerable discussion, most of it related to the means of paying for the project. A written ballot was taken, and purchase was approved by a vote of 112 to 7.

This was a great advance and a real opportunity. Not only did it meet the immediate needs for more church school space, but more importantly it broke the barriers that confined us and constituted an opening wedge toward expansion into the entire city block.

Because of his expertise in building matters, Frank Griswold was put in charge of the remodeling of what came to be known as the annex, converting the warehouse space into large classrooms. Associated with him was Willard A. Morse, who was involved in all the building projects of my ministry. It was thought that perhaps some of the front area could be rented for office space, but this was never accomplished. An immediate appeal for $29,000 was sent out in the summer of 1954 to pay for the expansion. This was forthcoming, and an indebtedness of $90,000 voted by the trustees to cover the total project. It was planned to amortize this over eight years by items in the annual budget. The actual cost of renovation came to $59,000, making the total investment in the annex $139,000. By 1959, just five years later, this had been largely paid off.

It was not until spring of 1955 that the "big shift" to the new church school annex came when six large rooms were ready, and our educational program moved into the expanded facilities. Ruth Bailey had assembled an outstanding corps of teachers to inspire our many children and youth. In my first year at Plymouth I had three young people in my confirmation class: Jean and Dawn Skarnes and Doreen Jacobson, all of whom married and whose families have remained active at Plymouth. By the time of the "big shift" we had nineteen in confirmation class, and from 1955 we went on to grow rapidly to classes of fifty and more confirmands.

For twelve years we made good use of the large rooms in this annex until we demolished the building in our final expansion program of 1967-68.

Simultaneously with the Walgreen project, other property expansion was taking place through the farsighted eyes of Frank Griswold and Frank Bean. The former spotted three dilapidated frame houses in the Nicollet Avenue block north of us, where Eighteenth Street, coming west from Abbott Hospital, runs into Nicollet but does not go beyond. Our area was in a slump at this time. The neighborhood was deteriorating. Mr. Griswold and Mr. Bean purchased these three lots in November of 1954 for $25,000 and had the eyesore structures demolished. The area was blacktopped in the spring of 1955 and leased to commercial operators for weekday parking, with our people having free access on Sundays. This acquisition was another pivotal advance. Within a few years, through trades and land swaps, Plymouth was able to provide a large park-

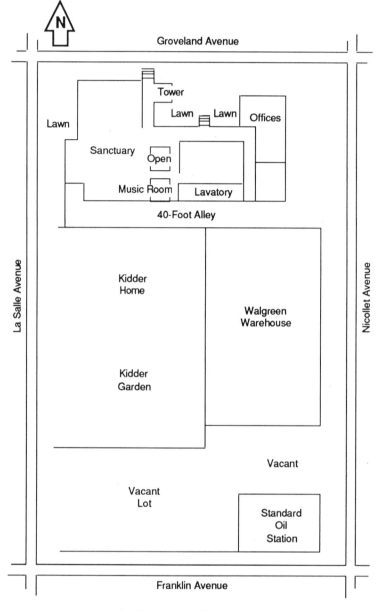

The Plymouth Plant in 1944

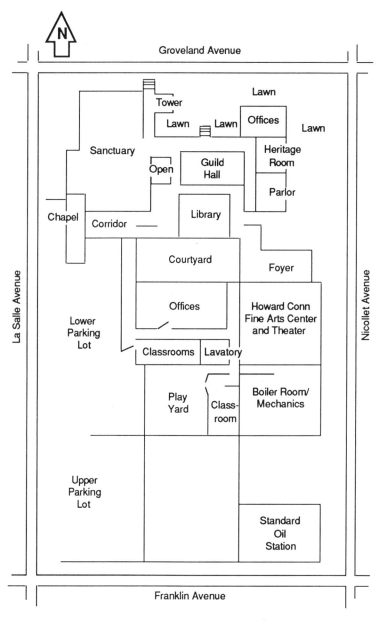

The Plymouth Plant in 1976

ing lot immediately across the street on Groveland from which it derived substantial income through partial renting to Red Owl Stores.

During these years we were constantly involved in improving our facilities. In 1952 the trustees replaced the slate roof on both the sanctuary and the original parish house. That same winter Merlin L. Pugh provided funds to panel with knotty pine the large basement space under the chapel to make an attractive room for the Boy Scout Troop.

Over the summer of 1953, Mr. Griswold and Mr. Morse supervised a complete redecorating of Plymouth's lovely Tudor-Gothic sanctuary. Because of high ceilings this is a major task for any church. A forest of scaffolding has to be built to enable workmen to reach the ceilings. New Gothic sanctuary lanterns were designed by Dale McEnary and Cecil Branham to be hung from the ceilings, to replace the original circular iron fixtures with exposed bulbs. Red carpet was put on the aisles and the chancel. Some $30,000 was expended on this project. On September 27, 1953, nearly a thousand friends packed the sanctuary for a Reconsecration Service. Everyone seemed delighted with the fresh brightness of our lovely house of worship. Harold G. Cant, who was then moderator, surprised me with the presentation of a new pulpit robe, that the minister might also be "refurbished"!

In December of that year, the wooden announcement boards facing both Nicollet and LaSalle were replaced with permanent stone bulletins made of the same seam-face granite as the buildings. The glass area is opened to put in the weekly announcement of Sunday services.

Seven years after the chapel was dedicated, Frank Griswold donated funds to install a pipe organ in that place of quiet beauty. The gift was in honor of Professor Arthur B. Jennings, our beloved organist, and was to coincide with Plymouth's Centennial. The contract was with the Moeller Organ Company of Hagerstown, Maryland, and the instrument was designed by Mr. Jennings to be especially effective for weddings and small devotional services. Previous to this Mr. Jennings had used an old-fashioned reed organ, and for more triumphal occasions had played the sanctuary organ with the doors open for the music to be heard in the distance.

The new organ has 933 pipes, thirteen ranks and three manuals. The console is placed in the balcony, where choir stalls and tiered pews were added. The pipe chambers are in the chancel walls, where space was provided at construction. Dale R. McEnary designed two lovely organ cases for the side walls to match the design of the reredos. As one of the main events of Centennial Sunday, April 27, 1957, Mr. Jennings gave the inaugural recital on the new instrument. To accommodate the crowds, duplicate recitals were given at 2:30 and 4:30, with Mrs. John Lane Sprague and her social committee hosting a Guild Hall tea from 3:30 to 6:00.

The year 1957 was a spectacular year for Plymouth, being its Centennial. In the week after Easter we had a tremendous celebration with over one hundred new members affiliating, the Hivales visiting from India, and a memorable banquet for which guests came from afar to mingle reminiscences of the past with dreams of the future.

But 1957 also brought the second dramatic breakthrough in our dreams of expansion. This was precipitated by a death, as was our first opening in the summer of 1945. This time it was the death in February of our neighbor, Lorraine W. Kidder. It may seem inappropriate to speak again of the Hand Always Above My Shoulder providing good fortune through the death of another. In this world of complex relationships, it often does take the death of a pivotal individual to open avenues of advance. Mrs. Kidder had earlier blocked Plymouth's property expansion to the south, though as a property owner and resident she had every right to do so. Her husband, William A. Kidder, was a gentle, kindly man who appreciated the situation of the church. He saw the growing programs of Plymouth, as he and Mrs. Kidder had united in membership earlier in my ministry. He recognized that we had acquired the Walgreen property directly behind his. He came to us in the fall of 1957 and said that the house was too big for him alone, and he was sure we would like to have it. He offered us the 150 feet on LaSalle for $75,000. I thanked him for his thoughtfulness, and assured him that indeed we would want to make the purchase. A business meeting on November 19 unanimously approved the recommendation of the trustees that we do just this.

Mr. Kidder's offer of his property to Plymouth was of momentous significance, because it meant that we now would have the use of the entire block except for the Standard Oil station on the far southwest corner of Nicollet and Franklin. I decided to make a dramatic event of this acquisition, and challenged the congregation to bring a "Miraculous Offering" on the second Sunday of Advent to raise on a single morning the $75,000 purchase price. It would indeed be a miracle if that sum were contributed spontaneously and quickly. But because of the generous response of Plymouthites on many previous appeals, I had faith in "miracles."

Yet "miracles" do require preparation! Not only are we dependent upon the Hand Always Above the Shoulder, but all of us need to do our part in attaining a goal. Fortunately, throughout my years Providence has provided "angels" to cap the generous giving of hundreds of dedicated members whose affluence was not as great as theirs. After announcing this offering, I went to these special friends to lay our needs before them. Atherton Bean is the older son of Frank and Bertha Bean, a Carleton College graduate and benefactor, a Rhodes Scholar, a patron of the arts and all things worthwhile. He is one of the ablest and finest men I have ever known. He is not a member of Plymouth, but he has respect for the Congregational principles of freedom and openness, and an appreciation of his father's love for Plymouth. He has helped us on many occasions, always with the quiet anonymity that characterizes the philanthropy of this family. Atherton recognized at once the importance of acquiring this adjoining property, and made a substantial commitment of $25,000.

Another of my "angels" was Merlin L. Pugh, who with his wife Phyllis had come into membership during my first year. By 1957 "Bob" and Phyllis Pugh had built a home in the Minnetonka area for their growing family, and had transferred their membership to Wayzata Community Church. We remained good friends, and they looked upon the wealth that had come from Bob's skillful development of the Franklin Transformer Company as a trust to be used to help others. They are among the most conscientious people I have known. I went to Bob with our opportunity, and he said at once, "Of course Plymouth has to have that property." He too made a gift of $25,000. I asked Willard Morse to help with the Sunday offering, for he was a part of all the property programs throughout my years. He responded with $5,000.

When the December Sunday came, we had substantial under-writing in hand. If the rest of us would extend ourselves a bit we could bring the remaining $20,000 that morning. And so we did! It was thrilling to feel the excitement and enthusiasm of an expectant congregation making another historic advance. "Miracles" indeed do happen!

The large Kidder house was set on the northern part of the 150-foot property, and we left that intact. It was already divided into first- and second-floor spacious living units. For twelve years we used these as residences for the young ministers we brought in as assistants. These were largely young men and their wives who came to us directly out of seminary and spent three years in something of an apprenticeship training. Most of them were outstanding, and were an inspiration to our youth for whom they had special respon-sibilities. After a few years, they generally went on to good parishes of their own. The basement area of the house was also spacious and sufficiently well decorated that it could have been used as an apart-ment. We decided to convert it to a youth center. It had an outside entrance at the rear, which we painted to dub the place "The Green Door." This was utilized for several years for our high school pro-gram.

The southern portion of the property had been used by the Kidders for a garden. We blacktopped seventy-five feet of this to provide parking, which had ready access through a rear door into the annex, and from there into the main building. We were indeed fortunate with this arrangement for many years, though the exterior front of the annex required frequent repairs and had no aesthetic charm. It had been constructed for industrial purposes of manufac-turing and storage. Behind this poor exterior we had spacious rooms to accommodate Sunday school classes, but even they were clearly renovated warehouse space. Though we made the best of this acqui-sition, we recognized that at some future time we must replace the building with a more appropriate structure.

As one looks back over these years, it is astounding to realize how one new project followed another, so that we seemed in a con-tinuous process of acquiring and remodeling property. A minister is primarily an inspirer and teacher of the spiritual life of a congregation, but it is helpful also to have sound business judgment for the material side of parish life. In a congregation like Plymouth there are many, many business and professional leaders, but they come to trust the guidance of a minister who has creative imagination to explore the future, who understands business exchanges, and whose enthusiasm never outruns fiscal responsibility. Through all the years I enjoyed my relationship with the able men and women who constituted our boards.

Amid all our growth we did have one aborted effort that must be recorded. In the late fifties there was a burst of activity among religious groups to develop retirement homes or health care facilities for the elderly. This movement was facilitated by the Hill-Burton Act, through which sponsoring groups could obtain federal financing for this worthy purpose. There were provisions to assure that facilities constructed through such funds be open to the general public and not confined to a special group.

The family of Bertha Alden Morse dreamed of creating a Plymouth Residence that would provide the graciousness of a club, the comforts of an apartment, the convenience and assurance of an infirmary, and the mutuality of a religious community. The Morse Foundation generously gave $100,000 in 1960 to form a nonprofit corporation known as Plymouth Residence. Some thirty-five Plymouthites were named to a board of directors, from whom were chosen an executive committee. This was constituted of Willard A. Morse, president; Richard B. Thomson, vice president; Alan M. Struthers, treasurer; Mrs. James A. Ross, secretary; Mrs. Herbert F. R. Plass, assistant secretary; with Clarence R. Chaney, Fred Clausen, Wellington W. Tully, Mrs. H. Glenn Wyer and myself. This was an able group who took their charge seriously. Other foundations added to the treasury. A successive row of houses on the south side of Ridgewood Avenue, beginning at Pillsbury Avenue, were purchased. This was an ideal location, just two blocks from the church and down the street from the Protestant Center building.

The executive committee advertised for an administrator, and brought from Massachusetts Mr. Allen H. Mathewson, a cultured and sensitive gentleman in his late fifties who was ideal for the position. The architects Armstrong and Schlichting prepared preliminary sketches, a financial rate chart was established, and an attractive brochure was printed to invite applications. These endeavors went on for nearly three years.

The problem that finally aborted the project was financing, and the person responsible for the negative decision was myself. The directors were conservative individuals who balked at government financing. They would not apply for Hill-Burton funds because they wanted to guide the residence on their own terms. The cost of such a project was staggering, even in the pre-inflation days of thirty years ago. We presumably could have obtained a mortgage of $600,000 from Twin City Federal, whose founder and president was Roy W. Larsen, a former Plymouth trustee. But to obtain such a loan we would first have to raise gifts of $800,000.

It was at this point that I demurred. I have always enjoyed fund raising and am optimistic as to possibilities. I like to challenge people to extend themselves, but am realistic enough to evaluate what is truly possible. I will not be led into an attempt about which I have serious doubts. I questioned whether such a sum could be raised in a canvass. Even if it could, I believed that such a campaign would drain the resources of the congregation, and make impossible any further development of our own facilities. The result would be a case of the tail wagging the dog! Plymouth Residence would be dominant, and the church would have to trim its activities to accommodate. This would jeopardize the inherent ministry of Plymouth Church, which is directed toward a liberal religious atmosphere and the nurture of persons of all ages into a meaningful and useful life of Christian service. If the directors would not apply for government funds to launch the project, I would not go along with a financial campaign among our members.

This ended the Plymouth Residence project after nearly three years of effort. We did have a responsibility for Mr. Mathewson, who with his wife had come west in October 1961 for the glowing promises of administering an ideal retirement home. One of our members, Mrs. Wadsworth A. Williams, was a member of the Andrus family whose benefactions included the John E. Andrus Memorial, one of the nation's finest retirement homes located at Hastings-on-Hudson. Her sister was active on the board of that home, which then was seeking a new administrator. Through this connection the New York home hired Mr. Mathewson, and he left

Minneapolis on April 1, 1963, for a much better position than we could have provided.

The residence directors were able to sell all the property on Ridgewood, and able to return in full all the foundation gifts that had been given for the project. Willard Morse was understandably quite disappointed, and for a time was provoked with me for making the crucial decision not to support a financial canvass. The Morse family members have been devoted Plymouthites for more than half a century. Willard soon forgave me and continued his helpfulness. With Willard and Mary Morse I enjoyed a close friendship over the decades. In 1987 I was called from retirement to conduct the memorial service for Willard when he passed away in his ninety-second year.

During these 1960-1963 deliberations of the Plymouth Residence board, the church proper was involved in other real estate negotiations as opportunities arose. As already mentioned, Mr. Griswold and Mr. Bean had purchased three old houses on Nicollet where Eighteenth Street runs into it. In 1955 the buildings were demolished, the area blacktopped and leased for weekday commercial parking and our use on Sundays. That gave us a foothold in the block north of us.

On the Groveland corner directly across the street from Plymouth's original parish house was a well-maintained brown residence, owned by a Mr. and Mrs. Harold Olson. In the Dewey era he had been chauffeur for the Van Dusen family, and she a dressmaker of considerable skill. They were now elderly. In good weather they often sat on their porch, which faced our lawns. I frequently walked downtown for lunch, and as a person who enjoys people I often stopped to chat with them. One day I said, "I wish you would let your lawyer or children know that when you are finished with the use of your house Plymouth would like first chance to buy it." I had no way of knowing how seriously they took my suggestion, but when they did pass away their lawyer did write that they had instructed him to contact the church.

By this time our neighborhood work with Emerson School children was outgrowing the facilities of our basement. We were also in discussion with Hennepin Avenue Methodist Church about combining in a joint community effort. The Olson house provided space for such a program. In 1960 we bought this house for $40,000. Again, I went to my "angels," including this time John S. Pillsbury, and they provided the funds. In January of 1961, we moved our neighborhood work across the street into this attractive brown house, and a Girl Scout professional was hired as full-time director.

Not only did this purchase provide immediate housing for our service to the needs of the neighborhood, but it also firmly anchored us in the adjacent block north. We owned the corner and a 150-foot plot in the middle.

Within the year after we and Hennepin Avenue Methodist had formed the Loring-Nicollet Center and located it in the brown house, a group of real estate developers known as Bradley Properties, Incorporated, approached us with the proposal for a land swap. They proposed to construct a shopping center on the west side of Nicollet, the principal occupant to be a unit of the Red Owl grocery chain. At the annual meeting in January 1962, Mr. Philip S. Duff, chairman of our trustees, outlined our involvement. A few months later, a special business meeting was called to get congregational approval of the transactions as recommended by the trustees. They involved the sale, exchange and lease of properties owned by Plymouth in the 1800 block.

In this deal Plymouth exchanged the lots we owned and leased for parking in the middle of the block for a like amount adjacent to our corner house. The four contiguous houses we then owned were to be demolished, and a parking lot laid out. This area would then be leased back to Bradley Properties on a twenty-year increasing-rental basis. It would serve as a parking area for the shopping center constructed by them on the lots we traded to them. This transaction was a real gain for Plymouth. It removed several houses in bad repair, upgraded the neighborhood with an attractive shopping center, gave us additional parking directly across from our buildings, and provided us with steady annual income from the lease.

In this transaction the house we were providing for Loring-Nicollet Center was demolished, but Plymouth immediately purchased a large old residence at 1920 Pillsbury for $40,000, across the street from the Protestant Center and just two blocks from the church. It was larger, with more opportunities for expansion than the Olson house. We donated the use of this house rent-free to the

Loring-Nicollet Center until 1987, when it was sold for $140,000. Half of the profit was divided by the church with Loring-Nicollet-Bethlehem Center, which had then relocated to better quarters.

The consolidation of many building improvements and expansions came in the 1967-1968 project, which gave us a new building with 23,700 square feet of interior floor space and unified all our advances into a complex that architecturally matched the beauty of the original 1907-1909 edifice. This was the dream I had when I resisted the overtures of the Plymouth Residence board five years earlier. All the devotion of more than a century of Plymouth members had been directed to making this congregation one of the viable places of worship in downtown Minneapolis, and a base of strength for the free churches of Congregationalism nationwide. We were now to take a decisive step in the embodiment of this dream.

The movement toward this development followed an orderly process. In the fall of 1964, the deacons launched "Project 1974," to undertake a study of the needs and hopes of Plymouth Church. What did we want to be doing in 1974? What should our fellowship be like a decade hence?

Over two hundred persons were involved in studies of nine areas of concern, under the general chairmanship of Philip F. Sherman, Mrs. Harold N. Rogers, Robert Ragsdale, and William J. Erickson. As interpreter and guide the project engaged Dr. Thomas C. Campbell, a member of the congregation and dean of United Theological Seminary of the Twin Cities. After a year of studies, all findings were presented at a church meeting in May 1965. These were discussed at a round of Colony meetings in the fall of that year.

From these discussions came a recommendation approved at the 1966 annual meeting that we demolish the Walgreen and Kidder buildings and construct more modern facilities on the same land. The trustees were authorized to launch a campaign to raise funds for the project.

Merrill S. Finch became chairman of the 1974 Capital Improvement Fund Campaign. One of the officers and builders of the Nash-Finch Company, wholesale grocers throughout the Upper Midwest, Merrill was a gentleman of deep spirituality and dedication, one of the dearest friends I ever had among the financial leaders of Plymouth. He understood the unique role we played as a liberal congregation with a broad, universal outlook. In an extended bout with cancer he derived from religious faith the strength to go forward without bitterness. He said to me that if he had the strength he would devote his last years to acquainting more people with the vibrancy of the open faith proclaimed at Plymouth.

The trustees decided that though the estimated cost of the project would be $750,000, the campaign should seek to raise only $500,000. The balance should be put under a mortgage in order that the younger families coming into the church to use the facilities should bear a portion of the cost. A special dinner was held at the Minikahda Club, to which were invited the families from whom larger contributions could be anticipated.

That was a memorable evening I shall never forget. Mr. Finch presided and presented the program as outlined by the trustees. He then opened the gathering for any questions or discussion. Edgar F. Zelle rose. He had been moderator at the time of Plymouth's Centennial, and one of our most generous benefactors at every stage. He was loved and respected by all. Edgar said that he would make a $15,000 pledge to the program as outlined, but he would gladly do considerably more if the campaign were to raise the full amount. Plymouth had not had a mortgage since 1875, and we should continue the policy of raising the funds before proceeding with any building. After Mr. Zelle spoke another respected elder, Frank Struthers, arose and concurred with Edgar's offer. He too would do more if the goal were to attain the full amount. It soon became evident that these on whom the load would fall the heaviest were committed to the higher goal. It was a heart-warming expression of long-standing and deep affection for Plymouth, and we went home that evening thankful once more to be associated with such committed men and women.

A hundred canvassers under three team captains—John F. Finn, Jr., Roland W. Chambers, and James G. Peterson—went to work. Merrill Finch himself made many strategic calls, patiently and pleasantly waiting until the family agreed to a larger gift than they had originally intended. The full sum was obtained.

In the spring of 1966 a building committee was appointed, selected for their competence and experience in the specific elements of parish work the program was designed to meet. Members were:

Frank W. Griswold, Wallace T. Bruce, Merrill S. Finch, Donald E. Fraser, Mrs. Paul Guzie, Miss Elaine Marsh, Mrs. James G. Miles, Mrs. James E. Thompson, Richard B. Thomson, Lynn George Truesdell III and myself. As architects the committee selected Armstrong, Schlichting, Torseth and Scold. Claire Armstrong was a Plymouth member whose firm was prominent in school and church architecture throughout Minnesota. They had designed the Protestant Center building just two blocks from Plymouth. The design was presented to the annual meeting of February 14, 1967, and approved by the congregation.

Demolition of the two properties came in the fall of that year and opened 150 feet of land back to back between LaSalle Avenue on the west and Nicollet on the east. The contractors were able to secure seam-faced granite from the same quarry near St. Cloud used in the original 1907-1909 construction and again in the 1948-1950 chapel addition. Thus on the exterior Plymouth presents an attractive, harmonious appearance.

The area nearest LaSalle was designated for parking, allowing for four rows of cars. The entrance and corridor to the first building is set back pleasantly from the street. Two of the 1950 main floor classrooms were brought together to form a spacious and attractive library. In the new building two floors of classrooms were added, adjoining an attractive administrative unit to house the offices and staff. This looks out on an inner courtyard across to the library. At the Nicollet end is a handsome theater that seats two hundred, with a large foyer for receptions that opens into the inner court. Corridors are designed with lights and fixtures to hang artwork in changing monthly displays. This whole complex is called the "Howard Conn Fine Arts Center," and is used by many community groups.

A gala week of dedication was observed in November of 1968.

The final building project of my years was the Guild Hall restoration. In the original parish house of 1909 the only large room was called "the chapel," down the corridor from the sanctuary. It was constructed with similar heavy oaken beams and trusses to form a cathedral ceiling. The three side windows have the same stone tracery design. At the eastern end was a balcony faced with oak panels. The western end had a large undecorated wall, beneath which was a slightly raised platform. Originally it was quite a handsome room. In the 1940s the balcony had been walled in with plasterboard, and a floor put over the declining seat area in order to provide Sunday school rooms. At the time of one of our building projects, we had removed the platform and the heavy brown linoleum floor covering. We had replaced the linoleum with heavy solid oak planks, a handsome improvement at a substantial cost.

In the more than fifty years' use of this room, which in my time we called the Guild Hall, no one had come up with any suitable design to fill the large space of the west end wall. From time to time suggestions had been made, but nothing done. After the completion of our Fine Arts Center in 1968, the Rev. Miss Elaine Marsh, our talented associate minister, and Mrs. Paul Carson began to talk together about possibilities. Mary Carson was a specialist in textiles and weaving. These two artistic ladies came up with the idea of creating a large tapestry hanging for this area.

They were attracted to the design work of an Englishwoman, Pauline Baynes, who had done illustrations for books of J.R.R. Tolkien and C.S. Lewis, and texts on British heraldry. On a trip to England, Dr. and Mrs. Carson visited Pauline in her home in Surrey to enlist her interest in the project. Later Miss Marsh and her friend Alice Huston also went to see the artist to discuss the subject matter. It was to be "Churchmen in the New World," the story of Congregationalism and its contribution to American history. A price was agreed on and a contract made.

Mary Carson and Elaine Marsh recruited some fifty women in the Plymouth congregation to become "Needlers." They were trained in skills of crewel embroidery and tested by standards of the Needlework Guild of America. A smaller group studied the history of Congregationalism and detailed events that might be depicted in the design. The artist is an Anglican and claimed she never did understand why the Pilgrims left for America! However, with a skill that can be regarded as nothing short of divine inspiration, she did produce a design that captures the spirit of our history with brilliant color and charm. The next task was to blow up the three-foot drawing into cartoons that would be the exact size of the work when transferred to a tapestry whose general dimensions are twenty-five feet by sixteen feet. Dr. Carson, a dentist and an artist in his own right, was familiar with precise measurements. With a camera strapped high on the beams of an old barn, he was able to photograph sections of the drawing to the desired size.

The Needlers worked regularly in two large rooms set aside in our educational wing for their purpose, and section by section, in three years they completed the tapestry. It is now the largest crewel embroidery in the United States, and at its dedication was described and pictured in the *Smithsonian* magazine. Mrs. Glenn Wyer helped generously with the financing of the project, and made it possible to bring Pauline Baynes and her husband Fritz O. Gasch to Minneapolis for a week of festivities when the embroidery was hung and dedicated on October 13, 1974. It is now one of the scenic wonders of the Twin Cities that tourists come to see.

To beautify the room in every respect and make it hospitable for this tapestry was the incentive for the Guild Hall project of 1974. The old partitions of 1940 which closed off the balcony were removed, and the original beauty of the east end restored. A massive Tudor table was designed and built by Leonard Lampert of Woodmasters to sit in the middle of the large space. Later Donald Pomeroy donated an elegant buffet from his family home. Pauline Baynes designed drawings of Minnesota birds, fish and animals, which the Needlers needlepointed into coverings for the large oak settees along the outer walls. Willard A. Morse was the chairman for this restoration project, which provided Plymouth with a large baronial hall appropriate in its design and most useful for receptions and after-service coffee hours. Guild Hall reflects the artistic good taste of the original builder, and radiates the warmth of our hospitality.

Always we retained appreciation of the good taste of the 1907 building committee. We were grateful for what we had inherited and used its beauty to attract a new generation to an inspiring house of worship. As younger families responded to the open search for meaning, we sought ways to enlarge our plant to serve a growing congregation. Over the thirty-two years of my ministry, new opportunities seemed to fall into place through the Hand Always Above Our Shoulder. We were continuously in real estate and building projects that moved us from confinement at one end of a city block until we expanded to encompass nearly the entire area. These material developments were symbols of a deepening commitment, a more universal understanding, and a greater opportunity to serve.

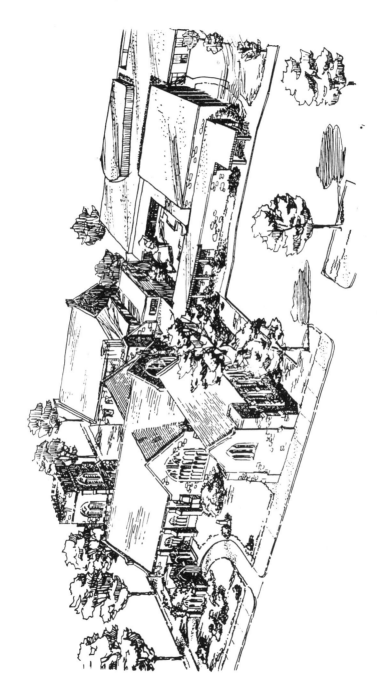

Plymouth Congregational Church Minneapolis

14

Creating an Endowment Fund

MY INITIAL FEELINGS ON GOING to Minneapolis were a combination of amazement and trepidation. It was indeed a dramatic move for a young minister of thirty-three to go to a major congregation. Yet after the first trial year, the response of the people was sufficiently positive to give the assurance that we could lead them forward. From that point on my vision became thoroughly long term. I identified myself completely with Plymouth Church, and never doubted that my life ministry would be to serve and to build that congregation. The only tempting offer to do otherwise came in the spring of 1947, only three years after my arrival, and was the invitation to join the faculty of Yale Divinity School.

Thus my concerns always had the dual perspective of the immediate and the long range. What do we do currently, and how will this affect the future? From the outset I began to worry about the future of Plymouth Church, while at the same time trusting that the Hand Always Above My Shoulder would provide wise and beneficent guidance. Frequently I remarked in a facetious manner that Plymouth would probably prosper as long as I kept both worrying and trusting!

My worries rested in part upon the precarious situation of downtown churches. My ministry had begun in New England and had exposed me to vital parishes in metropolitan areas. I had seen that shifts in residential populations had left many churches stranded in once-prominent locations. Only those survived that had large endowment resources with which to provide programs to attract members from considerable distances. One example was Broadway Tabernacle, our large Congregational church in Midtown Manhattan, which ceased to exist.

As the post-war era began, the movement toward the suburbs fast gained momentum. In our own Minneapolis area, the expansion of Wayzata Community Church and the establishment of Edina Colonial, to name only two, occurred after my coming to Plymouth. In addressing the future, it was clear that we faced a challenge quite different from our secure past, when Plymouth was a comfortable neighborhood for wealthy families living near downtown.

Yet we had no reserve resources with which to meet that challenge, as the older generation of millionaires was moving to Minnetonka. When I arrived in 1944, Plymouth's invested funds were $65,000. I early set about to change that situation, and on my retirement these endowments were but a few thousand less than one and a half million.

At the time of Plymouth's 125th anniversary in 1982, Miss Agnes Lewis who joined in 1946 wrote this estimate of our efforts in this direction: "I recognized what you were doing. You changed Plymouth from a church of wealthy people to a wealthy church. If you had not, Plymouth would not be in business today."

My first move came in 1945 to establish a memorial endowment fund to which at a time of funerals friends could send a donation in lieu of flowers. An attractively printed acknowledgment would go to the donor as well as an announcement to the family. This idea took hold quickly, and quite changed the practice. I encouraged burial an hour or two prior to a memorial service. Following that burial, attended by the family only, we returned to our beautiful chapel for a thanksgiving remembrance of the loved one, with no casket present. It became truly a worship experience, with a family-chosen centerpiece on the communion table. The gaudy display of uncoordinated floral baskets was eliminated, and money previously spent for such became part of a living endowment. By 1952 annual gifts to that memorial fund were $2,160, and in 1956 they were $3,246. By the time of my retirement in 1976, the fund had reached $75,000, all of it "flower money," the income of which was used to support the program.

In 1952 Plymouth received $28,000 from the estate of Mrs. Edward A. Strong to establish the Edward A. and Robert Seldon Strong Memorial Endowment Fund. This was a family long active at Plymouth, but all members of which were gone by my time. This legacy brought our invested funds to $100,000, and I began talking with the trustees and writing in the *Chronicle* of the importance of people leaving bequests in their wills. The suggestion plants seeds in the minds of people who might otherwise never think of it. Without some encouragement, the average person tends to suppose that bequests come only from families of recognized wealth. My experience is to the contrary. The old named families of wealth never left legacies to Plymouth. Most of them had established family foundations and given their offspring the responsibility of allocating gifts from these trusts. We were able to tap into a few of these trusts for specific help on several projects, but Plymouth never received direct endowments from these major sources. Our legacies for the most part came from members in more modest circumstances— retired school teachers, single persons with no descendants—whose imagination was stimulated by a word from their pastor to see themselves as perpetuators beyond their lifetime of a church precious to them.

Perhaps the most fruitful endeavor of this kind was a small pamphlet I wrote and circulated in January 1952. It was entitled "Letter to An Unknown Friend from Howard Conn," which was printed on the outside in reverse blue. Inside was this letter, most of which text I include here:

Dear Unknown Friend:

Though we have talked together many times, I must address you as "unknown" because I do not know which one of the Plymouth people you are! You are a friend who, without my knowledge at this writing, will provide in your will for a substantial bequest to Plymouth Church. By the time I learn of this fact it will be too late for me to express my appreciation. I therefore want now to say with all my heart, "Thank you!"

The future of Plymouth requires that we have a large Endowment Fund, the income of which can be used to maintain a strong program. The story of downtown churches is the same across the country. Families with means move farther and farther

out to the suburbs. Young people send their children to neighborhood parishes. An inner-city church like Plymouth can survive
only if it has a strong program to attract people from a distance
and to serve the transient groups nearby. Having lost its old families, it cannot afford such a program without heavy endowment
income.

I love Plymouth Church very much. I want to feel that twenty-
five or fifty years from now, regardless of sociological changes, she
will be making a strong witness for the liberal, free, democratic
religion of Congregationalism.

Your bequest—large or small—will help significantly in this
direction. I thank you for it. Plymouth today has by far the smallest
endowment of any of our downtown Minneapolis churches.
Everyone of us should leave something to her in our will.

Your bequest—be it $1,000 or $100,000—will continue perma-
nently your support of the Plymouth we love. I thank you personally, and future generations will be grateful.

May God bless you richly.

Faithfully yours,
Howard Conn

The next step to promote permanent funds came as we looked
forward to Plymouth's Centennial in the spring of 1957. Four years
earlier we conceived the idea of creating a "First Century Fund" of
$100,000 as a gift from present members to those of the second cen-
tury. We announced this plan early, and in the year 1954 gifts came
to $27,684.

In 1955 the will of John Lane Sprague left $25,000 to the church,
the first large bequest of that size from one who was a dear friend of
mine. His mother, Mrs. Frank W. Sprague, was one of the first older
women of the congregation to take me under her wing and guide
me in my early years. She became the first woman trustee. Jack
Sprague's widow Margo is one of my closest friends, with whom I
sponsored several tours to the Far East, and who is one of the three
Bell sisters prominent in our history.

A full-scale approach to the First Century Fund was launched in
the spring of 1956, a full year before the Centennial of April 28, 1957.
A Committee of One Hundred was named to assure that the
$100,000 goal be reached by that date. Ellwood H. Newhart was
named chairman by the moderator, Edgar F. Zelle. An attractive
brochure was printed, suggesting that gifts be made in units of one

hundred dollars. As the campaign was launched, $30,000 had already been contributed. Names of friends who gave units were printed in the *Chronicle* of May 31, 1956, and a further list in January of 1957. Some two hundred fifty families made unit gifts, so that the final tabulation for the First Century Fund came to $141,000. This was a smashing success and another indication of what people working together can accomplish beyond what any single one by himself or herself might do.

At the annual meeting following the Centennial celebrations, in February of 1958, Mr. J.A. Ross, our venerable treasurer, introduced a resolution to create a Second Century Fund to which donors could make gifts toward permanent endowments. In speaking for the resolution, which was adopted, he promised not to be on hand to initiate a Third Century program!

In recalling Plymouth's finances, we owe a tribute to two very special persons who served over thirty years each with unusual devotion and competence. Miss Hazel Fraker became Dr. Dewey's secretary in 1921, and was a key person through years of staff development until her retirement in the summer of 1957. Through the years she became financial secretary and business administrator. For her it was not as much a job as a devotion to Plymouth Church. Her guidance and support of me were crucial. She was a person of few words, direct in her approach, but of sound judgment and kind intentions. The enhancement of Plymouth was uppermost for her.

Working with her as a volunteer was James Archibald Ross, who was first elected treasurer of the society in 1927 and served for thirty-five years. He was married to Anne Bovey Ross of the prominent Bovey family, and was an officer of Northwestern National Bank. He was an old-school aristocrat, but a warm and friendly person. After retirement from the bank, he had a second career for twenty years as an investment broker with Harris Upham & Company. He was usually in the church office a late afternoon or two a week. He and Miss Fraker opened all the contribution envelopes, which she recorded, and together they prepared the financial reports for the trustees.

Mrs. Ross was a genial, friendly person with a fine sense of humor. Anne and Archie were married fifty-four years. Vi and I were often in their home, and we enjoyed their friendship. Mrs. Ross died in 1960. A year later Mr. Ross asked me if I thought it would be fair at his age to ask Miss Fraker to marry him. I gave my enthusiastic blessing on such an idea, for they had worked together so congenially over the decades. They came north to our cabin on Burntside Lake, where our family was summering. We went across the water to a beautiful chapel I had built on Pine Island, where they exchanged wedding vows in an idyllic setting. All of us then returned to the mainland, where Vi had prepared a happy luncheon for the bride and groom!

They had seven years of great joy together before Archie Ross died of a heart attack. That day in 1968 I was in Boston attending the graduation of our daughter Janet from Wellesley. When Hazel phoned me I immediately set out on the return drive to Minneapolis. Hazel Fraker Ross lived on until 1984. These were two fine people who loved Plymouth dearly, and the memory of whom will always be cherished by those who knew them.

By 1960 the endowments had grown to $400,000. Mr. Ross felt that the proper investment of a sum this size was a responsibility that the trustees by themselves should no longer assume. He persuaded them to transfer these assets to a trust account with Northwestern National Bank, with the bank giving supervisory and custodial care, though the trustees reserved the right to final approval.

In 1964 a new system of accounting and investing of Plymouth's permanent funds was developed. Three persons were instrumental in establishing procedures. Miss Norma Nyquist had been made business administrator on the retirement of Miss Fraker seven years earlier. She was a quiet, efficient and loyal accountant who was an active Lutheran churchperson, and who served us faithfully through the nineteen remaining years of my ministry. In our membership and trustee group were two of the city's outstanding accountants: Harold M. Solstad, resident partner of Peat Marwick & Mitchell; and Walter M. Bury, resident partner of Ernst & Ernst. Both Harold and Walter were active members of the church. They devised an accounting system whereby dollar gifts to endowments are translated into units. At the end of each year the unit value is calculated. With the passage of years and inflation, new money coming into the funds will buy fewer units than the earlier dollars of greater worth. I am not an accountant and do not fully understand the intricacies, but we are fortunate to have a system that can be maintained far into the future while giving weighted value to economic changes along the way.

Another important distinction was introduced regarding funds in which the principal is nonexpendable, as in cases where bequests specify that they may be given for endowments or for specific purposes. Other gifts are interpreted to permit the principal to be expendable if they are left to Plymouth Church without specific designation.

Throughout my ministry I have been interested in investments, both my own and those of the church. I have actively participated with the trustees at their meetings and was always made a member of the investment committee, which met regularly with the officers of the bank trust department handling Plymouth's endowments. I was also a director for thirty-four years of Ministers Life, a Minneapolis-based insurance company that is one of two in the nation designed specifically for persons in the religious professions. During most of that time I was a member of the five-man investment committee that handled all the assets of that company. My experience is that most ministers of large churches do have managerial skills and training in investment strategies. They do have a responsibility for the development of their institutions.

Through constant reminders in our monthly parish paper I kept before people the need for remembrance of the church in wills, so that a person might contribute to the future strength of the fellowship they had enjoyed during their lifetimes. Many more people than we imagine come to the end of their years with a comfortable accumulation of assets, with no immediate descendants nor close relatives to whom to bequeath their estate. A minister, a lawyer, a friend may properly make suggestions as to dispositions that will help sustain constructive influences in the community far into the future. Throughout my ministry I tried to stimulate this concept among parishioners, while respecting the freedom of each individual to make his or her choice.

The only dramatic encounter of this kind that did bring significant gain to Plymouth is my relation with Miss Edna Crabtree. She was the only daughter of a prominent tobacco wholesaler who had been in the Park Avenue Congregational Church which returned to Plymouth in 1937. She was a semi-invalid, limited somewhat in activities by a heart condition, but was an active member of several of the women's groups in the church. She tended toward a negative view of most situations, probably because she was lonely and perhaps brought up to be suspicious. Yet she was a kind and generous person who wanted to be helpful. Early in my years at Plymouth she was pointed out to me as a lonely person who did appreciate attention. She had engaged the architect Dale McEnary, who had been a friend since their youth, to design a lovely colonial house for her on south Fremont in the Washburn district, a house with an elevator to enable her to go up and down without strain on her heart. I called on Edna more often than on most members, because she seemed to appreciate attention and was always cordial. Often when out in that neighborhood I dropped in for a brief visit. I discovered that she had no close relatives and that the circles of Plymouth were her major scene of activity. One of her first gifts was money to install an elevator at the Nicollet Avenue entrance to the parish wing, where one had to go either a half-floor down to the basement of a half-floor up to the main level.

One afternoon I said to her, "Edna, what is going to happen to this lovely house when you are gone? It would make an ideal parsonage for the church. Vi and I live in this huge mansion by Lake of the Isles, but when our girls finish high school it will be much too large for us. When you are gone this house would make an ideal home for one of Plymouth's ministers." She took favorably to the suggestion. Her attorney was Harold G. Cant, the chairman of the committee that had brought me to Plymouth, one of our earliest moderators, and a thorough Christian gentleman respected by everyone. She asked "Casey" to put this in her will. When she died in 1961 Plymouth did receive the house. At that point we were not ready to leave the Kenwood area, so the trustees sold the property for $42,000, which went into the unrestricted endowment as a bequest from Edna Crabtree.

From July of 1959 to February of 1960, the church gave us a sabbatical leave during which Vi and I took our two daughters on an extended trip around the world. Throughout Asia we stayed in college dormitories, mission hospitals, and church guest houses through contacts I had made through work with the missionary enterprise in Japan, Thailand, India and Turkey. Edna Crabtree was one of a few persons who had made generous gifts to underwrite this journey. We were appreciative of this opportunity to go together as a family while our girls were of high school age.

On my return I realized that Edna was not well, and I tried to think of aspects of Plymouth that might entice her to make further bequests. I mentioned the ministry to shut-ins. Would she consider establishing a $50,000 fund to support the parish visitor? No, she didn't care to have someone like that popping in. Another day I tried the appeal of youth work, how important it is to the families of our congregation. No, she didn't care particularly for young people.

Finally I said, "Edna, you know how much our sabbatical trip meant to our family. You are the custodian of funds that could be designated to carry on activities in which you have got some pleasure. Would you consider establishing a $50,000 Crabtree Ministers' Travel Fund, so that future Plymouth ministers might have opportunities such as you helped make possible for my family?" Without hesitation she replied that she would. I thanked her, and said through the future many others would be grateful for this thoughtfulness.

Within days of this conversation in her home she suffered a heart attack and was taken to Abbott Hospital. When I learned this I immediately phoned Casey Cant and told him that Edna had agreed to establish a Crabtree Ministers' Travel Fund of $50,000. I suggested that he draw up a codicil to this effect and take it to Abbott Hospital. He did so that afternoon. She died two weeks later. She had made bequests to several philanthropic and cultural institutions in the Twin Cities, with a small residue going to distant cousins somewhere in the midwest. She was a lonely person whose life never blossomed into the full enjoyments that might have been hers, yet at heart she was a generous, kindly person who was willing to use her money for lasting benefits to others. Because of my suggestions Plymouth endowments received $92,000. This is an illustration of the way in which I think a minister can give friendly counsel to parishioners whose imagination needs to be kindled toward constructive giving of their resources when their earthly life is over. I am ever grateful to Edna Crabtree for her love of Plymouth Church.

By the time of my retirement in the fall of 1976, Plymouth's permanent endowments had reached one and a half million dollars, the income from which made a substantial difference in the kind of program we could maintain for our own members and for the needs of people in the depressed neighborhood where we are anchored. As I write these lines some twelve years later in 1988, these funds now come to $1,822,310. Once the concept of legacies in wills is planted in the minds of churchpeople, such a program of giving will gain momentum and carry forward over decades to come.

A striking example of results that come from seed ideas planted earlier is a legacy received in 1989 from the estate of Dorothy and Miles F.P. Dallison. They were a couple from New England active in Plymouth when I arrived in 1944. Miles was a salesman for Bemis Bag Company. I recall two occasions when we held Colony meetings in their modest home. Dorothy was active in Marguerite Beach Circle and Plymouth Women's Organization. Miles served a term as deacon. He retired nearly ten years before I left Plymouth, and they moved to Arizona. They had no children or apparent relatives. In February of 1989, Plymouth received a letter from an Arizona bank serving as trustee. Miles had passed away in 1986 and Dorothy two years later. Their estate came to $1,600,000 and was to be divided among four religious or civic organizations. Plymouth received $400,000, the largest single bequest up to this time. Here is the dramatic harvesting of a gift from an idea planted in the minds of people who moved away from Plymouth twenty years earlier!

I consider the endowment fund one of the permanent contributions of my ministry.

15

Our India Family

ANOTHER MANIFESTATION OF THE Hand Always Above My Shoulder is our relationship with India. My interest in Eastern mysticism through a study at Harvard of the Hindu Upanishads found a channel for continuing growth when I was called to the ministry of Plymouth Church, for this congregation has long had an association with that country. During my tenure historical circumstances greatly enhanced that relationship, and forged a friendship with the Hivale-Barnabii family that is one of the closest of my life.

As early as 1888 Plymouth became interested in India. One of our members, Miss Anstice Abbott, an honored teacher in the Minneapolis schools, was commissioned by the American Board for Foreign Missions and went to Bombay. She founded a school for the blind, and worked tirelessly with children and child-widows. After seventeen years of service her health failed, and she retired in 1905. Two others went out to carry on her work, Miss Anna Millard and Miss Mary Etta Moulton.

Perhaps the most notable career in India of a Plymouth member was that of the Rev. Dr. Alden Hyde Clark. As a child he had been baptized in our sanctuary and had gone on to graduate from Amherst College and Union Theological Seminary in New York City. On May 25, 1904, he was ordained in Plymouth. He and his wife Mary Whitcomb Clark went forth to India as missionaries from our church. They became teachers at the Boys' School of the American-

Marathi Mission in Vadala, and in 1907 moved to Bombay to found a settlement house for work with the youth of that city. Here they had a distinguished career for twenty years, until in 1926 they were called back to the United States for Dr. Clark to become India Secretary for the American Board in Boston.

At that time there were no members from Plymouth to volunteer for service in India, so Dr. Clark asked our minister, Dr. Harry P. Dewey, if we would be willing to support as our representative an Indian national. He had in mind Dr. Bhaskar P. Hivale, who was then in Boston earning his Ph.D. in philosophy at Harvard, and whose wife Ruth was studying for a master's degree in dietetics at Simmons College. The Clarks had known this young couple in Bombay and had recognized their Christian dedication as well as their intellectual brilliance. The couple visited Minneapolis, charmed the people, and became Plymouth's official missionaries.

During their student years in Boston, three daughters were born to the Hivales, which conferred American citizenship on these young people and has contributed to their remarkable blend of Western and Eastern cultures. Upon receiving graduate degrees the Hivales returned with their family to India, where Dr. Hivale became professor of philosophy at Wilson College, a Scotch Presbyterian institution on the Malibar coast of Bombay. Once in the thirties he returned to the States to visit the people who provided his support.

Bhaskar Hivale was more than an academician, however, and while teaching philosophy at Wilson College he branched out into other endeavors. He was a man of dynamic energy who knew how to fashion his dreams into realities by hard work and good judgment. His keen mind had been trained at Harvard, but his warm heart had a compassion for people and a love for Jesus. He was no emotional evangelist but one who appreciated every approach to truth, while recognizing what Christ can do for human life.

With his background and vision, he rapidly became one of the most influential Christians in India. He edited the official weekly paper of seven denominational missions, so every week his thoughts were carried to Christian leaders. He became chairman of the Bible Revision Committee, and no change in translation of the Scriptures into native tongues could be made without his approval. This leadership was recognized by election to the presidency of the All-India Conference of Indian Christians, and in this post he had contacts with leaders of other principal religious groups, including Gandhi of the Hindus and Jinnah of the Moslems.

He was active in the Marathi Mission of Maharashtra, which the American Board had maintained since the mid-nineteenth century with social work, agricultural stations, and schools. Two of its centers are Vadala and Ahmednagar. While Congregationalists give witness to Jesus' love for all humankind, our missions are not basically directed toward evangelizing or proselytizing. We think in terms of humanitarian service that will enrich the quality of life. The mission had operated a boys' school in Ahmednagar, but that had been abandoned and the property left in a state of neglect.

Dr. Hivale dreamed of starting a college for the youth of the Deccan, the agricultural plain above the western ghats or hills. This is a depressed area with little opportunity for young people. The Second World War involved India as it did most of the globe. Indian nationalism increased during the tensions of that period, and there was a growing call for independence. With the end of armed conflict it became likely that Great Britain would grant that independence. The Congress Party let it be known that at such time Hindi would become the official language, and that any new institutions of higher learning would be obliged to replace traditional English as the language of instruction. This national ferment intensified Dr. Hivale's anxiety to begin the college of his dream, and made clear his need to come to the United States to secure the support required for such an enterprise.

In the confusing days of the war's end, travel for civilians was difficult. Dr. Hivale had contacted the American Board officers in Boston to ask their help, but they had indicated that no help would be available for his project of another college. At that moment the various mission boards of the Congregationalists were primarily supporting the Committee for War Victims and Rehabilitation. Dr. Hivale never took no for an answer but found ways to persevere toward his goal. He was determined to come to the States, confident that his friends would help.

A second hurdle was to obtain a travel permit to leave the country. The central government refused him. There was a strange custom, however, by which local state governors in rotation had authority for one day to issue permits. The governor of Maharashtra was an acquaintance, and on his day Dr. Hivale went to his office and was granted the visa.

A third challenge remained, to find a ship that had accommodations. In Bombay port was an American cargo vessel that had room for only one passenger. Dr. Hivale submitted his credentials along with his request. The ship's captain looked over the list of applicants and said, "I will take that Harvard Ph.D.!" Thus in the summer of 1945 he was on his way to secure the means to found what has become recognized as one of the finest colleges in all India.

My first meeting with this dynamic Christian who became one of my dearest friends was in Boston that same summer. Our family was at our Berkshire farmhouse when Mrs. Harry P. Dewey and two of her daughters, Mrs. Gardner Perry and Miss Eleanor Dewey, invited me to come to lunch. They had never met me, but of course were interested to make the acquaintance of the new young minister at the church that was so dear to them. To this luncheon they had also invited Dr. Hivale. For me it was a rich experience to meet all four of these friends whose lives were as intertwined with Plymouth as mine was to be. I found Dr. Hivale to be charming, an excellent conversationalist as well as a man of real substance. We responded well to each other from the start.

The annual fall meeting of the American Board and its governing Prudential Committee was held in Bennington, Vermont. Though the leaders had originally advised Dr. Hivale not to come to this country, they recognized his presence and said that he might make a presentation. Though he was a "national" rather than an American foreign missionary, he had been associated with the American Board for sixteen years, and his standing among Indian Christians was recognized. After listening to his plea, the Prudential Committee voted that while they could not channel funds to him at that time, they would make available the abandoned campus in Ahmednagar of a boys' school previously operated by the Marathi Mission. Thus was begun the first step on this man's dedicated pilgrimage.

I had invited Dr. Hivale to come to Minneapolis to renew his ties with Plymouth. He spent two weeks with us, preaching on Sunday,

September 30, and meeting with various groups. We had the chance to talk about philosophy and to share his dream for his new college. We promised him our full support, and the assurance that Plymouth would be a founding partner with him. As a first step we made the offering on Christmas Sunday to be a gift to Dr. Hivale for his undertakings, that we might give $1,700 to the American Board to purchase an automobile for his use. In order to pay for passage to the United States, he had sold his old car and borrowed on his insurance policies.

On leaving Minneapolis he had gone south to St. Louis in the hope that he might secure the third element needed for his dream. To obtain a charter for a new college, the government of India required the deposit of one hundred thousand rupees as evidence of responsibility. In American terms this was the equivalent of $33,000. Though the American Board was giving him property and Plymouth was promising support, the securing of such an outright sum was a formidable third hurdle. St. Louis was the headquarters of the Ralston-Purina Company, founded by William Danforth, a philanthropist of sincere religious interests and Congregational ties. He had written a small inspirational volume to encourage youth to conscientious efforts toward achievements, and this book had been translated into several languages around the world.

Dr. Hivale phoned the Danforth office for an appointment, but the secretary of course knew nothing about this inquirer. He said that Mr. Danforth was too busy to see him. A man never to be put off, Dr. Hivale was quick in his response. He said, "When Mr. Danforth came to Bombay to ask me to translate his book into Marathi he was not too busy to talk with me." The secretary was taken aback, and inquired further as to the identity of the caller. He asked where he could be reached, and was told at the YMCA. After a short interval he phoned with the message, "Mr. Danforth is sending his car for you."

In this interview Mr. Danforth pledged the full sum needed for deposit. Dr. Hivale was able to return to Bombay with his mission accomplished. Two years later, in June of 1947, Ahmednagar College officially opened. In November of that year, Dr. Hivale was back in the States to raise $31,000 toward paying off debts incurred in clearing the property of brush and readying buildings for use.

In the next few years Dr. Hivale came back to the United States almost annually to secure funds for his growing institution. He stayed in our home when in Minneapolis, and we felt that it was a valuable educational experience for our two young daughters to have this engaging Indian a part of our family.

Dr. Hivale had risked his future to fulfill his dream. In order to raise funds to start the college, he invested all his savings and had cashed in his retirement equity in the "Provident Fund" of Wilson College. I recall a 1947 telephone call from Dr. Raymond Dudley, India Secretary for the American Board in Boston, who explained to me the risk that Dr. Hivale was taking and who asked if I would promise that Plymouth Church would underwrite the living expenses of Dr. and Mrs. Hivale as long as either of them lived. I gave my word that we would do so, as fifteen hundred American dollars would translate into a comfortable annual living in India. We kept our promise, and after Dr. Hivale's death in 1961 we continued this support for Mrs. Hivale until her death in 1977. This annual stipend enabled her to live in their large house, to have a car and driver, and to pay for medication for her health problems.

Their oldest daughter Manorama is a brilliant woman who has inherited the talents of her parents. After graduation from the University of Bombay in 1945, she too came to America and obtained a master's degree at Radcliffe. She returned to India to join the faculty of her father's new college. She married Thomas Barnabas of a long-time Christian family. The lives of Tom and Manorama have been intertwined with mine for more than forty years, and each of us counts the others as our closest friends in all the world. We have been together frequently, and they have come to Minneapolis for the major celebrations of my ministry. In the decade of the eighties, Manorama has taught at Boston University School of Theology and Tougaloo College in Mississippi. She then joined the staff of the United Board for Christian Higher Education in Asia as Executive Associate for Women's Educational Concerns. As an attractive and intelligent woman of Asian background who has demonstrated independence and familiarity with Western ways, she is uniquely qualified to speak on women's issues anywhere in the world. In her official capacity she traveled extensively in the Far East, visiting universities in Japan, the Philippines, Thailand and

Taiwan. This kept her commuting between the New York office and these foreign ports, with intermediate stops for her and Tom in Chicago with their two sons, who became practicing physicians in that city.

Until Manorama assumed these teaching posts in the United States, we funded in major part the travels of the Hivales and Barnabii to this country because we had become one caring international family. In the fall of 1949, Thomas Barnabas came to the University of Minnesota to do graduate work in chemistry, which is his field. Manorama was chairperson of the philosophy department at Ahmednagar. Their first child, son Satish, was born that year. Early in the spring of 1950, Manorama joined Tom in Minneapolis, leaving Satish to the care of her parents. On September 12 of that year Dr. Hivale suffered a heart attack, and a cable came to the young couple asking that they return to India.

I well remember the discussions we had as the two wrestled with a difficult decision. Being somewhat of a pragmatist, I argued that Dr. Hivale's condition was probably not as serious as the cable suggested, and that since they had embarked on graduate study they should continue for an advanced degree. The earnestness of Asian Christians was clear in Tom's response, that he had dedicated his life to Dr. Hivale, and that whatever the latter asked he was committed to follow. There was no real hesitancy in the decision to return, and in December the couple sailed on the *Queen Elizabeth II* for Europe on their way to India. My surmise that Dr. Hivale's illness was not fatal proved correct, for he lived another eleven years and made two more trips to the States. However, it was a wise decision for the Barnabii to return home, as they were to play a pivotal role in the academic growth of the college.

During those early years after the founding of the college in 1947, two Plymouth members went to Ahmednagar to lend a helping hand. In the second year Dr. Hivale invited Mrs. Willard A. (Gertrude) Stevenson to come to be a matron for the women students. She was a warm-hearted, sensitive person with a flair for dramatic speech. She came home with vivid tales of snakes and insects encountered in clearing the abandoned campus for its new residents. She was an eloquent speaker, and for several years was a helpful interpreter of Ahmednagar in Minneapolis. Later Ruth E.

Bailey, our director of Religious Education, and her mother spent several months at the college.

In 1951 Ahmednagar graduated its first four-year class. Its academic standards were so high that its students soon began winning honors among the several colleges that constitute the University of Poona. India follows the British pattern of separate colleges being grouped into a central university. At the opening of the academic year in the fall of 1951, Tom Barnabas became principal, and over the next twenty-five years demonstrated unusual administrative talents. Under him the college expanded rapidly, honors were achieved in several departments, and Ahmednagar became recognized by the Indian government as a model institution. Part of this recognition came from the rural development work instituted by Professor Mickey Hulbe, who had earned his Ph.D. at the University of Texas. He trained corps of students to go to neighboring rural areas to study village needs, train residents in cooperative work, dig water wells, plant new crops, market produce, and establish health centers.

Other members of the family dynasty made their contributions to the college, and also came to the United States for educational opportunities. Tom's younger brother Joseph has been chaplain and provost since the founding. He is married to the youngest of the four Hivale daughters, Sarala. In the late fifties, this attractive couple were in New Haven where Joe received his Divinity degree from Yale, and Sarala a Ph.D. in English. Over the years Joe has given wise leadership to the Church of North India, in which he was offered election as a bishop. He preferred to remain outside the institutional structure and to continue his important role in the college. In the fall of 1975 I arranged for Joe, Sarala and their two teenage children to come to St. Anthony Park Congregational Church in St. Paul while the minister was exchanging a visit at the college, and with the help of the American Board brought the family for an experience in Minnesota.

The second Hivale daughter, Vimala, married a Gujarati, Kanti Bhagat. He too earned his advanced degree in the States in political science, and chaired that department at the college. In the early sixties Vimala and Kanti spent a year in West Hartford as associates on the staff of the Congregational church. Later they left Ahmednagar when Kanti became principal of Hyslop College.

The third Hivale daughter, Indira, became a physician in eye care. While a student at Vellore Medical College in Bangalore she married a Pakistani fellow-student, a Christian named Henry Luther. We brought them to the University of Minnesota in 1960, and in one year both of them earned advanced degrees in ophthalmology. They returned to Quetta, where Henry succeeded his father as head of a Christian hospital. They had one son, Andrew. Each summer they conducted an eye camp at Sholapur, where they treated great numbers of poor people for cataracts and other eye diseases. Prominent ophthalmologists from the United States volunteered to assist them for short periods, for as one of them said to me when I visited, a surgeon could get more experience there in a week than at home in an entire year. Unfortunately, Indira died at an early age. She was a lovely, gracious person, quieter in manner than her sisters but equally talented.

After giving up the principalship to Tom in 1951, Dr. Hivale devoted himself to fund raising and to enlarging the physical plant. He was no architect, but he knew how to design rectangular buildings to provide needed classroom space. Stairways to the second floors were attached to the outside so that no area inside was lost. These were not beautiful structures, but they were functional. They were constructed at a minimal cost by primitive but efficient methods. Tribal groups experienced in such work were available. Dr. Hivale hired them as a unit, paying the men a rupee and a half per day (32 cents) and the women twelve annas, or 15 cents. At these wages an American dollar goes a long way! I watched a group of one hundred artisans construct the Dewey Library. Workers formed the bricks, mixed the concrete, and built the window frames. Women—many of them seemingly elderly—carried the cement in large trays atop their heads from the supply to the building site. It was incredible how much construction could take place in a day. Dr. Hivale was building dormitories and classrooms, while Plymouth and the American Board were providing funds for various projects.

The summer of 1954 was a momentous time for me. Harper & Bros. published my book on *The Hope That Sets Men Free*, with an introduction by Elton Trueblood, the distinguished Quaker writer who had been publishing articles of mine in *The Friends Magazine* from the early days when I was at Glenbrook. The impetus for my writing was to offer an alternative to the World Council of Churches, which was meeting in New Delhi under the theme, "Jesus Christ the Hope of the World." I wanted to suggest a more universal basis for hope than the Christian dogma.

In the summer of 1954, I also made the first of my seven visits to India to see at first hand the country whose philosophy and art I had studied with such appreciation. On July 1, I sailed from New York on the *Andrea Doria* and landed at Naples eight days later to be met by Hulda Stettler of the Congregational Committee for War Victims and Rehabilitation, and who was later to introduce me to the magnificent Santi family whose orphanage in Portici was to become another of our basic overseas concerns. It was a two-day flight with stopovers on TWA from Rome to Bombay. At the airport I was met by Dr. Hivale, Tom Barnabas, and Peggy and Ross Thomas. The latter was head of the American Board work in India. I did not sleep very well. I was put in a garden bedroom on the Thomas compound. Outside the wall I could hear people retching, and was made aware of the poverty of the folk out there.

The next day, the fourteenth of July, our entourage took the train to Ahmednagar with a leisurely noontime layover at Poona, during which Tom took me out to see the 400-acre campus of the University of Poona. It was evening when we reached Ahmednagar. Mrs. Hivale and others of the family were there to meet us and to garland me with the traditional Indian leis.

The several days following were busy with meetings and dedications. Dr. Hivale had timed events very well. There was a ceremony for the opening of the Ahmednagar School of Theology on a site near his home, with an elaborately carved granite stone with the inscription that the school had been opened July 16, 1954, by Dr. Howard Conn. A missionary council of some fifty clergy guests of the area had been assembled for the occasion. My address covered three contributions that religion offers: an understanding of man's place in the universe, guidance in moral conduct, and the power to achieve our goals. The next day we had the dedication of the Plymouth wing of the men's residence. On these occasions I met some very interesting people.

Among them was the Rev. Joseph Moulton, an American Board missionary of many years who with his wife Florence had a nice home at Supa, about twenty miles from Ahmednagar. After less than a week he drove Tom Barnabas and me to Bombay in his station wagon, which was a gift from the churches of Maine. Tom and I flew on a whirlwind trip to South India, where I was to make friends with some outstanding missionaries. We had excellent contacts in Madras, where we stayed at the Hotel Connemara, and took excursions to Kanchipuram and Mahabalapuram to see beautiful ancient artwork in temples and raths. Before leaving home I had carefully studied Kenneth Morgan's collection of essays on *The Religions of India*, and in Madras we were able to have interviews with two of the Hindu professors who had written chapters for that book. One of these was Dr. V. Raghavan, who had translated the Hindu Scripture for the Morgan book. He thought there was a religious awakening, for every day lectures are given on Vedic classics. When I asked him what form of Hinduism the street-corner temples represent, he replied, "The lowest!"

Professor Raghavan directed us to a Mr. Chenchiah, a retired judge who lived on Halls Road, Egmore, in Madras. We visited him in his home and had a thrilling conversation with him. He was clearly a devout, sincere and earnest Christian. He asked about the state of the Church in America. How far does it penetrate into American life? He feared that when people speak of a "Christian" solution to a problem, they actually mean to borrow the solution from the secular environment. Why do we not have direct contact with the Holy Spirit rather than go back to a book two thousand years old? When one asks a minister a question he answers by quoting Scripture. We have thus a system of lakes for storage, but we have forgotten the rains! Perhaps these are not broken cisterns, but we are working with cisterns. They provide a system of order, but it is a system cut off from basic inspiration. Historically, Christianity is associated with the lavish prodigality of the Holy Spirit. Why is it no longer so in our day? Man is not using his spiritual resources. In our world science and the secular state are so powerful that it becomes difficult to believe in spiritual powers at all. The challenge to the Church is to provide a fellowship that is life changing.

He saw Christianity's contribution to India as the Kingdom of God. Christianity is interested in the whole process of "becoming" as well as in the ultimate goal. Christ is the embodiment of creative perfection, and Christianity is seeking to turn the whole world into the Kingdom of God. First we must become children of God, and then the Kingdom will follow.

We also went to the Ramakrishna Center, one of the more contemporary forms of Hinduism, where I talked with the editor of their English publications. He emphasized that the essence of Hinduism is unity, quoting from the Rig-Veda: What is truth is one, but sages call it differently. To him Ramakrishna, Jesus and Mohammed are all incarnations of God. Hinduism has no difficulty understanding Christ, because he played a tune that has been there all the time. I asked if Jesus' understanding of suffering is not unique? His response was that suffering is an illusion. If one gets into the proper posture, one is not affected. This answer is the non-attachment of the Gita, but is certainly not the position of Jesus who voluntarily accepted crucifixion in the trust that loyalty to principle would bring ultimate victory.

On the twenty-second of July Tom flew back to Nager and I took the night train south. Early the next morning the Rev. Richard (Dick) Keithan got me off the Trivandrum Express at one of its stops, and took me to the home of the Rev. Sam Devapragasam at Tirimangalam.

I had previously met Dick Keithan at church camps for youths when he was home on furlough. He was a native Minnesotan and a graduate of Carleton College. Later I was instrumental in calling attention to his distinguished career to the faculty of the college, who conferred on him an honorary degree. Dick was quite different from the usual Congregational missionary. His was a radical, independent spirit. Rather than reside in a comfortable mission bungalow with servants, he and his physician wife lived in a small untidy house that they might identify with the local poor. The night I stayed with them they sent me to a bed in their fruit shed, and warned me not to be upset if I heard the four-footed creatures that also inhabited the shed! Dick had worked as a partisan for the movement for Indian independence, and had even been imprisoned at one point by the Colonial government. In his jeep he drove me to two villages where a single woman with few facilities was serving as a nurse. His ministry was to show compassion and helpfulness in the spirit of Jesus.

A moving experience of my seven weeks in India was a visit to a nearby ashram where the Congress Government after Free India had established one of four rural life training centers. Nurses, teachers, social workers and village leaders were brought to Gandhi Gram for courses to train them better for service. The program is directed toward village problems. Its educational concept is that people learn not from books, but by doing the basic things that need to be done day by day. The director is a saintly man long identified with the freedom movement. We had tea in his home. Pointing to three portraits on the wall, those of Gandhi, Tagore and C.F. Andrews, he said, "These are my saints." Such a trilogy witnessed to the universal spirit of this remarkable man. In our conversation he put a test of spirituality to me, and the ensuing result I have since regarded as one of the major experiences of my lifetime. I reserve the telling of it to the chapter on ecumenism.

Breakfast and lunch that day with the Devapragasams in their Tirimangalam home was the beginning of a friendship that was to last through several trips until the deaths of Sam and his wife Nesam in the early eighties. I was impressed with the dedication of this couple, and the work of the Devapragasam Orphanage in the outskirts of Madras. It is now carried on by son Arthur and his wife Sakkhu, and has become one of the continuing items in the benevolence program of Plymouth Church. Sam was originally spotted as a promising young national by Ruth Isbell Seabury of the American Board, who provided a scholarship for him to study at the Chicago Divinity School several years before my first meeting with him. Later in December 1961 Plymouth provided funds for Sam and his wife to come to the United States to tell of their endeavors. They spent several weeks in our home.

From the Dindigal area I went to Madurai, where the American Board had several missionaries working in schools, villages and hospitals. I stayed with Lloyd Lorbeer and his lovely second wife Olive. Lloyd had a life-long career in India and was respected as one of the deans of the distinguished company of American Board representatives around the globe.

In talking with thoughtful people on this trip, I asked the same question: What do you regard as Christianity's distinctive contribution to India? From Hindus I generally got the same answer: that it had brought material help in the form of schools, hospitals, agricultural stations, to improve the physical lot of the people; but that it had brought no spiritual aid. Such an answer is not surprising, for Hinduism looks at the physical world as an illusion from which enlightenment brings release. Hence the involvement of missions with the physical needs of people can be regarded as helpful service to their immediate situation, but is of no assistance in the recognition of the unity of their spirit with God.

As somewhat of a mystic myself, I regard philosophical Hinduism as the most spiritual of the world's religions, and to a degree I can appreciate this response. Yet the sad fact is that the masses of the Indian people are not living on this exalted plane. They are caught in a cycle of poverty and hopelessness, which the Christian concept of the incarnation of deity in human souls might alleviate. Also in this standard Hindu answer I detected a note of cynicism and jealousy. Almost always the respondent went on to condemn the United States for the materialism of its culture. A tinge of Third-World inferiority was latent as more and more of India strove to emulate the technology of the West. People wanted material comforts. In seven visits to India over twenty-two years I saw great strides in westernization. More cars were on the road, more skyscrapers were being built. In the big cities old bamboo scaffolding was giving way to huge industrial cranes.

From Christians I got different answers to my question. To Dick Keithan the unique contribution is the Church. This is a surprising answer for one who is an independent soul, a political activist and reformer, and indicates the depth of his thinking. Christianity is unique in the fellowship which the Church offers, and Keithan felt that even profound scholars like Radhakrishnan have never grasped the full import of this. His Hindu friends say that it is too bad that he feels he must stay within the Christian Church, because he is so much like them in spirit. But they do not appreciate the concept of the Church. There is no corporate fellowship in Hinduism, but its temples are like bazaars where throngs of individuals are performing separate acts of worship, such as burning candles or incense, or offering flowers. Keithan must stay in the Church, because that for him is the Body of Christ. On the other hand, his Christian colleagues do not understand how he can associate so closely with non-

Christians. Another missionary, Emmons White, expressed the fear that Keithan was in danger of obscuring the fact that Christianity is not just a way among many, but *the* one true way.

Lloyd Lorbeer's view of Christianity's contribution was "victorious living." It has shown the Indians that life is not something from which to seek escape, but that it can be lived fully and joyously. Each year during Holy Week the mission schools at Pasulamai perform an outdoor Passion Play depicting the life of Jesus. Thousands come each night.

The return from South India was timed to have me present for the special event that was the official reason for my trip to Ahmednagar, the dedication of the new Dewey Library. This was one of Dr. Hivale's building projects to construct adequate facilities on the campus. He had received $50,000 from the Harvard-Yenching Foundation, whose work in China was now curtailed. It had selected nine colleges in southeast Asia for substantial grants, and Ahmednagar was one of them. After seven years of operation, the college now had 1,400 students who were gaining recognition for academic, scientific and athletic achievements. Dr. Hivale had elongated the Sherwood Eddy Auditorium building with this addition. Classrooms were on the ground floor, and the Dewey Library on the second. The stairway projected out in three directions from the main space.

The day before there had been so much work yet to be done that I thought it impossible to complete on time. But the hundred men and women tribal workers put on all the finishing touches and cleaned the grounds so that all was ready. The board of overseers met on the morning of August 3, and Manorama gave a luncheon for them and the American Board missionaries who had been invited. One hundred of them came, and with the students comprised an attendance of seven hundred. As the official guest I was brought over at 5:30, climbed the stairs, was garlanded, and then cut the ribbon as I declared the Dewey Library officially open. The guests followed to fill the room. At the front of the room was a garlanded photo of Dr. Harry P. Dewey, with the words that he was "Pastor Plymouth Church, 1907-1935." After a musical number Tom introduced me as the chief guest speaker. I began by saying that it was appropriate that the college library should be named after Dr.

Dewey because he was a scholar with a keen mind and rich spirit. I then asked what is this Plymouth Church of which you hear so much? I described it as a fellowship of people organized around six basic ideas. Since these ideas have universal validity, I hoped that the college might likewise pursue them.

1. Education is the best method to bring individuals to fulfillment of their highest potential.
2. Freedom is the rightful heritage of every human being.
3. Man should be tolerant.
4. We are all brothers around the world
5. Man attains his highest stature as a spiritual being.
6. Our happiness lies in service to one another.

The address seemed well received. The member of parliament from the Ahmednagar District came up afterwards and said that more talks like this would build understanding between our countries.

During the remainder of the week I spoke at various gatherings of students. Manorama invited to the bungalow porch some of the more articulate students for an exchange of ideas. I always find give-and-take conversations to be the most stimulating form of communication. On my last Sunday morning, August 8, I spoke at the college chapel at eight o'clock, then went with Joe Moulton to the village church at Jamgaon. It was a moving experience. Some people were waiting for us when we arrived, and others came shortly. Some had walked four miles. Forty-five men and thirty-five children were crowded into a small room, with thirty-five women on the side. I preached briefly, with Joe translating sentence by sentence. We had communion, with people taking the elements very devoutly. This service made an impression to which I have referred many times on World-wide Communion Sundays. Though we did not speak a common language, we experienced a common love in the heart.

A week after the dedication of the Dewey Library, I left Ahmednagar with Tom Barnabas to explore further this fascinating country of India. It was an emotional farewell because I had made many new friends and had participated in so many college activities. Chairs had been arranged outdoors and a professional photographer engaged. I was garlanded by a group of the students and then by representatives of the workers. Mid-morning a 1941 Lincoln Zephyr arrived to take us the one hundred fifty miles to Aurangabad. Tom and I sat in the back seat, along with the registrar of the college, Pramed Gadre. He was a fine, cultured young man who came from a high Brahmin family that had converted to Christianity. Our destination was the caves of Ellora and Ajanta some distance from Aurangabad, where in the jungles are hidden these art treasures of the fifth and sixth centuries. Carved out of stone cliffs are temples and monuments at Ellora, and murals in caves at Ajanta depicting scenes from Hindu mythology. Gadre was a talented artist himself, a good guide for our excursion. Later he sent me a magnificent watercolor he had painted, showing the artisans of those earlier centuries painting the murals that visitors can see today. I treasure this very much.

After three days the others returned to Nagar, while Tom and I took trains that carried us to Agra, Fatipar Sikri, Benares, Delhi and Simla. To travel on Indian railways is to open oneself to varied experiences. Along the way we met interesting people, and in Delhi had interviews with missionaries, American aid workers, and embassy staff.

A high point of our contacts was a visit on August 20 with Dr. Sarvapali Radhakrishnan, a former Oxford professor who was India's best interpreter of the Hindu spirit, a scholar whom I regard as the most knowledgeable student of religion in the twentieth century. On three trips to India I was invited to his home, the third occasion being at the presidential palace in 1963.

I told him of my study of the Upanishads and my acceptance of Divinity as a universal spirit rather than a sectarian God. He responded that all religions in their highest insights recognize the same truths. I asked if he would be favorable to a Christianity that did not insist on one unique historic revelation. He answered in the affirmative, and said that he considered himself a Christian and part of the Invisible Communion. He has spoken in Hindu temples, Moslem mosques, Buddhist retreats and Christian churches without ever feeling any compromise because he embraces the spiritual truths to which all of them witness. He thought the world was moving in the direction of such universalism. I told him that the Neo-Orthodox teachings in the United States were contrary to that view, and quoted what Reinhold Niebuhr had said to me at the Claremont General Council meetings in 1952, that the study of comparative religions was of interest only to decadent liberalism. Radhakrishnan told me not to be discouraged because my position was undoubtedly the correct one, and the only one offering any hope to the world.

While I accept that ultimate reality is spirit, I have been troubled by the Hindu claim that the material world is an illusion. I asked him if in immortality individuality and personal attitudes would be preserved. He said yes, and quoted Sankara as having said that as long as the sun shines in the heavens, so long will souls retain their individuality. We cannot say what the final state will be when all creation has reached its consummation in the perfect harmony of God.

I told him of my visit to the current Sankaracharaya at Kanchipurum, and my disappointment that a supposedly learned man offered more show than substance. He advised me not to try talking to various holy men, because I have the true spiritual outlook. He had addressed a group of them recently and told them that they should take off their robes and dress as common men because they are not fulfilling their role as spiritual teachers.

After a momentous seven weeks in India, I bade farewell to Tom Barnabas as a beloved brother at the Delhi airport, and flew to Bombay and then on to Turkey to visit Plymouth's missionaries at Talas. After more than a week with friends in the Near East Mission, whom Vi and I had met on our 1951 trip, I went on to Europe and down to Naples to make my first visit to Casa Materna and the dedicated Santi family, which then became one of Plymouth's ongoing benevolence centers.

While at Ahmednagar we had discussed the possibility of someday building a Plymouth Chapel at the college, as the small Christian chapel currently used was much too small for the growing student body. In 1955 the Indian government offered to give the college an adjacent thirty-five acres for expansion, to provide an athletic field, but it would not allow a Christian church to be erected on government property. Dr. Hivale decided to accept twenty-two acres as a gift and to ask Plymouth to buy the other thirteen acres on which he could construct whatever buildings he wished. This agreement was entered into, and Plymouth Minneapolis sent $15,000 for this. We used funds that we had begun to accumulate for a future chapel. In the years since several important buildings—science departments and a modern library—have been erected on this land.

Dr. and Mrs. Hivale made their last trip to the United States in the winter of 1957, when he taught for a semester at the Pacific School of Religion. This visit was timed to bring them to Minneapolis for the Centennial observance of our church. A gala anniversary banquet was held on April 26, 1957, which climaxed a year of various observances. The Hivales arrived a week earlier because Ruth Hivale wanted to give a luncheon as an expression of appreciation for the thirty years of support the church had given them. She had brought with her herbs and spices with which to prepare a thoroughly Indian meal. Gertrude Stevenson gathered a group of women who worked in the kitchen for two days preparing the ingredients.

The next direct contact with our India family came two years later when Vi and I and our two daughters went on a seven-month sabbatical trip around the world. At that time Judy was a junior in high school, and Janet was a middler in junior high. It was an educational adventure for all of us. Throughout the trip we stayed in mission hospitals, schools and homes of American Board career missionaries. We sailed from San Francisco on July 4 on the *President Wilson* of the American President Line. We reached Ahmednagar on October 6, where we stayed for a month. Janet was sick on our arrival, as she had not been eating well in Asia. Dr. Tholar, a trustee of the college and close friend of Tom and Manorama, put her to bed and gave careful medical attention as she gradually regained her strength. During our visit we had an official photograph taken in the Barnabii living room of all the members of our families. Only Indira, Henry and Andrew were missing, as the other three Hivale daughters, their husbands and children were present.

During our stay we had a formal "opening" of the Plymouth Annex, the thirteen-acre tract we had purchased for $15,000. Later Tom Barnabas went with our family on a flight to Kashmir, where we stayed on the houseboat *California*, a deluxe accommodation owned by Hagi Karina Ramzan Goroo, a pleasant Moslem entrepreneur. On the return flight Tom and I made a stopover for two days at Chandigarh, a new city built on the plains below the foothills of the Himalayas. This is the new capitol of the Punjab, where four renowned architects headed by M. LeCorbusier had laid out the city and designed modern buildings to speak to the tomorrows rather than the past. By this time it was clear that we in Minneapolis would build a Plymouth Chapel on the annex we had purchased. We wanted it to be more than a functional rectangle such as Dr. Hivale had been building, and to be something distinctive that would reflect a forward vision. We were impressed with the freshness and openness of the new city of Chandigarh.

After our visit Tom engaged the Bombay firm of Gregson, Batley & King to be the architects, and a brilliant young Parsee, Mr. Pheroze Kudianwale, prepared the design. The white cement structure is surrounded by a moat crossed by a small bridge, so that one entering the chapel is conscious of passing from the common earth into a special realm. The roof rests on two long beams supported by columns. These 120-foot beams had to be cast in position, the first such construction done in the Deccan area. Light comes from two long rows of high nave and clerestory windows, in addition to narrow cross-shaped lancets recessed in the walls. The atmosphere of the sanctuary is one of light and air that blends the worship with the vast outdoors. While the plans were being formulated, Plymouth insisted that the cost be kept within $45,000. Construction took place in 1962.

Mr. and Mrs. Merlin L. (Bob) Pugh contributed $20,000 to the project on condition that the congregation raise the remainder, which we did through three Easter offerings.

Dr. Hivale passed away peacefully in his sleep the night of September 7, 1961. Word passes quickly in an Indian community, and by morning crowds of people began coming to the house. The funeral was held at four that afternoon, and was attended by six to seven thousand people. It was impossible to tell how many, as the streets were completely crowded as far ahead as one could see. It was a fitting testimonial for a man whose work had touched the life of the entire Ahmednagar community, regardless of caste or creed. He was a scholar with a brilliant mind, but with a heart for people that inspired one practical achievement after another. Certainly I shall always remember him as one of the most dynamic Christians I have ever met.

One of the thrilling climaxes to these long associations with our India family was the dedication of the Plymouth Chapel at Ahmednagar on March 10, 1963. I took a party of fifteen on a forty-five day tour of "Ancient Civilizations," and also to attend this dedication. Twelve of us were Plymouth members: Mrs. John Lane "Margo" Sprague, Mr. and Mrs. Matthew C. Madsen, Mrs. Ralph Madson, Misses Naomi and Ruth Liljeberg, Mr. and Mrs. Gordon W. Wittich, Neal Bailey, Miss Grace Barker, and Mrs. Fred Carleton. My sister and brother-in-law, Wilma and Phil Prescott, and two of their daughters joined us in India for this part of the tour.

Our group made a pilgrimage to the grave of Dr. Hivale, where Gordon Wittich laid a wreath on behalf of Plymouth. On Sunday morning, at the cool hour of 9:00 A.M., the dedication service was held. Men in white suits or shirts, women in brilliant-hued saris, made colorful the chapel already festooned with a profusion of flowers.

Mr. Matthew C. Madsen and Miss Naomi Liljeberg brought greetings from Plymouth. Mrs. Hivale spoke for the family, and a moment of silent tribute was paid Dr. Hivale. Dr. Kanti Bhagat spoke for the faculty, two youths for the students, and Principal Thomas Barnabas for the college. I preached a dedicatory sermon on "The Glory That Transfigures," showing that both Hinduism and Christianity belong to the universal religious spirit that gives men and women a clearer insight into the meaning and purpose of life. The service ended with the congregation singing "Mine Eyes Have Seen the Glory."

My last visit to India was on my five-month saunter around the world after my retirement in August 1976. Tom and Manorama had come from India to be with me on that occasion, as they had on previous significant days. On this last trip I arrived on January 15, 1977, in Delhi from Kabul with my good friends Ruth and Terrance Hanold, who had met me in Istanbul on New Year's Day. This was their first trip to India, and they could only stay ten days. On this visit I was busy filling speaking engagements that Tom had made for me, at the Church of North India on Malibar Hill out of Delhi, at the De Nobili Jesuit College in Poona, and the Union Theological Seminary at Yeotimal, associated with the University of Serampore. I also made a trip to Madras to visit Arthur and Sakkhu

Devapragasam and their orphanage.

Mrs. Hivale had suffered a stroke on January 19 and was failing in Dr. Tholar's nursing home during the weeks that I was in India. We realized that she was not going to recover, and we prayed that she might be released while I was still at Ahmednagar. Vimala came to join her sisters, and each day the three daughters went to the hospital to visit with their mother and give her some care. In India the family members of hospital patients are expected to feed and care for their loved one.

Tom and I knew that we had to leave for Delhi on Thursday, February 24, as I had a reservation to fly on the twenty-fifth to Bangkok and he to a meeting of college principals in South India. Vimal had to return to her teaching post at Nagpur. The Hand Always Above My Shoulder must have been watching, for at 4:15 in the morning of February 23 the end came, the last day that all of us could be present. The hospital phoned. Tom and Manorama, Joe and Sarala went and brought the body home at 5:00 A.M., bathed and dressed her, and at 6:00 A.M. took her to the Plymouth Chapel, where she rested on a stretcher in the chancel. Though she had been active in the Ahmednagar Congregational church, she had requested to be buried from the campus chapel because her life had revolved around the college.

Tom got a crew of college groundspeople to go to the Christian cemetery at 8:00 A.M. and dig a grave four and a half feet deep. The cemetery is a bleak place, no grass, no flowers growing in the hard soil, though Dr. Hivale's grave is under a tree. Another group was instructed to build a coffin. This was ready at noon, and the body placed in it with the lid left off. There are no undertakers in India, so the family must make all preparations. There is no embalming. Because of the heat funerals must be held immediately.

From early morning groups of students kept vigil in the chapel, groups seated on the floor singing bhagans, religious chants with rhythmic style something like folk songs. A constant stream of visitors came and went. The service was scheduled for one o'clock. The chapel was filled to overflowing. Joe Barnabas, the chaplain, presided. Three local ministers read the Scriptures prescribed by the Church of North India ritual. I gave the only talk and was brief. I referred to the long association of Ruth and Bhaskar Hivale with

Plymouth Church from 1929 to 1961, their four daughters and their families, and their sacrifice to make possible the dream of a college education for the young people of the Deccan.

Though Tom is ten years younger than I, he retired according to Indian regulations at about the same time that I retired at sixty-five in 1976. In the fourteen years since, we have seen each other nearly every year. Because of Manorama's teaching and her position with the Christian Board for Asian Education, they travel frequently between Ahmednagar and the United States. With their two sons both in medical practice in Chicago, we can arrange visits. Over forty years of association across oceans, continents and cultures, we have remained each others' best friends.

And all the members of Plymouth have been enriched by a hundred years of Christian love and service in India. Our India Family is a precious part of the record.

16

Neighborhood Involvement

PLYMOUTH HAS A LONG RECORD of concern for the community. At the turn of the century when Scandinavian immigrants were coming in large numbers, our church members started several Sunday schools in north Minneapolis, in part to help children become fluent in English. Over the decades a number of settlement houses were established to serve the needs of people not connected with our church. Among these were Northeast Neighborhood House and Elliot Park Neighborhood House. Neither of these is in existence today. The latter later changed in name to Waite House, in honor of Judge Edward F. Waite of Plymouth who had served for decades on its board. The most enduring of these settlements has been Pillsbury House.

One more of these service enterprises was formed during my days, and grew from a program in our basement to become an independent organization that in the late eighties is one of the major social agencies in Minneapolis. The Loring-Nicollet-Bethlehem Center, with a 1988 budget of $767,900, is an expression of the social consciousness of our people, and the story of its growth deserves to be told.

My experience over the span of half a century indicates that when a church serves the larger community, it establishes a reciprocal relationship. It is not a one-way street. The motivation of concerned Christians is to reach out beyond one's circle to try to meet a human need, but as a congregation does this it attracts new adherents who notice this dedication. Many persons are looking for churches that are more than self-serving groups of complacent believers. At the conclusion of the Second World War, the Twin Cities, like most metropolitan areas, witnessed an explosive movement of the population toward the suburbs. Many of the strongest congregations today in Edina, Minnetonka, White Bear Lake, Burnsville and around an expanding circle were not even in existence when I came to Plymouth in 1944.

This shift has constituted a challenge for the downtown churches, and the large inner city congregations of the major denominations have met that challenge well. Over the years I expressed to my ministerial neighbors that we were not competing as much as supporting one another, for we were creating programs and services that kept many of the civic and cultural leaders coming downtown in their religious affiliations. We needed to challenge our communicants that by their participation they are keeping vital the moral and spiritual life of a great metropolitan area. They earn their money downtown and go home to comfortable areas in the suburbs, but we need them to return to inner city churches that are serving less affluent neighborhoods. Plymouth occupies a block on Nicollet between what would be Nineteenth and Twentieth, with Seventh Street probably being the center of the business district. We are six blocks south of Grant Street, which marks the end of the Mall. We are in a deteriorating area of old apartments and former mansions converted to board-and-care homes. Our neighborhood accommodates low-income families, mentally retarded in boarding homes, many of the gay community, long-time elderly residents who cannot afford to move. Our Sunday congregations include very few of these, but our weekday outreach program is directed toward them. Hence we have been able to appeal to young families of idealistic vision, creating a warm fellowship of their peers and challenging them to blend their good fortune with service to the needy. Many times we say, "We raise our money from the suburbs and spend it in the inner city."

Our involvement in direct neighborhood work began in the fifties. During that decade Plymouth had taken a leadership role in the attempt to curtail some of the practices of the Council for Social Action in our national denomination. That is a significant enough story that I am devoting a chapter to it. Gideon Seymour, executive editor of the *Minneapolis Star and Tribune*, our second moderator and one of the finest laymen I have ever known, had served as a member of the board of review appointed by the Congregational General Council to study the program of the CSA. Mr. Seymour said that inasmuch as Plymouth was objecting to a national group taking a specific stand for all Congregationalists, it would be appropriate for us to show concern for social questions by creating a group within our congregation to discuss current issues from our viewpoint.

In response to his suggestion, a committee was formed in the spring of 1952 to ask the deacons to create a Committee on Social Problems. Attorney Wellington Tully was chairman, joined by Lloyd Hale, Terrance Hanold and Mr. Seymour. This resulted in the creation of Plymouth Forum to meet one Sunday evening a month, with Gideon Seymour as chairman, Mrs. Herbert F.R. Plass as secretary, with additions to them on the executive committee of Professors Roland Vaile and Henry Allen, Mrs. Stanley Platt and Terrance Hanold. After the untimely death of Mr. Seymour in 1954, leadership of the Forum passed to Philip F. Sherman, another devoted layman who was secretary and counsel for Pillsbury Company.

Out of the Forum discussions came the impetus to start a neighborhood project. The February 20, 1955, meeting centered on the questions: Should the church attempt to provide day nurseries, or group work, and recreational activities for less privileged neighborhoods not far from the church? Or should we leave all these activities to tax-supported agencies and the Community Fund, and eliminate social action, confining ourselves to our own membership? The discussion that evening clearly called for participation by Plymouth, and four areas of concern were defined. The most urgent was that we begin a recreational program for the children of single-parent and low-income families in our immediate area. At the next meeting Professor and Mrs. Henry Allen were named to get such a program started.

Initial activity began with the September 1955 school year. The nearby Emerson Elementary School had a dedicated Methodist layman as principal, Mr. Robert G. Christman, and he welcomed the overtures of Plymouth. One of the three celebrated Bell sisters of our church, Mrs. Claude Osgood (Ruth), was school counselor at Emerson, and aided in the selection of the youngsters. Mrs. Allen's advisory committee enlisted the help of two social work professionals from Elliot Park, Donald Johnson and Phyllis Baker. Volunteers from our congregation were Mrs. Robert Finch (Marilyn), Mrs. Thomas G. Colwell (Phyllis), and a retired school principal, Claude D. Siehl. David Warden helped with a baseball team.

Mr. Christman selected the youngsters whom he regarded as most needful of help, and nearly a hundred of them came two afternoons a week to our basement from 3:30 to 5:30 P.M. Mr. Arch W. Goldman, new director of Waite House, soon became interested. In 1958 he pointed out that the Plymouth Center was the only place in Minneapolis where a church, a public school and a settlement house were working together. This cooperation continued for six years, with more and more members showing interest until a new step was taken.

In 1958 we considered this program so much a part of Plymouth that on May 25, a special meeting of the congregation voted to create the Plymouth Center Board as a fifth official board authorized by our bylaws. Mrs. Donald Mathison (Mary Lou) became the first chairperson of the twelve-person board.

After six years in the basement of our building, Plymouth Center moved into a house of its own in January of 1961. This was a brown frame house across the street at Groveland and Nicollet, which the church had purchased from Mrs. Harold Olson in 1960.

Several Plymouth families and three hotels responded to a plea for furniture, so that the house was almost completely furnished. There was a lounge and two activity rooms on the first floor, and boys' and girls' clubrooms plus a large handicraft room on the second floor. The youngsters of the neighborhood responded excitedly at having a house of their own. They scrubbed walls, painted the kitchen and arranged the furnishings for their meetings.

Just as we moved the Plymouth Center across the street to the brown house a significant development occurred. Our neighbor at the other end of Groveland Avenue—Hennepin Avenue Methodist Church—said they had watched our program and wanted to start something similar for their congregation. When they came to us for counsel, we suggested that rather than start another program they join us in a work that was destined to grow larger than any single church could handle. They were receptive, and we invited other sister churches of the area to join in a common neighborhood program. Westminster Presbyterian, Wesley Methodist and St. Mark's Cathedral joined Hennepin Avenue and Plymouth in founding what we called the Loring-Nicollet Center, with its activities in the house at 1830 Nicollet, which we owned and provided for group use. At the same time a joint committee engaged as a full-time director Miss Courtney Bell from the staff of the Girl Scouts in Detroit. She had a master's degree in social work, and was a charming and dedicated person. I well remember sitting at a meeting to discuss these moves of our Plymouth Center board under the chairmanship of Mrs. Stephen H. Baxter, Jr. (Marjorie) when word came of the assassination of President Kennedy.

After providing the use of the brown house for a year and a half, Plymouth became involved in the exchange of properties on Nicollet Avenue that resulted in the creation of a three-hundred-foot parking lot leased to Red Owl Stores. This necessitated the demolition of the house we were providing for Loring-Nicollet, so we found and bought for the use of the center a larger brick house at 1920 Pillsbury Avenue. Again, we retained ownership of the property and donated its use to the center. We paid $40,000 in 1962 for the new location. The building underwent several renovations over the next twenty-five years as the program constantly expanded, until Loring-Nicollet-Bethlehem bought a large property at 1935 Nicollet in 1987. We sold our house for $150,000 and gave half the profit to the settlement house. The large budget of Loring-Nicollet-Bethlehem is financed by grants from government agencies, the United Way, and a constituency of supporters, as well as the founding churches.

After the creation of the Loring-Nicollet Center and the 1962 move to our house on Pillsbury, that agency became independent from Plymouth with its own board of directors, though we continued to make substantial annual contributions as part of our benevolence program. Two Plymouthites over a period of more than twenty years gave active leadership to the Loring-Nicollet board: Merrill S. Finch and John Sandbo. The Finch family was generous in financial aid for building improvements.

In the late sixties Loring-Nicollet joined for summer projects with Bethlehem Community Center out of Bethlehem Presbyterian Church on Twenty-fourth Street. This led to a merger of the two to form the more encompassing Loring-Nicollet-Bethlehem Center.

When Plymouth gave independence to this new settlement house, the church did not lose interest in area work. Our fifth board changed its name to the Neighborhood Board, and for twenty-five years has created and sustained programs for area residents. The fireplace room on the ground floor of our educational wing was designated as a drop-in center, open two afternoons a week for our neighbors in the board-and-care homes for mentally and physically handicapped. Once a month afternoon Bingo parties were instituted, to which residents from these homes were bused to our dining room. Many volunteers from PWO Circles acted as hosts.

In 1967 we brought to our staff for our customary three-year period a brilliant and articulate graduate from Yale Divinity School, Roger W. Paine II. He was particularly concerned with social issues focused in the Vietnam War, and did a great deal to stimulate interest in member participation in service projects. He arranged a largely attended series on volunteerism and social needs. Under his leadership the Neighborhood Board engaged Anne Newhart Trucker to assist him in a fourfold program. The trustees remodeled the unused area under the sanctuary to form a youth center named One Groveland. A drop-in center for youths was opened five nights a week, with bands brought in for weekend dances. Tutoring at Emerson School was reinstituted, and visitation on neighborhood elderly was begun. Roger was an excellent organizer and administrator as well as a stimulating preacher. Since leaving Plymouth in 1970, he has been director of youth homes in Colorado and Texas, and more recently director of a retreat center near Boston, called InterFace.

The Neighborhood Board continues as one of the vital parts of Plymouth Church, operating a food shelf assistance in One Groveland and studying the operations of many small groups that address special needs. In 1987 it sent $59,000 of Plymouth benevolences to thirty-three outside agencies.

The Loring-Nicollet Community Council is another agency that was formed out of the neighborhood involvement of Plymouth Church. Over the decades there was a continuous effort to keep saloons and liquor stores out of the area, in which are located several hospitals, schools and churches. To fight liquor had been a traditional activity of churches. After Frank Griswold had bought three lots and demolished slum houses where Eighteenth Street runs into Nicollet, the trustees leased the lots to a parking company. In 1961 merchants applied for a liquor license to open a store adjacent to the north end of this lot. Our trustees and deacons voted to petition the License Committee of the City Council that no permits for package liquor stores be granted south of the then proposed Interstate 94 cut across Nicollet.

A group of us called on Frank Moulton, long-time powerful councilman, whose wife was a Plymouth member. After listening to us he spoke quite an indictment of our narrow interests. He said that churches were always protesting liquor licenses, but frequently ignored other issues. He challenged us to form a cooperative council of neighborhood institutions that would develop a general program for area improvement.

In January of 1962, Robert C. Miller, administrator of Abbott Hospital, and I gathered representatives from twenty-three non-profit organizations within the area to found the Loring-Nicollet Community Council. Committees explored freeway development, traffic control, fire prevention, area security, licensing, housing and zoning. A retired florist, Mr. Edward Peterson, served many years as the paid executive of this group, which still continues at the end of the eighties.

Plymouth has been a strong and vibrant religious center through all the years since its gathering in 1857. There have been four foundations for this strength: its New England Congregational heritage as an independent congregation linked with other free churches in fellowship; its liberal open theological stance, which encourages freedom to think; its warm, caring fellowship within its membership; and its practical service to the surrounding community.

This chapter tells the story of this neighborhood commitment over the last fifty years.

17

The Social Action Controversy

AT THE SAME TIME THAT DEVELOPMENTS and expansions were taking place in our parish life, Plymouth Church gained national attention through involvement in two major controversies that rocked Congregationalism in the decades of the fifties and early sixties. The first related to the authority and function of the denomination's Council for Social Action, and the second was over the proposed merger of Congregationalists with the Evangelical and Reformed Church to form the United Church of Christ. In both of these matters Plymouth Church played a pivotal role, but in the end was unsuccessful in making its viewpoint prevail.

To be on the losing side of the major conflicts of my time of course colored my ministry. An observer may ask why the Hand Always Above My Shoulder did not assure victory to my side, or at least prod me to choose the winning positions. My concept of divine guidance recognizes that God does not play favorites but grants wisdom and courage to all who seek. Individuals must respond as they interpret this guidance, and the blessing lies in integrity and humility more than in victory. Since so much of my life has developed favorably, I think I gained precious insights through losing these battles. One comes to appreciate that there are different ways of looking at the same problem, and that solutions are possible when each side is allowed the means to function on its own terms. This clarifies issues that heretofore were hazy and undefined, and leads to separations which, though painful, may be necessary for the integrity of each party.

Throughout two decades of controversy in which I played a leading role on both issues, I was strengthened by the full support of our Plymouth membership. I am grateful that Plymouth has continued to be the liberal, responsible, caring church of my ideals. Our position was largely misunderstood on the national scene, basically because we were making carefully delineated distinctions that people on a crusade ignore as not being important. As I reflect on my life and tell the story of Plymouth, it is essential to recall these two controversies and again to set forth our position.

The social action controversy involved the basic question of the relation of local congregations to national agencies, and was bound to arise sooner or later. It did come through the chance attendance in 1948 by Dr. Donald J. Cowling at a Congregational laymen's retreat in Minnesota. During his thirty-seven years as president of Carleton College, Dr. Cowling had an active role in the denomination. He was a member of significant commissions of the National Council, as the coordinating body was called until its change in 1931 to the General Council. In 1921 he chaired the group to raise the Pilgrim Memorial Fund, which adds annually to the pension accumulations of ministers. As a strong believer in individualism, he thoroughly understood the freedom principles of Congregationalism. Upon his retirement from Carleton, he and Mrs. Cowling moved to Minneapolis and united with Plymouth Church in November 1945.

At the laymen's retreat the program leader was a staff person from the national Council for Social Action who discussed the lobbying activities of that group as they testified before congressional committees as to their position on various social questions. Among these was Federal Aid to Education, which the CSA supported and Dr. Cowling strongly opposed. He was shocked to learn that an agency of Congregationalism was speaking in behalf of a principle that he as a life-long educator saw as a threat to academic freedom. He came home and shared his distress with a number of laymen who had been associated with him at Carleton. Among them was Frank Bean, who as chief executive officer of International Milling Company had a research secretary on his staff. Soon he had gathered yearbooks, minutes and publications from the denominational offices. The CSA was publishing a *Labor Letter* and an *Agricultural Letter*, plus a monthly magazine that took stands on specific issues. Members of the staff were appearing before congressional committees, implying that they represented Congregationalists and speaking for or against proposed legislation.

From this awakening a group of laymen, largely in Plymouth, formed a committee to alert lay members to what they regarded as a violation of Congregationalist principles on the part of the CSA. Soon they were joined by others across the country, especially in Los Angeles, Milwaukee and Detroit. They took as their name the Committee Opposing Congregational Political Action, but later, when it became evident that this controversy was spilling over into the merger debate, they enlarged it to become the League to Uphold Congregational Principles.

One of the complaints of the Minnesota Lay Group was that the denomination provided no way to protest the actions of national agencies on issues with which they disagreed. One possibility might be for financial contributors to withhold funds as a form of protest. However, a policy of the denomination nullified such an attempt, for the Missions Council practiced what was called "equalization." Each of the national agencies was assigned a percentage of the contributions from the churches and conferences. At the end of a fiscal year, if one board had received less than its quota, the amounts were "equalized" within the total so that each group received its assigned proportion. Thus no amount of withholding could penalize a board.

This was a way of saying that the national agencies have the final determination, and the actions of individuals or congregations are not effective. The Minnesota Lay Group and Plymouth protested this policy, and in the spring of 1952 the Executive Committee of the General Council heard the complaints and abolished this system. Here was one small victory that our efforts did accomplish.

By March 1952 the controversy had become so heated that the General Council Executive Committee appointed a board of review to study the matter and to make recommendations to the 1954 General Council as to the role of the CSA in the denomination. This was a blue-ribbon committee of nine persons of national reputation. It held its first meeting on May 17, 1952, a second one on July 18-19, a third on January 26, 1953, and a fourth and final session to formalize its report on September 21, 1953.

At the June 1954 General Council meeting in New Haven the report of the board of review was presented and adopted. It contained a section on "Findings," which found the CSA operating within its charter, yet taking positive stands that made it appear to be spokesman for the denomination rather than an agency within it. "Recommendations" were nine, the effect of which was to recognize the importance of the CSA but to curtail the degree to which it is an advocate. It is to "devote the principal part of its resources of personnel and money to the education of members in the denomination on the Christian viewpoints in social issues. . . . Most of the publications should be in a form which can be widely used by pastors and individuals and groups within the churches . . . It is recommended that in its statements regarding political, economic, and other social issues, the CSA present the principal positions on which Congregational Christians may fairly differ. It is expected that it would include a statement of its own position or positions in such a framework." Another recommendation was that the eighteen members and its two hundred fifty associates be chosen to represent all segments of background so as to maintain balance and breadth of viewpoint.

Gideon Seymour, executive editor of the *Minneapolis Star and Tribune*, one of the nine members of the board of review, wrote an addendum that was attached to the report: "My only misgiving is whether the restraint of the Report and its general terms make sufficiently plain the sharpness of the controversy which prompted it, and the forcefulness and unanimity with which the board of review agrees on the need for drastic reforms in the conduct of the Council's work. I concur thoroughly in the opinion that it is not the Charter of the Council which needs revision, but the interpretation given to the Charter by the staff, an interpretation so slanted that the purpose of the Council has often been scarcely recognizable in the activities of recent years."

Mr. Seymour's misgivings were well-founded, because the general attitude of the clergy and laity involved in denominational affairs was to bring what they deemed a Christian perspective to the fore without regard for the restraints of historic polity. Congregationalists have always been socially minded, concerned with the issues of contemporary society. In their enthusiasm for a witness, the national board members were unable to make careful distinctions, and hence misunderstood or ignored the position of concerned laymen and of myself.

The most disillusioning experience of my life came on Saturday afternoon, June 21, 1952, at the General Council session in Claremont, California. Mr. Frank W. Pierce, a director of Standard Oil of New Jersey and chairman of the board of review, arranged and presided over a presentation of the Council for Social Action issue. There were three speakers for the position of the CSA: Dean Liston Pope of Yale Divinity School, Miss Ruth Isbell Seabury, a beloved American Board missionary, and Emerson Hangen, pastor of the large Long Beach church and a concerned Christian. I was one of three to bring the criticisms of the Council's actions. I agreed with ninety percent of what the three proponents said, because I regard myself as a social gospel minister. Of course we have concerns for all the issues which the proponents have expressed, but we think that within our polity restraints must be exercised by national agencies. This distinction simply was not heard. I resented that it was not even acknowledged by the other three, all of whom knew me personally and what I stood for.

When that afternoon session adjourned, Boynton Merrill, an elder minister whom I greatly admired and whose friendship my wife and I cherished, came over to console me. I said to him, "If ministers don't have the wisdom and the courage to make fine distinctions, perhaps I ought not be in the ministry." He put his arm around me and told me not to be discouraged.

At the Monday morning business session, a motion was introduced that "the report of the CSA, including 'Stewardship of the CSA,' be approved with commendation." The moderator, Dr. Vere V. Loper of First Congregational Church in Berkeley, ruled that "the vote on this motion will therefore constitute a close approximation to a vote of confidence, or no confidence, in the CSA." When the balloting took place on Tuesday morning, there were 689 ayes, 31 nos, and 19 abstentions. In an atmosphere charged with such commitment to social betterment, there was no possibility that any voice of restraint would be heard.

The impression prevailed that the laymen who objected to CSA procedures were political conservatives who wished to stifle reforms, that Plymouth Church was a wealthy, reactionary congregation, and that I am opposed to the social dimensions of the gospel. These were inaccuracies that need to be corrected.

As for the laymen in the league, they included varying viewpoints. We know that there have been and are today powerful men in the right-wing conservative faction of many denominations who have opposed any liberal advance. They have used religion to justify their opposition to social and economic change. When a group such as the Minnesota-based League to Uphold Congregational Principles is formed, there will be reactionaries who join it as a means to their end. This is inevitable. I was unhappy with some who joined forces with us, such as Dr. James W. Fifield of First Congregational Church Los Angeles. He was an archconservative with whom I had little in common. The men whom I knew in our Minnesota group were not of this extreme, but felt that the staff and boards of the CSA lacked experience in the business community and were not qualified to make judgments concerning its problems. Furthermore, they considered that the advocacy of specific issues rather than presenting various views was a violation of Congregational independence. As Gideon Seymour once said, "I believe that God is concerned with the problems of American agriculture, but I doubt that he has a position on the Branham Plan."

As for Plymouth Church, I doubt that there are many congregations more involved with social issues than we. At the very moment when the CSA controversy was taking place, Plymouth organized the Plymouth Forum for monthly discussions of controversial issues. Gideon Seymour was the first chairman, and after his death he was followed by Philip F. Sherman of the Pillsbury Company, and later Attorney Wellington Tully. These meetings discussed public housing, race discrimination, world order, welfare systems, and the like. I have mentioned earlier that on the Sunday after the death of President Roosevelt, the deacons presented a resolution to be forwarded to the San Francisco Conference forming the United Nations in which we pledged support for a world body, and 804 persons in the congregation came forward to sign. Through the years we have maintained an active adult education program, both before worship on Sunday mornings and on a weeknight. At these, speakers on a wide variety of topics make presentations and lead discussions. We are a civic and politically minded congregation that reflects a wide and liberal vision toward contemporary problems.

The position of Plymouth was expressed in resolutions passed at its annual meeting in January 1952:

> Resolved, that Plymouth Church recognizes and shares the concern of the Christian Church for the social order; that Plymouth Church approves the work of the Council for Social Action in those instances where it has tried to awaken and stimulate that concern by factual and balanced reports of social problems communicated solely to our churches and membership; that Plymouth Church vigorously disapproves the lobbying activities, the weighted editorial presentations, and the attempts to represent or to apparently represent our churches, of the Council for Social Action, and registers its vigorous disapproval with the General Council; that Plymouth Church requests the Council to establish an agency to stimulate through our churches constructive social action by individual members, and expressly to withhold from such agency authority to represent or seem to represent in any manner or degree our churches.

This resolution may have had some impact on the national staff, because that spring the Executive Committee of the General Council did recognize the problem and did form the board of review to examine the role of the CSA.

My own position on the social gospel has been clear throughout my ministry, though during these years of controversy with the CSA it was misinterpreted, probably intentionally, by those who wished to discredit any murmur of dissent. I regard myself as a fiscal conservative and a social liberal. I believe that social concerns are an integral part of Judeo-Christian ministry. A Congregational minister is concerned with every aspect of life, and as preacher and teacher he is both free and responsible to express his views according to the wisdom God gives him. If he has made clear to his congregation that he speaks with no authority other than his own judgment, and that his parishioners are free to disagree, then there can be a healthy interchange in which both he and his people may grow. Significant growth and action on any issue must come from public sentiment at local levels as citizens are stimulated to view national and world affairs from a moral perspective. Because we Congregationalists believe that the covenanted community is the local church, we cannot authorize or permit any overall agency to speak for us or to exercise judgment over us. This is a matter of ecclesiastical polity, not of any lack of social vision.

During my first years in the ministry, when I was on faculties of summer conferences for our youths, the course I taught was on the prophets of Israel. This was a focus on prophetic ministry to social and economic problems, and I have carried this through the years. At the Ecclesiastical Council which examined me for installation as the twelfth minister of Plymouth Church Minneapolis on February 1, 1945, I discussed four demands of the human soul which Christian faith fulfills. The fourth of these is the demand for righteousness. I said:

> The Church holds the key to the rebuilding of civilization insofar as it will call society and its members to a hearty repentance and to a new commitment to righteousness. It is the task of Christians to become involved in the social and economic issues of the time in order to bring to bear the ethical demands of Jesus Christ, which demands, because they are woven into the very fabric of the universe, simply cannot be ignored. . . . If the good society is to be built, the Church must become increasingly articulate in social problems. We dare not content ourselves with pious phrases and comforting thoughts when there is a real campaign against darkness and injustice that must be waged.

In my preaching schedule I tried to make one in four sermons relate to social and moral problems. The most effective technique I developed was to speak on the first Sunday of January or the last of December on the "Ten Most Important Events of the Year." I made this annual summary for forty years, and began the practice before the religious columnists started a similar one. These became some of my most popular sermons. Because the Minneapolis newspapers usually carried the story, people outside our parish came on this special Sunday, and members of our congregation tried to anticipate by forming their own lists. This year-end analysis became the hardest chore of my ministry, because it involved keeping an enormous file of newspaper and magazine clippings.

The point to make is that this practice is a highly effective teaching tool. The minister is selective, and he can choose events that dramatize moral dilemmas and social concerns. He can discuss an issue on which his people may largely disagree with his viewpoint, because he is not primarily arguing his case but reporting a specific happening.

When the controversy arose over the denomination's Council for Social Action, I became a spokesperson for the critics. I may have disagreed with some of the political stands, and I certainly believed that the members of the council's staff and board were partisans who did not represent a cross-section of the people in our churches, but these were not my basic points. My opposition centered in the polity issue, that within the Congregational theory of free and independent churches, no national agency is permitted to take a stand on controversial matters. This was misunderstood and maligned, and I was judged a reactionary, opposed to social vision.

To try to clarify our position, I wrote a nineteen-page pamphlet in June 1950, entitled "Congregationalism and the Social Gospel." I pointed out that from colonial days Congregationalists have been concerned with social issues, and that as minister I have tried to follow this heritage. I quoted the words of my Harvard philosophy professor, William Ernest Hocking: "The Christian Church needs the courage to believe in its pertinence to every social situation, and its partisanship to none. It has still to define and exercise the function described by its own genius, that of bringing to the questions which it has no competence to settle, the moral postulates without which there can be no settlement."

I stated again my opposition to the CSA policy of taking stands on specific issues, and encouraged it to do educational and research work to help laypeople in our congregations to inform their own judgments.

Spokesmen for the CSA attacked my pamphlet: Dean Liston Pope of Yale Divinity School, and later chairman of the CSA; Ray Gibbons, executive director of the CSA; and Ernest Lefever, a graduate student at Yale Divinity School. Their criticism was dismaying, because they accused me of wishing the CSA to speak positions with which I agreed and to be silent with what I disagreed. That was an obvious misreading, because I referred to no specific item. They claimed an inconsistency in my calling for the church to lead, yet objecting when it did. My objection was to the manner of the leading. The major criticism they had was at the point of the function of the CSA. They saw it as empowered to act by taking stands on social questions, whereas I considered its function to be educational.

This is a basic difference which involves Congregational polity. My interpretation is that all authority resides in the local church, and that no outside agency may speak for it. This is a distinction that was incomprehensible to the delegates who heard the 1952 debate at Claremont.

In my paper I had a section to which none of these critics replied. To make clear that I was not attempting to silence the church, I had a concluding section in which I defended the right of the Federal Council of Churches and the National Catholic Welfare Assembly to take stands on issues. They are operating under different rules. Their charters do permit them to speak.

This is still my position, often misunderstood and probably difficult to accept. I am happy to have the church give leadership on social issues. I am helped by listening to documents of the Roman Catholic bishops, to positions of the Methodist Church, and to the officers of the National Council. All of these have a polity that authorizes them to speak, and the rest of us can be influenced by their analyses. But Congregational polity does not permit a similar voice, because we are not a centralized church but a free fellowship of independent churches.

The controversy over the CSA thus was a foretaste of the simultaneous debate over the merger. They are not two separate controversies, but a moving development about the nature of Congregationalism. In a very real sense, the formation of a unified United Church of Christ legitimized partisan stands on public affairs. Both in the sequence of time and in the issues involved, the one controversy led to the second. The same lines were drawn in both.

18

The Merger Controversy

A LANDMARK EVENT IN THE YEARS of my ministry was the formation of the United Church of Christ through the merger of the General Council of Congregational Christian Churches with the General Synod of the Evangelical and Reformed Churches. Leading up to this union were heated debates and legal battles for two decades, until the final consummation in June of 1961. When the controversy was over, many friendships were broken, old associations severed, and new alignments made. To record or to read of these struggles as past history can in no way evoke the emotions and deep feelings of those of us who were participants.

Of the five thousand Congregational churches, some four thousand voted to enter the new denomination, while over a thousand took no action. One hundred formed the National Association of Congregational Christian Churches in 1956, and three hundred fifty others have joined the fellowship in the ensuing years. Now at the end of the eighties we have four groups instead of the two before the merger: 6,400 UCC churches, 450 CCC/NA churches, 89 Conservative Congregational churches, and about 800 that have remained outside. It often happens that attempts at organizational union produce new divisions.

This merger had special significance for ecumenists because it brought together two groups with differing polities. The very name of the Congregationalists witnessed to one of the three New

Testament traditions; namely, the independence of local churches. The Evangelical and Reformed were a German ancestor group who followed the tradition of presbyterial relationships. Other unions of the past forty years have involved consolidation of branches within the same denominational lineage. It was hoped that this new venture would become a uniting as well as a united church, and demonstrate how differing polities can function together.

The controversy covered the second and third decades of my ministry and involved me actively in issues about which I feel strongly. As a birthright Congregationalist, I am proud of our heritage and its historic role in defining freedom in the United States. There is a direct line from the Mayflower Compact through the Fundamental Orders of Connecticut to the Constitution. A wariness against authority has made us cautious about structures.

From my ordination in 1936 by the Fairfield County Association of Connecticut, I was fortunate to have the friendship of our denominational leaders, so I was intimately involved in the workings of the General Council and of the Board of Home Missions. As is often the case, the move toward union was initiated from the top by clergy involved at the national level as administrative officers. They appealed to the grassroots sentiment for union that swept the country in the ecumenical spirit that followed World War II. People involved at these higher levels have a different perspective than laity in local congregations. They want to support each other in programs that they see as enhancing their effectiveness toward worthy goals. During the two decades of controversy, there were many well-known ministers and laypeople who raised questions, urged delays, encouraged further study before action. These came to be regarded by the majority as troublemakers or stubborn, and every question raised added to the momentum of those who wanted to proceed with the union.

The opponents were outmaneuvered and persuaded by the enthusiasm of the majority. Many reluctant clergy went along because of fears as to what their prospects might be otherwise. My esteemed mentor, Dean Rockwell Harmon Potter, who was the very embodiment of Congregationalism, said to me, "You will find that 'out' is a very big place when you are in it!" All his life he had been at the center of conferences and gatherings; he could not picture himself outside the fold.

When the final division came, only six of us who had held national posts chose to cast our lot with the National Association of continuing Congregationalists. They were: Henry David Gray, who earlier had been secretary for youth work and student life of the Board for Christian Education, the founder and executive secretary of the National Pilgrim Fellowship, a member of the Executive Committee of the General Council, and during the controversy minister of the large Oneonta Church in Pasadena; James E. Walter, one-time Project Secretary for the Missions Council, and then president and builder of Piedmont College in Georgia; Harry Johnson, superintendent of the Rocky Mountain Conference; Neil Hanson, executive of the Chicago Congregational Union; and myself. All the other founders of the National Association were local ministers, college professors or laypersons outside the mainstream of denominational life, but willing to take risks to preserve the Congregational way.

It is not my intention to record all the details and legal moves during these decades of controversy, but rather to recall my own involvement, that of Plymouth Church, and my reasons for rejecting the United Church of Christ.

The principal architects of the union were the two top-ranking officers of our denomination, both brilliant and able leaders. Douglas Horton was our chief executive officer as Minister of the General Council, a post he had held since 1937. Truman B. Douglass was Executive Vice-President of the Board of Home Missions, our largest administrative agency and the one that held the major endowment funds. I knew both of these men quite well, and was associated with them in many programs. Though both looked toward the consummation of the union, I felt that by temperament their motivation differed.

Douglas Horton was a gentleman through and through, always gracious and charming. He was a scholar with a keen intellect who spoke and understood Latin as well as other languages. He made the first American translation of Karl Barth's *Epistle to the Romans*, which reflects his high view of Christ and the Church. He was very much at home as official visitor to the Second Vatican Council, sharing in the day-to-day development of that council. At heart he had the vision of the Church of Christ being one and unified, and

strove to find ways to attune independent Congregationalism to that
larger union. Some of us said in jest that if Douglas could be given a
cardinal's hat he might happily become a Romanist!

Years later, after the UCC had come into being, he said that its
ecumenical spirit is the "great gift which our communion has to
make to the future." Writing in the Spring 1965 issue of *Minister's
Quarterly* he said:

> I myself would be happy to see a fixed date for reunion with
> Rome, say four hundred years hence, and measures taken, by dia-
> logue and even more systematic means, to build up mutual under-
> standing and sympathy which would lead in the direction of that
> high, far off, divine event. That it will someday take place I have
> no doubt at all—and I believe that we (the UCC) are designed to
> have a part in it.

In the merger debates no one mentioned ultimate reunion with
Rome, and certainly many who supported union would have
demurred if they had thought that was the direction they were moving. Yet these later words reveal something of the motivation of this
good man.

A step toward rationalizing this direction was given by Dr.
Horton in his Minister's Address at the 1950 General Council held in
Cleveland. This address came more than three years after the official
document, *Basis of Union*, and a year and a half after the General
Council had approved it in February 1949. In it he modified tradi-
tional thinking by distinguishing between what he called
"Congregationalism A" and "Congregationalism B."

Under "A" the General Council, boards, associations and conferences are basically controlled by the local churches. They are expressions of fellowships, instruments to do the will of the churches, and
are not free agents to make their own decisions. This has been the
understanding of those of us who cherish the complete independence and centrality of local churches, and why we protested the
practice of the Council for Social Action in taking stands without
regard for the opinion of local church members.

Dr. Horton pushed in the direction of centralization by introduc-
ing "Congregationalism B," in which these denominational bodies
are regarded as having independence. Their members are elected by

delegates from associations and conferences. Once constituted, they are as free as local churches, and they may act without reference to what church members may wish. These bodies have their own constitutions, which are not merely charters under which local churches work together.

In his address he stated that these higher bodies are not churches, but in his mind he must have been regarding them as equivalent. He gives them the same freedom as local churches. The subtleties of his mind become evident as one reflects on the years of his leadership. An earlier act before the merger controversy was his recommendation in 1937 that the title for the paid executives of the state conferences be changed from Conference Superintendent to Conference Minister. In those early years as a delegate to General Council meetings I voted for this proposal, not realizing that for Douglas this was more than a polite change of nomenclature. The titular head of our denomination was called the General Secretary of the General Council, and the Conference Administrators were Superintendents. These titles signified persons selected by the churches to carry out specific functions. The change to Minister has overtones I did not immediately sense. As a minister a person is chosen by a congregation to be its pastor and teacher. Congregationalism A holds that there is no church beyond the local church. A decade before he was to introduce Congregationalism B, Douglas Horton's mind was conceiving of superstructures as churches. And, indeed, the Constitution of the United Church clearly transfers the locale of the church from local congregations to the national body: "The name of this church shall be the United Church of Christ," in which parishes are units.

Dr. Horton resigned as Minister of the General Council in June of 1955 to accept the post of dean of Harvard Divinity School. This was a fine recognition of his scholarly standing and distinguished churchmanship. After the death of his first wife, he had married Mildred McAffee, former president of Wellesley College and head of the Waves during World War II. She was equally charming, and the marriage brought together two highly regarded thinkers and administrators. Vi and I were entertained in their summer home at Randolph, New Hampshire.

We had a friendship that developed from my participation in the

234   *The Merger Controversy*

programs of the General Council. On a trip to New York from Great Barrington, before I went to Minnesota, I recall going to Dr. Horton's office to tell him that I had been called to Plymouth Church. This was news to him, inasmuch as the appointment had not passed through denominational channels. I vividly recall his comment: "We have always thought of Plymouth as the chapel of the Grain Exchange!" That winter he came west to preach the sermon at my formal installation on February 1, 1945, symbolizing his recognition both of the church and of me.

My association with the second of the union architects was even closer. Truman B. Douglass also had a brilliant mind, which was coupled with a dynamic drive and administrative skills. These enabled him to fashion creative programs. After effective pastorates in two of our larger churches, Pomona and St. Louis, he became Executive Vice-President of our Board of Home Missions, the largest and best financed of our agencies. It encompassed many areas: church extension, home mission projects, education, American Missionary Association for work with blacks in the south, evangelism, pension funds.

As a bold planner Truman did not appreciate those who opposed him, and could be caustic in his comments. I felt that his motivation differed somewhat from the all-inclusive vision of Douglas Horton, in that he saw union as a means to power. At a private luncheon I once asked him why the cooperative way through church councils would not be preferable to insistence on organic structure. His reply was that he could more effectively act through one organization than through several. If he had to obtain approval of a number of executives of independent agencies, the process would be slow. If he were the executive of a unified body, he could proceed promptly to accomplish his purpose. To me this was a brazen bid for power, even though the high-minded leader that he was would use it for what he considered worthwhile advancement of Christ's kingdom. It was a frank admission of what I felt was his motivation.

Theologically he shared with Dr. Horton the high view of Christ and the Church. He emphasized what he called "the particularities" of Christianity, meaning its uniqueness and divine authority, and in many discussions opposed the universalism which I represent.

In 1948—at a time when my attitude was somewhat favorable toward the merger—the Home Board selected me to be on its Executive Committee, a body of twenty-four persons who met in New York four times a year to chart the course. Moreover, I was immediately put on the five-person Policy and Planning Committee, a powerful group that met with Truman to hear his agenda the day prior to quarterly meetings. No matter could be brought before the Executive Committee without the approval of the Policy and Planning Committee. I served the allowable two four-year terms, 1948-1956, all of which time I was on P & P, serving as chairman the second four years.

This experience put me in the midst of executives who were promoting the formation of the United Church of Christ, and permitted me to observe their attitudes and intentions. From this close association I became a firm opponent of union, for I felt that the national leadership was determined to have its way, and that their united church would give only secondary status to laity in local congregations. For me, this was a departure from classical Congregationalism, and I was not willing to sacrifice this heritage.

However, during my eight-year tenure I never opposed Truman on any practical matter of his administration. My interests are philosophical rather than in denominational politics, and I felt that as the chief executive officer of the board he should be supported in programs within his area. We were good friends, and I enjoyed associations with him and with other board executives. It was exciting to observe from the inside what was taking place. We differed in both theology and polity. As it became clear that I opposed the union and was to cast my lot with the National Association, Truman became increasingly critical.

I switched my views thrice. At the outset of the merger proposal, I was mildly favorable because I shared the general feeling that Christians should be drawn together. As an active participant in denominational life, I attended and was a delegate at all the biennial meetings of the General Council from 1940 through Claremont in 1952. When our wives were not with us, my Yale classmate George Haskell of Southern California and I roomed together. I was a zealous Congregationalist, proud of our denomination. However, I came to feel that our leaders were determined to pursue their own agenda regardless of the sentiment in local churches. This feeling was developed through the social action controversy in which the national officers took stands unacceptable to many lay members, and resisted efforts to reform such procedures. Another practice that appeared high-handed to me was that of "equalization." At the end of each fiscal year the Missions Council transferred benevolence receipts among the national boards to make sure that each received an equal share of its apportioned amount. This policy negated any effort by contributors to send their monies to specific boards and thus register a protest against any of whose policies they disapproved. This was a clear violation of the rights of local churches to decide where their gifts should go. We at Plymouth protested loudly, and the Missions Council did ultimately rescind this policy. But the intent to dominate at the national level was clear.

A critical event that furthered my misgivings was the decision of the General Council to proceed with union, even when it failed to receive the desired support from the churches. The Executive Committee of the General Council in January 1947 had approved the official document of merger, *Basis of Union*. It submitted this to the churches for acceptance or rejection, in an advisory vote, with the provision that when seventy-five percent of the churches voting responded affirmatively, the Executive Committee, in consultation with the Evangelical and Reformed Church officials, would take necessary steps to consummate the union. When the General Council met at Oberlin in June of 1948, the affirmative voting churches constituted only sixty-two percent. Plymouth Minneapolis was one of them. Up to that point I maintained my mild approval. In the February 1948 issue of our parish *Chronicle* I wrote: "Even though I personally believe in the Merger . . . I have been inclined recently to vote 'No,' on the ground that church unity cannot be achieved by any measure which has created the controversy that this has. . . . I therefore go to Cleveland confused and troubled. I regret that there is a division within our fellowship and I am ashamed at the bitter charges that have been hurled in this debate."

When the Oberlin General Council found that the recommended seventy-five percent affirmative response had not been obtained it voted to extend the deadline to the next January; and if the seventy-five percent was not forthcoming by then to call a special meeting.

By the closure date the approval level had risen to seventy-two percent, and the General Council delegates were called to a special
meeting at Cleveland. Though the established criterion had not been
reached, the enthusiasm among clergy and officials was so great that
the vote to proceed toward union was 797 to 172. I include clergy in
this statement because they comprise half the voting delegates in
any General Council. Though I do not intend to impugn the
integrity of my fellow ministers, nonetheless it seems to me that they
have a vested interest in developing a favorable relationship with
officials who conceive of the church as something more than local
congregations. The realism of a situation in which denominational
officials and all Conference Ministers favor the union requires considerable courage for a minister to stand against it.

The significance of this Cleveland vote for me was clear evidence that the national body was determined to have its way, even
without the support of local churches. To me this was a pivotal indication that the UCC was founded on a decision that did not meet its
own guidelines.

Two other actions of the General Council increased my awareness that the leaders were determined to proceed regardless of questions raised. No constitution had been written, and quite a number
of thoughtful ministers wanted further clarification. In 1950 a bipartisan committee was formed to study Free Church Polity and Unity,
and it prepared a summary of historic practices for submission to
the 1954 meeting at New Haven. But when the delegates arrived
they were given a letter from the lawyer of the General Council that
questioned the findings of the committee. The issue was sidestepped
by voting to circulate both the report and the letter without approval
or disapproval. Voices raised in honest questioning were silenced.

After silencing the report on Free Church Polity, in October of
that year the executive committees of the two denominations met.
The Claremont Resolution of 1952 had said that "if both approve,"
the two executive bodies should be responsible for preparation of a
draft of a constitution, to be submitted to the membership of both
communions for discussion and suggestion. At the October meeting,
however, the Evangelical and Reformed group refused to proceed to
draft a constitution, saying that there were already sufficient safe-
guards and that their representatives preferred to merge first and

write the constitution afterwards. Whereupon our Executive Committee took the position that since the condition of the Claremont Resolution, "if both approve," could not be met, the Executive Committee was free to proceed with the merger by a vote recorded at the 1949 special session of the General Council. Therefore, no further authorization was needed from churches or General Council to consummate the union.

These decisions I regarded as maneuvers from the top without sufficient regard for the people in the pews, and thus a bypass of the traditional focus of our polity. I thus changed from my original support to one of opposition.

There were lawsuits as to the rights of churches in national funds and about the power to form the united church. These went on for nearly a decade, but since I do not have a legal mind I did not follow them closely. The final decision did grant the General Council the right to consummate the merger.

With the authority of the 1949 General Council resolution, the Executive Committee in 1954 proceeded to negotiate with the Evangelical and Reformed representatives to form the UCC. A Uniting General Synod was held at Cleveland in June of 1957. What particularly distressed me was that Bishop Lesslie Newbigin of the Church of South India was invited to bring the keynote address. He was a Scotch Presbyterian who had turned Anglican and had spearheaded the union in southern India. His book, *The Household of God*, expressed the high church concept of divine union at the far end of the spectrum from free churchmanship, but was theologically consistent with the views of Horton and Douglass. To invite Newbigin to bless the formation of the UCC was a declaration that this merger was but a step to further union, and was an insult to those who hoped to retain some vestige of Congregationalism. Surely a more temperate and reconciling speaker could have been selected.

Following its legal formation in June of 1957, the UCC went ahead to prepare a constitution. A draft was submitted to the churches for study in the fall of 1959, and on July 7, 1960, the United Church General Synod unanimously approved the final document. The synod declared that this constitution would be in effect if at the close of voting on June 1, 1961, it had been approved by two-thirds of the Congregational Christian Churches voting and by two-thirds of all regional Evangelical and Reformed synods. These requirements were met, and the new constitution was declared in force as of July 4, 1961.

With this affirmation, the final consummation of the United Church of Christ took place in Philadelphia the first week of July 1961. Three days prior to this, both denominations held their last separate sessions in that city, and then met together as the General Synod of the new church.

Though I had been an active opponent of the merger during the last decade of the controversy and was not joining the UCC, I was selected to be chaplain for that concluding session of the General Council. I conducted four worship services with meditation, and on Saturday evening assisted my good friend, the Rev. Dr. Fred Hoskins, then president of the UCC, in serving communion to the delegates. I appreciated this honor, and deemed it a recognition that throughout two decades of controversy I had been responsible in my comments and respectful of those with whom I differed.

Turning now from the national to the local scene, I want to record briefly the strategic votes taken by Plymouth Church Minneapolis. I want to salute the members of our congregation for the fair and open way in which they considered the issues and choices over the period of thirteen years during which the merger controversy was waged. We had differences among us. In the early years the Minister of the Minnesota Conference, the Rev. Dr. Thomas A. Goodwin, was a member of Plymouth. Like all the state executives he favored the union. He and his wife spoke for the proponents at our business meetings. While discussions sometimes became heated, there was always an atmosphere of tolerance and goodwill that respected the right of individuals to differ. I strongly opposed the merger and undoubtedly influenced the congregation in this direction. I also spoke at state conference meetings and on invitation at quite a number of churches around the country. Always we sought to interpret what we thought classical Congregationalism to represent, to show differences from the UCC, yet always to avoid questionable claims and invectives against persons. I am especially grateful to four prominent laymen of Plymouth, who brought careful judgment and calm presentations to our people: Philip Sherman, Wellington Tully, Richard B. Thomson and Alan M. Struthers.

In the end, when the final decision was made not to join the UCC but to cast our lot with the National Association, only one family withdrew. This is a testimony to the strong ties of fellowship and responsibility that prevailed. I made it a point to see that those who had favored the UCC continued to be as much a part of Plymouth as ever, and that they be named to boards and committees as before.

Though the merger was first proposed at the Durham General Council in 1942, only six years later were the churches first asked to express their opinion. This was the advisory vote on the question:

> Do you advise the General Council to unite the Congregational Christian Churches and the E & R Church into the United Church of Christ, in accordance with the *Basis of Union* dated 22 January 1947?

Plymouth responded with balloting on Sunday morning, April 11, 1948, with polls open from 10:00 A.M. to 1:00 P.M. An affirmative answer was given, 315 to 159.

This election showed a surprising negative sentiment at an early stage before organized opposition had arisen, and despite an editorial by me in the February issue of our parish paper favoring the merger. As already noted, by the June 1948 deadline only sixty-two percent of the voting churches had been favorable, and the General Council extended balloting until January of 1949. When that date produced only seventy-two percent favorable, the special session at Cleveland voted this to be sufficient, even though it was short of the predetermined measure. It was then that I turned against the proposal because the national body was clearly determined to effect the union without regard for the wishes of the churches.

During the ensuing thirteen years of controversy and lawsuits, Plymouth Church members discussed the question at annual meetings, special meetings and in our official boards. At our annual meeting on February 16, 1950, the congregation voted that we take no steps to affiliate until a constitution was written and submitted to the churches. When the Omaha session of the General Council voted to proceed to form the united church prior to writing a constitution, our 1957 annual meeting reaffirmed our position. More than that, in conformity with a historic Congregational practice, Plymouth sent a "Letter Missive" to other Congregational churches, signed by Edgar

F. Zelle, moderator, Laura H. Miles, clerk, and Alan M. Struthers, chairman of the deacons. This letter reported the resolution adopted by our congregation. The key sentence was Item 3: "We intend to remain outside the proposed United Church of Christ until we are assured that under the constitution to be adopted we will continue to have not only legal independence, but freedom from imposed moral obligation to act in any way contrary to our own determination as to how we may best do the Lord's work as a church."

At our 1958 annual meeting the members voted favorably on a resolution distributed in advance by the deacons that Plymouth unite with the then three-year-old National Association of Congregational Churches. The vote to do so was approved 147 to 21. It was understood that we still kept our options open toward the new united church until it presented a constitution.

The General Synod of the UCC did present its constitution in the fall of 1959, with suggestions for revision to be made by year-end. By the following summer a final draft was issued, and all congregations were asked to vote their response by June 1961. In the Twin Cities an area-wide presentation of both sides was made at the Calhoun Beach Hotel on Tuesday evening, November 29, 1960. Plymouth created a bipartisan committee of both viewpoints to arrange and supervise our election.

Sunday morning, January 15, 1961, was the date for our definitive vote. The polls were open between 10:00 A.M. and 1:30 P.M. The question was:

> Shall Plymouth Church approve the constitution and become a part of the United Church of Christ?

The bipartisan committee reported to the congregation the following Sunday that the yes votes were 125; the no votes 1,020. Out of a roll of 2,047 members, 1,145, or fifty-five percent, actually cast ballots. An officially called meeting formally declared these results to be the decision of the congregation.

A year later the Minnesota Congregational Conference voted to become the Minnesota Conference of the UCC, and specified that all churches formerly in the Congregational Conference would automatically become members of the state body. Such a decision was actually a violation of the congregational principle that no outside

agency can impose any rule on a local church. At that time I probably should have requested our people to take a vote repudiating this
conference declaration, but my objective was to heal any wounds
left by years of merger controversy, and it did not seem diplomatic
to request another vote. Furthermore, we had in Plymouth membership six members of the faculty of United Theological Seminary.
They objected to a repudiation of the conference action because their
pension rights required that they be members of a UCC congregation. This obligation could be met technically by the unilateral action
of the conference. I acquiesced in their wishes, though this had long-
range implications that are unfortunate. Through the years the UCC
Conference has considered Plymouth technically to be a member,
though clearly we are "captive members," not by our vote but by the
unilateral action of the conference.

To counteract this situation, Moderator Ellwood H. Newhart
called a meeting of the Plymouth Church Council in September of
1962 that defined our relationships. First, Plymouth shall not pay
dues to an association or conference of the UCC, but may at any
time choose to contribute to and cooperate with such organizations
in worthwhile projects in which we feel an interest. Second, the
direction of interest, sympathy and effort shall be to the National
Association of Congregational Christian Churches, and any regional
development of this association. Third, staff and members of
Plymouth have complete freedom to work with and serve on committees of any organization that they deem worthwhile. This general
policy was approved at the annual meeting of 1963.

Before concluding this account of controversy engendered by
the merger proposal, I want to mention its repercussions in the
International Congregational Union. This was a gathering of various
national bodies around the world who adhered to the congregational polity, whose representatives met quadrennially for fellowship and the exchange of ideas. The General Council was the official
member from the United States. As the time drew near for the 1962
meeting, the National Association of continuing Congregationalists
followed the procedures to apply for formal membership. The
General Council Executive Committee had the authority to select the
sixty-five delegates from this country. They were thoughtful to
include five of us from the National Association in that roster: John

Alexander, Henry David Gray, Mrs. George Mead, Arthur A. Rouner, Jr., and myself. All five of us attended, but several declined to be accounted as delegates or to have expenses paid by the UCC.

The meeting was held in Rotterdam, The Netherlands, in early July 1962. The proceedings produced the rawest instance of organizational power in church affairs that I have ever experienced. We five appeared before the Executive Committee of the ICU to support the NACCC application for membership. Inasmuch as the ICU was essentially a fellowship body without any jurisdictional authority, we asked that it admit the NA as clearly a group of Congregationalists but with the statement that such acceptance in no way involved any judgment about the American disputes. This would give both the UCC and the NA fellowship in the international family.

At the final business meeting of the conference, the Executive Committee made its recommendation that the applications of the Bantu and Western Samoan churches be accepted, but that ours be rejected. What was astounding was the accompanying clause that our application be rejected without explanation! The presiding officer was Dr. Norman Goodall, then on the World Council staff, whose performance caricatured the British diplomat who smiles broadly all the while that he is denying your request. There were objections from Welsh Independents, but because the American delegates from the General Synod were the dominant group the recommendation passed. No explanation was given us or the general assembly.

Events of the next few years threw some light on the problem. In Britain a struggle among Congregationalists was going on similar to ours. The Congregational Union of England and Wales was being merged with the Presbyterians to form a Reformed Church recognizing common roots in the Protestant Reformation. When this act was completed the International Congregational Union ceased to exist and became a part of the World Alliance of Reformed Churches. If the National Association had been a member, we would not have gone into this presbyterial body. Our rejection may have been influenced by the recognition that as stalwart independents we would not have been congenial with proposals contemplated even in 1962.

To those who have united with Plymouth Church in the eighties and nineties, the foregoing history is unknown. To them the ongoing strength of the United Church of Christ may seem a preferable alternative to the continuing independence of congregations in the National Association. We who went through these earlier struggles hope that the story of them may stimulate sober thought about the easy loss of Congregational principles of independent churches before the allure of efficient organizations. Congregationalism arose in England four centuries ago as an alternative to powerful ecclesiastical structures, and its significance should be equally appreciated in modern times. Any Congregational church can at any time take any stand or move that its members wish, but once it becomes a unit in a larger ecclesiastical structure the members sacrifice the freedom to support only those decisions which they themselves make.

Although the UCC may run smoothly through decades to come, people with a yen for freedom need to recall that it was formed out of the overriding of the rules of its creators. The seventy-five percent approval of the churches was never attained, but delegates at the national level voted to proceed notwithstanding. At the 1954 General Council, the officials sidetracked the report of the Commission on Free Church Polity. Organizational expediency prevailed over the historic autonomy of local congregations, and one of the New Testament's three historic polities was subordinated to presbyterianism.

As we enter the decade of the nineties, Plymouth remains a strong, independent congregation with a caring heart whose benevolence outreaches enable it to cooperate with many community and world projects. Yet it retains its integrity and witnesses to historic principles of freedom that have molded the religious and civic life of our country.

19

Continuing Denominational Relations

THE YEARS OF CONTROVERSY ENDED with the early sixties when the United Church of Christ was securely established for those who wanted a new denominational structure, and the National Association had become the fellowship of those who wished to continue a classical Congregationalism. As I write in 1990, both of these bodies have been in existence more than thirty years. I feel that the Hand Always Above My Shoulder guided me in the decision I made. My choices were not for everyone, but they expressed my feelings about organized religion.

After these thirty years of existing side by side, I want to summarize my objections to the United Church of Christ and explain why the National Association expresses my ecumenical attitude.

First and foremost, in my judgment the United Church of Christ violates the basic principle of Congregationalism that the only visible religious structures are local congregations. The New Testament uses the term *church* always in the plural, referring to churches such as those at Ephesus or Corinth, except for references to churches in general, meaning the invisible body of Christ in faith community. As a denomination or fellowship, Congregationalism has never been a *Church*, but always a loose association of local churches. The General Council was never a Church but always a Council of Congregational churches in the plural.

In contrast, denominations subscribing to either of the other two

245

New Testament polities—presbyterian and episcopal—have deemed themselves in their corporate life to be a Church. For instance, there is the Roman Catholic Church, the Episcopal Church, the United Methodist Church, and the Presbyterian Church in the USA. These denominations have been able to speak with a coherent voice because they consider themselves to be an entity above and beyond their congregations.

Not so with Congregationalists. Our roots are in the Separatist movement, which brought the Pilgrims to New England shores in 1620. Here the freedom of the local church is in a covenant relation with God to develop full Christian responsibilities without dependence upon outside groups. In his *History of Plymouth Plantation*, William Bradford described it as allegiance "to the simplicity of the gospel, without the mixture of men's inventions."

The Constitution of the UCC begins with Article I: "The name of this Church shall be UNITED CHURCH OF CHRIST." This transfers centrality from local churches to a unified body and puts the UCC in the same category with other nationalized denominations that view themselves as a unity.

Defenders may say that this is merely nomenclature. On the contrary, it is a complete shift of emphasis. It enables the national body and its agencies to take stands on behalf of the whole fellowship. Article IV of the Constitution defines local churches as "units" in the superstructure of the UCC, and describes their relations. In Congregationalism local churches are the only churches, and they are self-defining and self-directing.

Second, though the UCC Constitution affirms that the autonomy of the local church is inherent, nevertheless it introduces moral pressures for it to follow the leadership of the national bodies. Article IV, Paragraph 20 states that local churches have "a God-given responsibility for that Church, its labors and its extension." Paragraph 22 states: "Actions by, or decisions or advice emanating from, the General Synod, a Conference or Association, should be held in the highest regard by every local church." Surely this undercuts traditional independence.

Third, within the UCC greater influence if not power is accorded the conference and national leaders. They take a more active role in guiding ministers and congregations. When I went to Minnesota in

1944, the Congregational Conference had two ministers and two office secretaries. Today that has proliferated into a Conference Minister with five ordained associates and a large staff of office workers. These are persons keeping watch over congregations, whose approval must be secured for the selection of parish ministers. A local pastor who seeks approval of the staff to be recommended for a larger church must be a cooperative conference-player. The independence and individuality of the ministry is seriously undercut. Bureaucracy has multiplied and is influential.

In the late 1980s the UCC formalized rules for the empowering of ministry that clearly define who and how clergy are to be selected by a local congregation. It published a 250-page *Manual on Ministry: Perspectives and Procedures for Ecclesiastical Authorization of Ministry.* These procedures are based on a 1984 revision of the constitution and bylaws. The premise is that ministry is a concern of "the Whole Church" in which there are several partners. "The ministry of the ordained or commissioned minister is a ministry of the United Church of Christ and not just a ministry of the person."

In my viewpoint, the concept of "the Whole Church" is a euphemism for the denominational executives, and thus gives them authority to say who may or may not be a candidate for a local pastorate. Only those clergy who have standing in the UCC may be considered by a local committee. Nor are UCC clergy permitted to serve congregations outside the denomination for more than a limited period. Such provisions encourage mediocrity and stifle creativity. They give enormous influence to the Conference Ministers and violate the independence of local congregations.

The history of organized religion is no different than that of any structure, for it tends to direct power toward the top. In all connectional denominations the central body exerts influence and pressure on the outlying units. Popes, bishops, synods determine the roles of local clergy. Only classical Congregationalism avoids these pressures by refusing to create superstructures. The National Association is a voluntary fellowship of churches that exercises no jurisdiction over ministers or congregations. Our annual meetings are largely fellowship opportunities to share with like-minded friends. Whatever commissions we establish are to promote activities in which we can join together for more effective service.

Fourth, the UCC attempts to define the theological outlook of this new unified Church. Paragraph 2 of the preamble of the Constitution has this sentence: "It (the UCC) claims as its own the faith of the historic Church expressed in the ancient creeds and reclaimed in the basic insights of the Protestant Reformers." Certainly Congregationalism, since the time of Horace Bushnell in the late nineteenth century, has had an open spirit, allowing for freedom of belief among its members. We have cherished diversity of thought. Among churches in the UCC there surely is diversity, but its very charter seeks to point a direction. Beyond that, recent writings in its publications suggest that the UCC needs to define itself more clearly by theological concerns. This need is a shift from the openness I cherish.

Fifth, these references to "regard" and "esteem" for denominational positions, and to the "claims of the historic Church," circumscribe the freedom of the spirit. I am a universalist who believes that men and women possess an inherent religious instinct by which as vulnerable human beings they reach out for some relationship with the Divine. Who are they? Where are they going? What is life's meaning? The human soul is in quest of answers. Historic religions try to impose special claims upon their followers, insisting that some uniqueness has authority over other revelations. Such claims limit freedom. Christianity makes such a set of claims. The UCC preamble accepts this exclusivism, whereas liberal Congregationalists have not.

We are of course Christians because we are born into western civilization, and Christianity has informed the culture all around us. We are raised with respect for the Bible and familiarity with its terminology. We say that for us Christ is Lord, but we give this a wide interpretation. We mean that the values which Jesus taught in the Sermon on the Mount and which he exemplified in his own unselfish life of self-sacrifice are revelations of the principles inherent in the universe. Liberals, however, do not accept the claims of the historic church about the person of Jesus. We cherish an openness about the relation of the individual with the Creator God. We cultivate a religion that enables us in adoration, thanksgiving and trust to develop our own prayer life, our own theology, and our own communities of faith. We invite people who are agnostics, people who may regard themselves as "nonbelievers," persons whose lifestyles may not conform to the rigid patterns of Christian traditions, to enter the fellowship of Congregational churches that we may mutually help one another in the search for a meaningful life.

Because we are an open fellowship, we cannot say that all Congregationalists share this view. We have liberals and conservatives among us, and in the spirit of freedom we must respect each other. My objection to the UCC on theological grounds is that its stated purpose places it within the Reformed tradition rather than in the openness of seekers. In our confirmation classes at Plymouth Church Minneapolis, we review the Bible and the historic creeds of Christendom, but we do not urge any doctrine on the confirmands. Instead, we encourage the young people to write their own statements and to commit themselves to a life-long quest of the deepest issues that confront the human spirit.

Though I personally do not consider the UCC to be a valid expression of Congregationalism, there are some four thousand churches formerly of our tradition in that body. Thus there are two national groups claiming the same heritage, each formed at about the same time. The United Church of Christ was officially formed in 1957, while the National Association of Congregational Christian Churches was organized in 1955. Each of these has declared itself to be the successor to the old General Council.

The protracted discussions and heated debates of two decades resulted in this division among Congregationalists. It is sad that most attempts at organic church union end in divisions that increase rather than reduce the number of groupings. We had to make a choice in the mid-fifties that altered relationships, severed many friendships and introduced us to new alignments. Both Plymouth Church and myself decided to identify ourselves with the National Association. I parted from friends with whom I had worked in denominational affairs, ministerial associations and seminary groups. I appreciated and respected them, recognizing that each must follow where the light of conscience leads. I became part of a new fellowship in which I have been happy, forming new friendships with colleagues whom I respect and love.

The National Association came out of a gathering at Hotel Fort Shelby in Detroit on November 9, 1955. It was called by a group of ministers and laypersons who realized after years of opposition that the union with its presbyterial polity could not be stopped. I was not present, but one Plymouthite, Attorney Stanley S. Gillam, did attend. I soon recognized that this was the group with whom I must affiliate.

That the National Association has survived is almost a miracle, since it was a small group of individuals and churches with no assets except loyalty to Congregational freedom and faith in God's guidance. When the division came, the old General Council and its national boards took the entire endowment funds of nearly a hundred million dollars into the UCC, and left the dissenters with no financial assets. We had to start with no backlog funds to build a simple structure for survival. Each year we have grown slowly, now numbering four hundred fifty churches, some of them the largest in Congregationalism. One of our wisest decisions was to establish the Congregational Foundation for Theological Studies, which enrolls college graduates to enter the seminary of their choice in preparation for ministry in our denomination. Financial grants and the counsel of a staff dean are provided. Twice a year enrollees are brought together for studies in our history and for the fostering of friendships that will last through their careers. This has proved to be an innovative way for channeling a flow of new young ministers into our fellowship.

Another strength has been the policy of annual meetings held each summer. These bring together more than seven hundred delegates and visitors, thus facilitating the development of friendships across the country. In conjunction with these adult meetings, the Pilgrim Fellowship holds a conference attended by three to four hundred high school and college youth that makes our program for young people one of the most attractive in the country. In nearly every congregation this summer pilgrimage of youth is well supported.

I have been active in National Association affairs. Twice I have served on the CFTS board and twice on the World Christian Relations Commission. I authored the "Moderator's Message" in 1968 and 1980, the two times when all the former moderators issued a statement of direction to the association. I prepared the draft of *A Statement of Ecumenical Intentions*, adopted at the 1986 annual meeting in Estes Park. I served a term as moderator in 1966-67. I was selected to give the first annual "Congregational Lecture" at the annual meeting at Pomona in 1965, which was a survey of the 1965 National Council. Again, in 1983, when the theme was Religion and the Arts, I gave the lecture under the title, "And Save the Soul Besides."

Along with the formation of the National Association, a similar development for Congregationalism has taken place on the world scene. The churches of England and Wales went through merger problems akin to ours. The majority joined with the Presbyterians to become the Reformed Church. Shortly thereafter the International Congregational Council, in which we were denied membership at Rotterdam in 1962, ceased to exist but entered into a new World Alliance of Reformed Churches. This left Congregationalists of the United States, Britain and elsewhere without any international expression. In the spring of 1975, sixteen Americans led by Harry Butman and John Alexander met with a group of Britishers gathered by Reginald Cleaves. The site was the Congregational Conference Center at Chislehurst, England. Together they produced a document known as the "Chislehurst Thanksgiving," which celebrated our free-church heritage. They also resolved to form an International Congregational Fellowship to meet every four years. The first assemblage brought several hundred attendees to London in 1977 who had the singular privilege of celebrating communion in Westminster Abbey, the first time since the Reformation that a non-conformist sacrament had been allowed in that sacred church. Subsequent gatherings were held at Bangor Wales in 1981, in Massachusetts in 1985, and at Leiden, The Netherlands, in 1989.

Those of us who cherish the freedoms of our Congregational heritage have thus been able at both the national and international level to continue the fellowship that is highly prized. We think of Congregationalism as the most ecumenical of all traditions, for as individuals and as local churches we are open to cooperation, affection and work with all Christians of other backgrounds. We do not claim any exclusive authority or privileged beliefs, but are ready in freedom and openness to join with others in common causes that will advance the truths of Jesus.

20

Ecumenism

ECUMENISM HAS BEEN ONE OF THE dominant notes of the twentieth century. The World Council of Churches has become a reality, and unions among denominations have brought Christians closer together. Conversations between Roman Catholics, Reformed and Protestant groups have occurred.

The term "ecumenical" comes from the Greek word, *oikumene,* meaning universal, "pertaining to the whole habitable world." My ministry has been open to this spirit in the fullest terms of cooperation. In the Plymouth Chapel we had the seal of the World Council placed in the center of the balcony's rose window. However, as a universalist, I have said repeatedly that I consider the formalized "Ecumenical Movement" to be the most deceptive program of my day. While claiming to bring people together, it defines Christian faith in such strict terms as to exclude multitudes; it constitutes a subtle reach for ecclesiastical control; and it has no vision of embracing other faiths in the whole habitable world.

If ecumenism is more than a legalism, it is a spirit of openness and goodwill that motivates us in our relations with people outside our particular parish or denominational group. I have always been active in community religious affairs. When I came to Minnesota I found the Minnesota Council of Churches to be a true expression of ecumenism. Its executive secretary, the Rev. Dr. Hayden L. Stright, was a buoyant American Baptist who had nurtured the Council for thirty-five years. He was supported by a group of active laypeople and some clergy from mainline denominations. These were people who saw beyond parochial lines and were happy to unite in projects throughout the state in which caring people have a common interest. They encouraged Sunday schools, fostered adult education, provided care for migrant workers in the agricultural fields, and chaplains to the court system. This was a spontaneous fellowship among caring Christians, and generated much goodwill. However, when the Federal Council of Churches on the national level was transformed into the National Council, it was essential to bring Lutherans into the process. The price for this was a more structured organization whereby the National Council became one of communions. On the state level, we in Minnesota had to shift likewise to a communion structure. This meant that our directors were no longer elected at large from cooperatively minded churchpeople, but representation was by denominations, with the executives of each validating their nominees. This has been an improvement in many ways: it has brought more denominations into the council and has given more leadership to programs and functions. This increased effectiveness has perhaps lessened the spontaneity we enjoyed in the less structured fellowship.

Hayden Stright was a visionary, always seeing ahead to goals some of us thought impossible. One of his dreams was the erection of a Church Center building to house denominational offices. In 1947 the decision to begin this program was made at a meeting of the directors held in Plymouth Church under the presidency of the Rt. Rev. Stephen Keeler, Bishop of the Episcopal Diocese of Minnesota. Bishop Keeler actively supported ecumenism. I was chairman of the committee that recommended the purchase of the Ropes mansion on the corner of Franklin and Pillsbury. We did make this purchase. The main house became offices for the Council, the Greater Minneapolis Council, the Methodist Board of Education, the Twin Cities Baptist Union, the Evangelical United Brethren, and the Disciples Conference. The spacious carriage house was remodeled to house the Congregationalists and the Presbyterians. This arrangement continued for more than a dozen years, during which period the Council acquired rundown and abandoned houses between Franklin and Groveland until we owned the entire block.

Then came the momentous decision to demolish all the houses, including the usable headquarters, and construct a $1,600,000 six-story Protestant Center building. I was active in fund-raising, and was vice-chairman of the building committee that supervised all the details. At the center of this accomplishment was Dr. Stright, whose vision and faith never wavered. When construction was completed in 1964, we had an $800,000 debt, but in the twenty-five years since that has been retired, and we have one of the finest headquarters buildings in American Protestantism.

Another vision of Dr. Stright was the creation of an endowment fund to support the work of the Council of Churches. A strong layman, Lawrence M. Brings, aided him in establishing the Minnesota Protestant Foundation, of which I was made vice-chairman. Mr. Brings as chairman, myself, and Philip H. Nason as treasurer are still serving as founding directors. The foundation now has assets over a half million dollars, and contributes about $40,000 annually to the Minnesota Council.

In 1952 I was elected president of the Minnesota Council for a two-year term. These activities indicate my interest in grassroots ecumenicity.

Already mentioned is the selection of World-wide Communion Sunday as the chancel window of Plymouth Chapel in the stained glass series on the "Seasons of the Christian Year." At the top of the central lancet are the words of the second-century Letter to Diognetus, "Christians hold the world together." The three medallions in each of the side panels represent ways in which Christians do this, with each depicting a scene from a different nation. Around the border are small figures to recall Biblical stories of crossing over borders: the Wolf that lies down with the Lamb (Isaiah 11:16); Peter on the rooftop seeing the vision of unclean beasts (Acts 10:9-16); the parable of the other sheep in the sheepfold (John 10:7-18); and the Good Samaritan caring for the Jew who had fallen among thieves (Luke 10:25-37).

Just prior to World War II the old Federal Council of Churches had suggested World-wide Communion for the first Sunday in October, and I had gladly embraced this concept of simultaneous goodwill as the start of a new church season. However, the creation of the World Council of Churches at Amsterdam in 1948 marked a dramatic shift from this concept of cooperative goodwill to one of the organic union of Christendom. Shortly thereafter came formation of the Church of South India, which was hailed as the structural union of various denominational groups that foreshadows what is desired on a global basis.

It is this shift from the cooperative-goodwill emphasis to that of organic union that to me constitutes the deception to which I have referred at the outset of this chapter. Laypeople have long asked the question, "Why can't Christians work together instead of being divided into so many competing groups?" They have been told that ecumenism will solve this problem, and accordingly have been encouraged to support unions and mergers. What they have seen is that this apparently innocent and commendable trend, as practiced at the top level, involves features that actually undercut the open goodwill that laypeople desire.

First, organic union requires precise definitions that exclude persons just as clearly as they bring them together. In his celebrated sermon at Grace Episcopal Cathedral in San Francisco on December 4, 1960, entitled "A Proposal Toward the Reunion of Christ's Church," Dr. Eugene Carson Blake said that "I am moved by the conviction that Jesus Christ, whom all of us confess as our divine Lord and Savior, wills that his Church be one." Such a conviction represents a high view both of Christ as Lord and of the Church, a view to which many Biblical scholars and religious liberals cannot assent. We are excluded by the first proposition.

Dr. Blake went on to say, "The reunited church must clearly confess the historic trinitarian faith received from the Apostles and set forth in the Apostles' and Nicene Creeds." The Yale University professor of history, Jaroslav Pelican, in his book *The Excellent Empire*, writes that the Nicene Creed is the only one genuinely entitled to the term, "ecumenical creed," and it confesses the church to be one, holy, catholic and apostolic. This is clearly the description of a majestic church whose unity and authority have come down through the ages. It is not one that a nonconformist would recognize as his church. Such a definition rules out evangelicals and liberals who constitute a significant portion of Christendom.

The second limitation on true ecumenicity is that such definitions provide the established clergy with continuing control. Dr.

Blake indicated this in his proposal: "The reunited church must have visible and historic continuity with the Church of all ages before and after the Reformation. This will include a ministry which by its orders and ordination is recognized as widely as possible by all other Christian bodies." This means more than acceptance of ancient creedal statements, for it implies recognition of the historic ordination process of "apostolic succession." The current discussions over the ordination of women indicate how strict some communions can be in interpretation. If the Bible does not tell of women clergy, then they will not accept such. To bring such groups into a reunited church would involve agreement on legalisms that are unacceptable to most of us. The freedom of the Holy Spirit to lead persons into the ministry would be nullified if left to the control of traditional clergy. Every lesser union of denominations in recent times has clearly defined who can be ministers, leaving the ordination process and the appointment process in control of the centralized bureaucracy. This is a deterrent to true ecumenicity.

In 1982 the Faith and Order Commission of the World Council of Churches presented a text agreed upon at a meeting in Lima, Peru. This is the basis for ecumenical commitment to a united church. A study guide is available for use with congregations, entitled "Growing Together in Baptism, Eucharist and Ministry." This booklet employs imaginary conversations of local churchpeople to illustrate what the text means in present situations. The assumption is that every Christian will want to be faithful to the historic church as defined by the ancient words of "one, holy, catholic (universal) and apostolic."

But a large segment of Christians today cannot subscribe to this formula, which again is the concept of a majestic church divinely instituted by a divine Christ. All the trappings of creedal orthodoxy and ecclesiastical power are involved. Neither liberals nor evangelicals view the institution in these terms, but affirm a more flexible flow of the spirit within individuals and congregations.

The third deception of the ecumenical movement is that its purpose falls far short of embracing "the whole habitable world." It relates only to Christians. Those of us who are universalists welcome a growing interest in world religions. If God is one, then he must have concerns for all creation, for peoples of all lands and backgrounds. The hunger of the world to know Deity is experienced in other faiths as well as our own. Each group has the freedom to prefer its own traditions, but preference should be made without claims to exclusivism. Inasmuch as in my graduate-student days I had exposure to Asian religions, I have been sensitive to the upreach of the soul, and have found kinship with poets and seers of other faiths. To me this is the true ecumenicity which is not appreciated by Christian church leaders who advocate unions and mergers. The only time I spoke face to face with Reinhold Niebuhr was at a small gathering after an evening program at the Claremont General Council in 1962. I asked him about the study of comparative religions, and he brushed the question off with the curt reply, "That is of interest only to decadent liberalism."

The contrast between universalists and ecumenists is illustrated by one of the memorable experiences of my life. The honor I most cherish is that my colleagues in the Congregational ministry selected me to be the chaplain for the final session of the General Council when in 1961 it passed into the Synod of the United Church of Christ. I cherish this honor because it was not a *quid pro quo* offer, which is as common in ecclesiastical circles as in civil politics, but a nostalgic recognition that though I opposed the merger and was parting from those who were entering the UCC, nevertheless I had maintained my witness with integrity and brotherly regard. This invitation probably was initiated by Dr. Fred Hoskins, a dear friend who was to become president of the UCC, and with whom I served communion at that final service of the Congregationalists before they went off the next day to join the Evangelical and Reformed brethren.

The theme of that 1961 General Council was "Jesus Christ: The Lord and Light of Life." As chaplain I had four meditations, and as lecturer Dr. Leslie E. Cooke, associate secretary of the World Council of Churches, gave three addresses. Leslie Cooke was an old friend. During World War II he was pastor of the Congregational church in Coventry, England, and was a guest in our home on the day of the Normandy landings, a day of great emotional significance for him.

The contrast between our presentations could not have been greater. Dr. Cooke followed the line of the World Council Assembly at New Delhi, which had asked the question: "Can we learn from the meanings of light in these other religions what it is that Jesus Christ claims to be?" The council answered with a firm no:

> "Christ's light does not shine like the light of other great figures; but He has given the Church, His body, and has entrusted to it the ministry of reconciliation. To accept this claim is difficult because of its exclusiveness; only through Him do men receive the light of life."

In one of his addresses, Dr. Cooke underscored this exclusivism by referring to Dr. Sarvapali Radhakrishnan. I regard Dr. Radhakrishnan as probably the most knowledgeable man of the twentieth century about world religions. He taught them at Oxford, authored many books on the spirit of Hinduism, and was a student of all the world's religious classics. When the World Council of Churches met in New Delhi, the members of the Executive Committee were invited to a reception given in their honor by this world-renowned philosopher, who was then vice-president of his country. Because he was sympathetic with Christianity and religious movements around the world, he had spoken to the delegates about universal brotherhood and the fundamentals of spiritual life that bind together all peoples in their quest for abundant living. Leslie Cooke, in his address at the General Council, reported on the tea that Dr. Radhakrishnan had given, and said that his remarks had sounded so warm and gracious that for a moment they had beguiled the delegates. But when they returned to their rooms and reflected, they realized that this universalism subtly undermined the sovereign lordship of Christ.

In contrast to this timeworn exclusivism of Christian theology, my meditations were on Christ as the Light of the World in inclusive rather than exclusive terms. I said that in the long run it was not going to make much difference whether we are Congregationalists in the UCC or outside the UCC, because ecclesiastical structures are secondary to the spiritual unity that exists among those of whatever name or creed who are born again into a spiritual relationship with God. The revelation of God in Christ would be suspect if it were so abrupt and so different as to be discontinuous with his everlasting giving of himself to those who seek.

The irony of the roles played by Dr. Cooke and myself should be comically apparent. They were a reversal of what should have been expected. Here was a leader of the World Council of Churches, a proponent of organizational union among churches, nevertheless pleading for exclusivism, and condemning a plea for unity on the part of a philosopher of another world religion. Here was I, not willing to be sucked into the structural schemes of ambitious churchmen, nevertheless speaking on behalf of a universal interpretation of Christ that could bring unity and brotherhood among all religions.

Another experience in my universalism I have referred to in the chapter on "Our India Family." On my visit to South India in 1954, Ralph Keithan took me to an ashram where the Congress Government after Free India had established one of four rural life training centers. The director of Gandhi Gram, as it was called, was a saintly man named Ramachandran. Keithan introduced me to him, and said that he had been impressed by my outlook and that I seemed to be in harmony with the Hindu spirit. Ramachandran said he had one simple test he liked to put to people, though most Christians failed it. I replied that I probably would also, but would be interested to hear it. He then put it to me: "Can you wish for me that I find my highest development and spiritual joy in my own culture without going outside my own faith?"

I thought a moment and said, "I am not sure I could wish that for you."

"You Christians never can," he responded.

Then I said that my hesitance was not because of any desire to bring him to my particular faith, but because his test was so worded that it involved the limitations of a particular faith, whichever it might be. I would not want him limited either by his faith or mine, but would wish for him the highest development of the Spirit wherever it may lead. "Ah," he said, "you have come very close, and I am going to ask you to speak at our devotional service this afternoon."

To relate to a spiritual leader in India who had a universal approach was an exciting experience for me. The worship that afternoon, with two hundred seated under an open-sided thatched canopy, was moving. There were scriptural readings from the New Testament, the Koran and the Upanishads. The spirit was truly one and universal.

The polity relationship of Plymouth Church was outlined in

September of 1962 by resolutions of the Church Council. The Minnesota Conference of the United Church of Christ was being instituted, and it voted that all former Congregational churches in Minnesota should be carried into the new UCC state conference, even though many of them had voted not to join the UCC. By this decree Plymouth became a captive member of the Minnesota UCC Conference without ever voting to be a part of it.

Our officers felt that this move altered our relations with the state conference, and that we should clearly define our status in three resolutions:

> I. It is the judgment of the Council that Plymouth Congregational Church not pay dues to an Association or Conference of the United Church of Christ, but may at any time choose to contribute to and cooperate with such organizations in worthwhile projects in which we feel an interest.

> II. It is the judgment of the Council that direction of interest, sympathy, and effort of Plymouth Congregational Church shall be to the National Association of Congregational Christian Churches, and any regional development of this Association.

> III. The Council reaffirms its traditional polity of granting complete freedom to staff and members of Plymouth to work with and serve on committees of any organization that they deem worthwhile.

We thus made clear our affiliation, feeling that the open fellowship of autonomous churches within the National Association gives us more freedom to be in a universal fellowship than do the restrictive provisions of the UCC. At the same time, we reaffirmed the openness of Plymouth in allowing ministers, staff and members to have other interests. We have no problem in having clergy of other denominations, provided they respect the basic orientation of Plymouth. This is itself an ecumenical witness.

Twice I have served as chairman of the World Christian Relations Commission of the National Association of Continuing Congregational Christian Churches. I largely authored the "Statement of Ecumenical Intentions" prepared by our commission and adopted by the 1986 annual meeting of the continuing Congregationalists. "We question efforts to forge Christian unity out of creedal tests, doctrinal purity, historical benchmarks, and organizational structure. We believe that the unity of Christendom is to be found in the celebration of God's great gift to us in the person of Jesus Christ, and in the hope we share of the glory to come through the gracious and redeeming love of a universal and caring God. We adhere to the covenantal relationship between the human and the divine, in which we mortals accept the covenant of grace so wondrously offered by the magnanimity of the Eternal One; and we bind ourselves beyond all differences to a mutual helpfulness as we seek to walk in the ways in which the Divine Truth, Beauty and Goodness are revealed to us. We see ourselves as a part of the historic continuity of the Christian Church through a common strand of devotion, yet ever expressing itself in freshness, creativity and wonder inspired by the outpouring of the Spirit.

"We of the Congregational Christian Churches extend an invitation to all individuals, churches and associations of whatever name to join with us in the effort to keep alive the rights of private judgment, the integrity of public worship, and the freedom of autonomous churches; and to labor for the inclusion of these rights within the ecumenical movement."

The ecumenical spirit is basically one of goodwill toward all persons and groups seeking to lead a meaningful religious life. This is an age of secularism in which the claims of the Spirit are easily overlooked. We do not advance the wider ranges of devotion by attempts to contract us into single organizational structure, when the challenge is to reach out in love and encouragement to all who seek.

The philosopher-statesman of India, Dr. Radhakrishnan, gives us a more universal concept of ecumenicity in his book, *Fragments of a Confession*:

> The light of eternity would blind us, if it came full in the face. It is broken into colors so that our eyes can make something of it. The different religious traditions clothe the One Reality in various images, and their visions could embrace and fertilise each other so as to give mankind a many-sided perfection:
>   the spiritual radiance of Hinduism,
>   the faithful obedience of Judaism,
>   the life of beauty of Greek Paganism,

the noble compassion of Buddhism,

the vision of divine love of Christianity,

and the spirit of resignation to the sovereign lord of Islam.

All these represent different aspects of the inward spiritual life which when brought together express the ineffable experiences of the human spirit. If religion is the awareness of our real nature in God, it makes for a union of all humankind based on communion with the Eternal.

21

Retirement Years

IN MAY OF 1975, I SENT A LETTER to the Plymouth membership telling them that I would reach the age of sixty-five in the summer of the following year, and that I intended to retire at that time. Though all was going well, I felt that forty years of active ministry was a full quota, and that a man should make way for younger persons. By giving advance notice, I thought the congregation would have time to choose a successor. However, the process took much longer as the people studied goals and discussed qualities to be desired in their next minister.

Through spring and summer of 1976 there were parties, celebrations and special speakers. Among these were two special friends, Howard Thurman of San Francisco and Walter Judd from Washington. Also there was an ecumenical program highlighted by former Roman Catholic Bishop James Shannon, and a retirement dinner in May at which the trustees presented me with a gift of $35,000.

During the summer my sermons were "position papers" on significant religious and philosophical issues distinctive in my approach. In one of these I said that it was possible, though not probable, that I might at some time in the future commit suicide. If I did, I would not be present to explain the act, so I wanted to say now that it would not be because of despair but of hope. I firmly believe in the continued existence of the soul in the spirit reality of Eternity. God created us with intelligence, and we have the right to use that intelligence to decide when earthly conditions no longer make physical continuance desirable. This comment made the newspapers and surprised people, many of whom disagreed. Of course I deplore teenage suicide among young people who are momentarily frustrated, because conditions for them will improve. They can overcome every obstacle. I was referring to the elderly who often undergo a humiliating process of senility and helplessness before death comes to release them.

My final Sunday was August 29, 1978, for which my long-time and efficient secretary, Peggy Widtfeldt, had prepared a twelve-page printed program with many photographs from "Thirty-Two Years of Memories." After the service there was a Congregational picnic by Lake Nokomis. At an earlier business meeting the bylaws were amended to provide for a minister emeritus, and I was elected to that post, one which I cherish and have held for fourteen years.

In order to be away when my successor arrived, I set out in mid-October on a round-the-world trip, but it was not until I arrived in Hawaii in mid-March of 1977 that I heard from the search committee that such a person had been selected. He was William Clyde Donald III, who regarded himself as an Interim Minister Specialist. He was an excellent speaker with a delivery free from manuscript. He served Plymouth well in that he understood that after a long pastorate a new face must come for a short time to accustom a congregation to a change. He did not attempt to put down roots or institute new programs. After two years he made way for a new search committee to seek a senior minister. During this period the associates on the staff—Elaine Marsh, Gary Reierson, and Timothy Barrett—carried a heavy load of pastoral responsibilities.

This second committee happily found the Rev. Mr. Vivian Jones of Wales to be my true successor. This connection came from another coincidence one may attribute to the Hand always guiding. A few years earlier Vivian Jones had visited Plymouth to see one of our then associates, the Rev. Budd Friend-Jones, who had been doing his divinity work at Princeton Theological Seminary when Vivian Jones had come to Princeton from Wales for graduate study. Realizing that I would soon be retiring, he had said to Budd that someday he would like the opportunity to minister to a church like Plymouth. Budd remembered this, and though he had left by the time of my retirement, he passed the suggestion to the committee. Vivian was invited to come for an interview. Everyone was taken by his charm, and he was officially called as the thirteenth minister of Plymouth. Vivian Jones is a Welsh Independent, and though his previous experience was with churches under a hundred in membership, he has demonstrated remarkable administrative skills. He has a marvelous sense of humor, an abundance of good sense, and a warm feeling for people. He is much loved, and under his wise leadership Plymouth has continued to grow and prosper. He and I have maintained cordial relations, and I am happy that he is my successor.

In May of 1978, I flew to California to attend the Fiftieth Reunion of our Fresno High School Class of 1928. As always on California trips, I went a few days early to visit my Yale Divinity classmate and closest friend in the ministry, Dr. George W. Haskell, and his wife Melva. The three of us were together in New Haven and have been close throughout the years. Like me, George and Melva are native Californians, but they had returned to the state for four good pastorates, the last two being San Bernardino and Whittier. They retired two years before I did, and had built a home in Del Mar. On the third and last day of my visit, as we walked past a real estate office, I went in and inquired if there were any properties in which I might be interested. Berta Hemsley, the agent, told me of a condominium townhouse in Del Mar Woods that was going on the market the next day. I responded that I would be gone by then, so she phoned to ask if she might bring me to see it. We went just before lunch, I liked the unit, made an offer that afternoon, and by nightfall had made the purchase. It was a lovely two-bedroom-and-den unit in a complex overlooking the ocean, just three blocks from the Haskell's home. I enjoyed it and spent several winters there before selling it in 1986. When I was not in residence, there were always renters to carry the costs. My years in the San Diego area were very pleasant, but the heavy traffic patterns became a problem.

In late summer of 1980, Dr. Erwin Britton, then Executive Secretary of the National Association, phoned me to say that Dr. Robert Crawford who was retiring from Bushnell Congregational Church in Detroit had requested an interim from among the continuing Congregationalists. Erwin said I was the person to respond because I had had experience in a downtown parish. This was a new venture for me, but I flew to Detroit for an interview and decided to accept the challenge. This opened me to some very happy experiences through four interim ministries.

Bushnell had been one of the strong Congregational churches of the country, founded in the late twenties by a beloved minister, Roger Eddy Treat, to serve the Rosedale Park neighborhood. It has a beautiful colonial style sanctuary and educational plant with its spire overlooking the Southfield Freeway at Grand River. At one time it had over two thousand children in its Sunday school, but after the racial riots of the sixties the younger families fled Detroit proper for the suburbs. When I came in 1980, there were no children to use the superb educational facilities, but there was a congregation of nearly a thousand members of middle age and older. They were as cultured and devoted a group as one could find anywhere.

At the time of the merger controversy, Bushnell was a strong bulwark for the UCC in the Detroit area, under the ministry of Dr. Eugene Bushong, who had been a colleague of mine on the Policy and Planning Committee of the Board of Home Missions. As time passed there was a sentiment for continuing Congregational principles, and the people had voted to have joint affiliation with both the UCC and the National Association. Among their last acts under Dr. Crawford's ministry, the congregation had voted to move to the suburbs and had purchased a ten-acre tract ten miles west on Meadowbrook Road in Novi. Already quite a number of members were residing in that area. As I surveyed the situation I was surprised that the vote had gone as it had, for there seemed as many people determined to keep Bushnell in its present location as there were eager for the move. I thus came to a divided congregation. My task was to unite them. This I accomplished by pointing out that any move westward was several years away, and that in the meanwhile they should retain the fellowship they had enjoyed over several decades. The sanctuary was so beautiful, the people so responsive, and the activities of Detroit so varied that I had a happy nine-month interimship. I rented an apartment in a large complex of eight-unit buildings known as Sutton Place, near the intersection of Lahser and Eight Mile Road in Southfield.

In the winter I contacted the Board of Education in Novi and arranged to rent the gymnasium of an elementary school near the new Bushnell property. Each Sunday morning from the first of March, Ray Ferguson, organist of our church and of Wayne University, and I went out to the school at 8:00 A.M. With the help of volunteers we set up chairs and a worship table. A talented artist in the congregation, Kay Crowell, made banners to hang. At 9:00 A.M. we had a worship service with fifty to seventy in attendance. At the end of those three months we took in forty new members, which was the launching of the Meadowbrook Congregational Church.

My second interimship was from September of 1984 through Easter of 1985 at the First Congregational Church of Beloit, Wisconsin. This, too, was a beautiful experience. The meetinghouse was built in 1862, seating twelve hundred to accommodate Beloit College commencements, and is on the register of historic buildings. It is true New England transplanted to the midwest. The sanctuary is all white with a central pulpit and a handsome balcony around three sides. The people are proud of their heritage and extend themselves to maintain their treasure.

I followed the six-year pastorate of a young evangelical minister, who had alienated some of the old standbys but had brought in a number of younger families. Within a few weeks these conservatives recognized that my brand of Christianity was not for them, and nothing I did would satisfy them. We started a Sunday Morning Bible Roundtable to meet an hour before worship in the hope that we might have dialogue with them, but none of them would come. The roundtable did become a precious experience, for we had some thirty regulars with whom we developed a spiritual kinship as we studied the Scriptures. A new warmth came into the congregation as many of the long-time members returned. This was the only experience in my years of ministry in which I encountered fundamentalist opposition, as all the congregations have been liberal in outlook.

That September of 1985 I accepted a third interimship for four months at the First Congregational Church of Royal Oak, Michigan, one of the northern suburbs of Detroit, which attracts many young families. This was like coming home, for I had spoken there many times and had many friends in this congregation who have been active in the National Association. Ten years earlier the Royal Oak church had called as its senior minister one of my associates at Plymouth, the Rev. Dr. Terence Elwyn Johnson. Terry is an excellent

preacher and a warm pastor. He and I had developed a close friendship through what for him was a transforming experience. He had
been ordained and had ministered in the conservative Church of
Christ, but had chafed under the restrictions of two pastorates. He
was disillusioned about its theology. He was ready to give up the
ministry when he responded to an advertisement for an associate
that Plymouth had placed in *The Christian Century*. I went east to
interview several candidates, and in Terry Johnson recognized a
potential waiting to be liberated. He came to Plymouth, studied liberal philosophy, had a genuine change of outlook and came alive as
a dynamic minister. After four years with us he was called to Royal
Oak, where he was greatly loved. The best insight into the spirit of
this man is his repeated and open acknowledgment of me as his
teacher and mentor. Most people are reluctant to say what they have
learned from others, but lay their development to themselves. Terry
is unique in these tributes, which express his own generous spirit.

After ten years Terence Johnson was called to be senior minister
of the Community Church at Margate, New Jersey, the residential
area of Atlantic City. I was invited to preach the sermon at his installation, and found this to be a most attractive parish with a beautiful
plant just a block from the ocean. Since both Terry and his wife Joan
had been raised in Miami, this was a happy return to the coast.

Royal Oak friends persuaded me to come for this brief period
before I left to spend the winter months of 1986 at my condo in Del
Mar. I had a happy experience with this active congregation, and
enjoyed contacts with Detroit friends from Bushnell. One of my
strong friendships in the Detroit area is with Mr. and Mrs. James
Morrison, who are among the loyal adherents at Bushnell.

On my drive from Minneapolis over the southern route to San
Diego, I detoured slightly to accept the oft-given invitation of Mr.
and Mrs. N. Peter Jensen to stop at Green Valley, a retirement community of fifteen thousand in the desert thirty-five miles south of
Tucson. The Jensens had come with their three teenage children into
Plymouth twenty-five years earlier over the merger controversy, and
had been active with me in National Association programs. Maude
had been chairperson of the Women's Commission, and their son
Mark had been ordained at Plymouth and is minister of one of our
strongest Congregational churches.

In this three-day visit I was captivated by the area. There is a serenity in the desert, a beauty of sky and landscape. Traffic is not congested as yet, the city of Tucson is nearby, and prices are exceedingly low in comparison with those of Southern California. After my first visit I returned a month later to look at houses, and purchased an attractive, spacious townhouse in Esparanza Estates, a block from the Jensens. That summer I sold my unit in Del Mar Woods for more than twice the purchase price in Green Valley. Over my lifetime I have been involved in twenty-seven real estate transactions, and have found this a profitable way to build assets. I have now spent four winters in Green Valley, and am happy with my decision to locate there.

In late August of 1986 I received a surprise telephone call in Minneapolis from Sally Nolen, Minister of Membership Cultivation at Plymouth Congregational Church in Lansing, Michigan. She said that I was urgently needed. Their beloved minister, Dr. Robert J.L. Williams, had been stricken with a rare heart ailment for which there is no cure. The doctors had ordered him not to undergo the excitement of any public appearances or work. This had occurred in the summer, so there had been no opportunity for him to say farewell to the congregation, though his resignation was to be effective October 1. Bob Williams was very much beloved by his people. He was a dynamic personality, trained in Jungian analysis, superb in one-to-one counseling, and an able administrator. He had been called to a bewildered congregation after a disastrous fire had destroyed its landmark building next to the State Capitol, had rallied them in a building program, and had infused his own spirit into what had become a thriving fellowship.

I was stunned by this request, but I recognized in the back of my mind that this could be a rare opportunity. Three years earlier the National Association had had its annual meeting on the campus of Michigan State at East Lansing. The worship service and communion had been in the new Plymouth edifice, and I remembered what a stunning building it is. The State of Michigan had desired the location of the burned Plymouth for parking, and had given the congregation in trade six acres of a park on East Grand River Road toward the university. With this gift of land, $1,250,000 from insurance proceeds, and a fund-raising effort, the church had built a unique

$2,000,000 edifice. It was designed by Arlan Dow Associates of Midland, and is a spacious circular edifice. An inner corridor goes around it, with offices, classrooms, parlors, music room, kitchen and dining room on the outer side, and with the sanctuary known as "the centrum" on the inner side. At the very center a cone of stained glass reaches to the sky out of a high-peaked wood-beamed ceiling. This spire is over a solid seven-foot-square altar. The floor is tile. The seats are not pews, but movable chairs handsomely upholstered in crimson. My way of describing the function of the centrum is to compare it to a baseball diamond. The choir and organ are in field positions, the altar is the pitcher's box, and the pulpit is home plate, with no guarantee that the preacher will hit a home run every Sunday!

The services are highly liturgical, with a crucifer, acolytes, and lay readers. All of these trappings were beyond the simplicity to which I am accustomed, but the worship is carried out with such beauty and sincerity that I found it uplifting. From my visit to Lansing I realized that Bob Williams had created a spiritual atmosphere in which it would be exciting to minister.

I said to Sally Nolen in this first telephone contact, "What does Bob Williams say?" She replied, "Dr. Bob says that if Howard Conn will come I know all will be well." With that assurance I knew that this was a call that I should heed.

"But," I said, "I have just bought and furnished a new house in Green Valley where I expected to spend the winter. I will come if you will allow me three weeks of January in Arizona." Sally thought that would present no problem, and indeed it did not.

The church trustees rented for me the East Lansing home of a retired Jewish rabbi who goes to Florida to serve a winter congregation, and whose absence coincided with the nine months of my tenure. The living conditions were excellent. The spiritual atmosphere of the parish was intense and caring. People felt sadness over the loss of Dr. Williams, but were responsive to an older minister coming to serve. The lay involvement through board structures was high. The church moderator was Edward Krause, a topflight business executive who had grown up in the parish, who loved it, and who was highly supportive. He and I had regular luncheon appointments to review operations.

My year at Lansing was a happy climax to four interim ministries that enriched my life and enlarged my perspective. Though I was at Plymouth Minneapolis so long that all its members are "family" to me, nevertheless these interims introduced me to many new friends and demonstrated that there are splendid, thoughtful and dedicated persons in every congregation. I look back with thanksgiving on all four of the parishes that I was privileged to serve briefly.

The capping event of my half century of ministry was the celebration given at Plymouth Minneapolis on the Fiftieth Anniversary to the day of my ordination on June 15, 1936. At morning worship that Sunday in 1986, I preached on the theme, "Learning Along Life's Way." In the evening a testimonial dinner was given at the Minikahda Club. My sister came from California, Tom and Manorama Barnabas from India, Jim and Dorothy Morrison from Detroit, and Crosby Willet from Philadelphia. A hundred seventy-five friends enjoyed the dinner and program presided over by John Sandbo, the Plymouth moderator. Speakers were the Rev. Gary Reierson, the Rev. Vivian Jones, Lynn G. Truesdell III, and Terrance Hanold.

At the conclusion of morning worship, the people gathered in Guild Hall for the unveiling and dedication of a stained glass window commemorating my ministry. Because of my long association with the magic of stained glass, Mr. Jones had thought this to be an appropriate tribute. The work was executed by the Willet Studios in Philadelphia, with whom I have maintained friendships for nearly forty years. Crosby Willet, current president and son of my dear friend Henry Lee Willet, came to pull the curtain at the unveiling and to pay tribute at the evening banquet.

The window fills the third of the three large lancets in Guild Hall, next to that which honors the music ministry of my dear friend and organist-choirmaster, Arthur B. Jennings. When I came to Plymouth in 1944, these were outside windows, but in our first building project of 1948 they were covered and today require artificial illumination.

The theme is built around one of my sermons, "A Faith to Match the Universe," and celebrates six aspects of my ministry: philosopher, universalist, mystic, friend, builder, preacher. The three major panels have at the center Jesus preaching the Sermon on the Mount, with Plato on the right for philosophy, and on the left an Indian in contemplation as a mystic. As I reflect, I wish that the Hindu Nataraj or Dancing Shiva had been selected rather than this ascetic, as there is nothing ascetic about me! In a gold band within these panels is my definition of religion as "a response of adoration, thanksgiving and trust which a person makes to the Unseen; out of the belief that at the center of the universe is a Being of intelligence, purpose and love with whom we seek to be in harmony."

Above these three major panels is a lovely depiction of the majestic sweep of the universe, our planet Earth moving in rhythmic pattern among the celestial bodies. Across the lowest panel is one of the oldest and most universal of all prayers, from the Upanishads:

> From the unreal lead me to the real
> From darkness lead me to light
> From death lead me to immortality.

As I reflect on these fifty years of ministry, and indeed on the nearly eighty years of my earthly journey, I am keenly aware of the good fortune that has been mine. A Hand Always Above My Shoulder has surely guided me into opportunities, friendships and appreciations that by my unaided self I could not have attained. I have enjoyed living not only in the broad perspective of a universal outlook, but also in the comfortable details of daily surroundings. One of my Stanford professors frequently quoted Julius Caesar: "I grow old, but I learn a multitude of new facts every day." It is not facts that make life worthwhile, but ever-expanding insights. The pursuit of understanding never ends, for each new glimpse becomes the threshold for a further advance.

I have been blessed in my professional life, having been called to Plymouth at a young age and allowed to grow along with a beloved congregation. In retirement I have enjoyed brief pilgrimages with the folk of four other churches, and for a moment have glimpsed their hopes. These opportunities came within a profession in which I do not fit the usual description. I think of myself more as a teacher than as a preacher. I often say that I do not have a drop of evangelical blood in my veins. I am not trying to sell an orthodoxy nor to argue listeners to a new position. Rather, I am witnessing to a philosophy of life that means everything to me personally, and am sharing this vision with others in the hope that in some of them it will kindle a flame that transfigures and empowers. I recognize that I have not been a powerful evangelist like Billy Graham, whose altar calls bring forward multitudes from their seats, but I have had the satisfaction of receiving word from many that through my ministry they have gained insights to walk steadfastly through what life may bring.

A minister is privileged to live in an intimate way with people through their joys and their sorrows. To share at the deepest level is one of the truest joys. In this regard I have been fortunate indeed in knowing persons beyond number who have enriched me by their presence, their caring and their courage. There is a wonderful couplet from William Butler Yeats:

> Think where man's glory begins and ends,
> And say my glory was I had such friends.

So I am daily grateful for the Hand that has brought me a philosophy to guide, a career to enjoy, friends to enrich, health and good fortune, and, above all, the serene assurance that when my earthly journey ends I shall return to that Whole that is God's love and Eternal Oneness.

The American Quaker, Kenneth Boulding, in one of his *Naylor Sonnets* entitled "There Is a Spirit Which I Feel," expresses this assurance so well:

> Can I, imprisoned, body-bounded, touch
> The starry robe of God, and from my soul
> My tiny part, reach forth to his great Whole
> And spread my Little to the infinite Much
> When Truth forever slips from out my clutch,
> And what I take indeed, I do but dole
> In cupfuls from a rimless ocean-bowl
> That holds a million million million such?
> And yet, some Thing that moves among the stars,
> And holds the cosmos in a web of law,
> Moves too in me: a hunger, a quick thaw
> Of soul that liquefies the ancient bars
> As I, a member of creation, sing
> The burning oneness binding everything.

Epilogue

AS I ENTER MY EIGHTIETH YEAR I feel the need to summarize the religious philosophy that has been the dominant theme of my life since college days. I have maintained a consistent world view throughout the decades, but in my later years I have had the courage to express it in less traditional terms.

I have always been thrilled by life itself, in the enjoyment of friends, the appreciation of nature, and the contemplations of the mind. All of us begin awestruck by the wonders and the beauty of the world around us. Too often, however, we are pressed into molds of practicality as the material aspects of existence make their claims. We want physical pleasures. We want social approval. We covet material wealth. We are trained toward careers and occupations that promise success. It is quite easy for multitudes of people to become absorbed in the everyday pursuits of conventional society.

But for some of us this is not enough. We catch glimpses of a vaster universe and behold visions of realities that transcend the immediate. We are quickened by the art and the music, by the wisdom and the poetry, by the philosophy and the prayers of seers and mystics who have gone before us. They give us intimations of a grandeur and a dignity that outlast the vulnerability of our transient lives. We know then that in our fragile existence we are somehow related to a vast Unseen. In the quest to discover that relationship are born both philosophy and religion.

Philosophy asks the questions. What is the nature of the universe? Is there a purpose and direction to creation? What is ultimately and abidingly real? In the Great Tradition in Philosophy that began with Plato many avenues are explored, most of which affirm that the Unseen is beneficent and dependable. Within that framework of reliability, religion arises in humans as a response of adoration, thanksgiving and trust. We want to relate to this Unseen in ways of intimacy, openness and companionship that will enable us in some measure to harmonize our own selves with this Glorious Whole. We may call this Unseen "God," but by this name we mean a reality vaster than the captured deity of our traditional creeds.

It is with this approach that my spiritual pilgrimage has been engaged. The magnificent literature and art of civilization deal with the themes provided by this basic contrast between human seeking and universal values—such themes as our hopes and yet our sense of lostness; trusts and betrayals; purity and sin; guilt and forgiveness; love and anger; loneliness and community. These themes explore the tensions in which all of us are involved. These rather than the creeds of our institutional churches ought to be the starting place of our religious pilgrimage.

In Chekhov's drama, *Three Sisters*, Masha is made to say "It seems to me that a man must have faith, or must search for a faith, or his life will be empty, empty. . . . To live and not know why the cranes fly, why babies are born, why there are stars in the sky . . . Either you must know why you live, or everything else is trivial, not worth a straw." This is a literary expression of a searching that has haunted humankind since the beginning of time. Humans have always experienced birth and death, growth and decay, joy and sorrow, health and sickness. These are challenges that prompt us to ask the deeper questions. If we ignore these for the scatter-and-miss policy of doing whatever seems expedient at the moment, we may end with the despair of a Macbeth for whom life was

> a tale told by an idiot,
> full of sound and fury,
> signifying nothing.

What I call the "metaphysical instinct"—the impulse to ask the basic questions about life—has for me been best expressed by

Matthew Arnold:

> But often, in the world's most crowded streets,
> But often in the din of strife,
> There rises an unspeakable desire
> After the knowledge of our buried life;
> A thirst to spend our fires and restless force
> In tracking out our true, original course;
> A longing to inquire
> Into the mystery of this heart which beats
> So wild, so deep in us—to know
> Whence our lives come and where they go.

This deep mystic longing, this common search for meaning, has characterized my life. Yet this may seem strange when all my working years have been spent within the Christian Church. I have had fifty-five years as an ordained Congregational minister. In 1986 Plymouth Church Minneapolis celebrated the fiftieth anniversary of my ordination by installing a magnificent stained glass window to depict six aspects of my ministry: universalism, philosophy, mysticism, friendliness, administration, preaching.

I do not, however, fit the clergy mold. I have always been reluctant to identify myself as a minister because people immediately assume that they know my beliefs and my judgments. They respond in terms of stereotypes and have no conception of individuality.

I did not go into the ministry because of Jesus Christ, neither because he had claimed my loyalty nor because I promised to serve him. Nor have I ever had any awesome respect for the Church as a custodial institution surviving through the centuries as a repository of truth, as a guarantor of sacraments, or as an ark of salvation. Nor do I take any pride in calling myself "a Christian" because of this historic legacy. My motivation was to find the Church a place in which I could share with people the insights that make life exciting, insights gained from teachers, writers, poets, mystics. I conceive of the Church as a place in the community where seekers in all stages of life can gather to learn, to share, and to relate to the eternal values of the cosmos.

What we have today are various denominations, historic overall groupings of Christians, such as Roman Catholic, Episcopal, Lutheran, Presbyterian, United Church of Christ. Each of these groupings claims to be a church instituted by God or Christ with a divine mission to perform. Actually they are all human-made, arising out of particular historic situations. Basically they are power structures. They have constitutions, regulations, administrative policies, creeds that define who and how clergy may function and how laity may respond. They operate on assumed authority exercised by hierarchies, dioceses, synods, conferences. While these denominations claim an ecumenical outlook that recognizes a unity as "the body of Christ," their practices contradict such universalism. They have rules to give special protection to their clergy and to bar outsiders from their sacraments. A great many people find comfort and security in the orderliness, the smoothness, and the certainty of these ecclesiastical structures. And most laypeople, concerned only with the routines of local parish life, have no awareness of the regulating powers of these denominational bodies.

As a lover of freedom and a respecter of individuality, I find these structures to impose intermediary restrictions between the individual and the religious search for fellowship with the Unseen. I grew up as a birthright Congregationalist without regard for the authority of superstructures. I adhere to the principle enunciated by the Pilgrim Fathers at the Cambridge Synod of 1648, that there is no church outside the local congregation. Every ecclesiastical authority has been established by human beings, and has no valid claim to represent the Spirit of the Unseen.

Though I reject all these supposedly higher institutions, I rejoice in each and every church that is a covenanted community of caring seekers. I have been happy to minister as "pastor and teacher" in three churches during the forty years between ordination and retirement, and in four parishes as an interim clergy. There can be no greater privilege than to live with people as a confidant and guide with no authority other than the love in one's heart and the reasonableness of one's thoughts. The minister in a community of caring seekers is not conferring some sanctified blessing on reluctant sinners, but is a friend sharing life and opening windows on the rich treasures of the Unseen.

We need happy churches. We may criticize creedal doctrines and institutional authority, but as human beings in search of the abundant life, we need to belong to a local company of people who can encourage one another, who can worship, pray, play and grow together. I love to sing the great hymns, to hear the majestic tones of the organ, to sit quietly surrounded by stained glass and beamed ceilings.

It seems to me unfortunate that before persons can be accepted into membership in a Christian church they are asked to affirm a creed which separates them from a large portion of humankind. The development of one's own spiritual life ought to be a process of continuous growth. Jesus called his followers to be seekers, askers, pilgrims. How earnest can be our search if at the outset we are obliged to subscribe to an ancient formula? In our quest even individuals in the same congregation may come to differing emphases. We can welcome diversity because we are a caring community of those who love one another.

In this broader Congregational view of the local congregation, I rejoice in the Church and I encourage people to participate. Plymouth Minneapolis is a happy church. Its strength lies in its openness, its warmth and its caring.

After making clear my appreciation of the Church, I come back to the philosophical outlook which prompts my religious response. It is a universal approach which surveys the wide panorama of humankind's seeking and recognizes that "religion" is broader than any of its historic expressions.

The religious pilgrimage is the most exciting adventure in which a person may participate. The civilizations of the past attest to the centrality of the search for meaning. Each of the historic religions of the world has developed a special insight and made a significant contribution. We today have the benefit of accumulated wisdom, but we ought not be required to accept as authoritative the particularities of any tradition. Like the ancient Greeks, we should seek "to see life steadily and to see it whole."

Universalism is the name best given to this broad outlook. It affirms that the relationship of persons to God is open to all human beings of any generation or any land. This relationship is not limited by the historical incidents, ritual forms or creedal statements of any particular religion. Universalism employs reason, intuition and tradition to arrive at understanding. On the basis of that understanding, the individual makes the response of adoration, thanksgiving and trust toward the Unseen. Universalism proclaims a mystery. It breaks forth into artistic expressions of music, drama, art, dance and liturgy that relate us to the divine scheme of creation.

I call my religion "Christian Universalism." Even though it goes beyond Christianity to include the insights of Asian religions, it is nonetheless Christian because it recognizes Jesus as the pivotal teacher. He had such a warm and intimate relationship with the Unseen that he referred to God as a Heavenly Father. He taught his disciples to pray. He himself prayed when in moments of direst agony he felt related to a universal center in whose ultimate acceptance and vindication he trusted. His understanding of the way in which the cosmos is organized is given in the Sermon on the Mount. Real Christianity is living the Beatitudes.

The gospel is indeed "Good News"—the Good News that God loves us, forgives us of our sins, and views us with divine mercy. It is the Good News that the universe cares about the needy and the destitute, and says no to many injustices of society. Jesus proclaimed this message apart from the particularities of atonement, judgment and redemption through the blood of a divine redeemer.

Unfortunately, the Christianity still taught by most mainline churches is that of the ancient creeds resulting from the distortions of St. Paul, who made Jesus a divine figure and shifted the emphasis from the teachings of the Master to a theology *about* Jesus. To me this is not tenable. Science today knows so much more about the universe than did the people of the fourth century, yet too many churches insist on the theology of that bygone era.

Throughout my ministry I have found Bible studies to be productive of ever-new insights, and consider the search for the Historical Jesus of supreme importance. How do we separate what Jesus actually said and did from what the early church taught about him? Though the Bible is precious, it should not be regarded as authoritative. Rather, it is the testimony of highly sensitive people as to their fears and anxieties, their assurances and hopes. We read it to illumine our own experiences, but we are free to interpret its wider implications.

As a universalist I believe that the religious impulse is native to all persons of whatever culture or generation and, therefore, that the presentations in our churches ought to be on this cosmic outlook rather than on the particularities of Christianity. It is more important that a person be in tune with God than that he or she be a Christian. In my ministry I have tried to impart the basics of pure generic religion as they apply to the living of people everywhere.

This is not to say, however, that all religions are the same. It is to recognize their common substratum before making distinctions among them. It does make a difference which of the historic world religions dominates one's thought patterns. Judaism emphasizes the separateness of a chosen people; Islam involves fatalism and a certain fanaticism; Buddhism encourages meditation and inwardness; Christianity elevates forgiveness from sins. Each has rituals of its own.

I am sympathetic to philosophical Hinduism, partly because I became familiar with it in graduate studies before I attended seminary, but also because I am a mystic with reverence for the Unseen. The Upanishads, written five hundred years before the Christian era, recognize Brahma, or God, as the guiding, caring, purposive force in all creation. Brahma makes the universe an intelligible and beautiful whole, alive with love. Hinduism identifies God with the universe and the self with God. Our prayers are offerings of openness through which creative powers may flow through us.

In contrast, both Judaism and Christianity make a sharp distinction between God and the world. The Bible portrays God as a sovereign deity separate from the world. In Genesis 2, 3, he walks in the Garden of Eden and issues his commands, then stands aside to judge conduct. This dichotomy results in the semantics out of which come the creeds of the first four Christian centuries. We get the concept of the Trinity. Can we today believe that there is a Triune Being out there in space? Prayer becomes a plea for a Being out there to intervene with natural events to do something for us.

Mysticism is not totally absent from the Bible nor from Christian experience. Scripture opens with the poetic vision of creation evolving from within itself. God is not a separate Being walking in the Garden of Eden but "the Spirit of God moving upon the face of the waters." This is process theology consistent with the findings of modern science.

This pervasive presence of God is celebrated in my favorite Psalm, the 139th:

> O Lord, thou has searched me and known me.
> Thou knowest my downsitting and mine uprising;
> Thou understandeth my thought afar off.
> Thou compassest my path and my lying down,
> And art acquainted with all my ways.
> For there is not a word in my tongue,
> But, lo, O lord, thou knowest it altogether.
> Wither shall I go from thy Spirit?
> Or wither shall I flee from thy presence?

I am not a Hindu but a Christian; however, I find eastern mysticism helpful to my devotional life. We need a "feel" for what is real. Intellectually I accept the philosophical tradition of Idealism, which recognizes mind as ultimate. Emotionally I need mysticism to relate me to God. Reality is one, though manifested in various modes. This provides a foundation for true ecumenism, for world peace, and for common respect among the world's people.

Many people today are waiting for this liberating message. When I completed a year's interimship, I received a note from a lawyer saying: "I've been a member of this church for nearly half a century, and at times during that period have had the uncomfortable feeling that my views conflicted with the 'correct' ones. You've made me feel legitimate again."

All of us need to remember that in religion there can be no certainty nor proofs. We are moving in a realm of mystery, living by intimations and surmises which are at the heart of our existence. They are personal affirmations we are happy to make but which we have no right to demand of other persons.

I have tried to record how I came to my position and to state my convictions. But like everyone else, I remain in this realm of mystery. My proper stance is that of Plato, who concluded an exposition of a philosophic doctrine with these words: "A man of sense ought not to insist that everything is exactly as I have described it; but he may venture to think that this or something like it is the truth about our souls. That, I think, is a venture fitting and worthwhile. Wherefore, let a man be of good cheer . . . and be ready to go forward on his journey."

Life has for me been an adventure fitting and worthwhile. I wish the same for you.

Joy on the journey!

Plymouth Church Moderators

1948-1990

Donald J. Cowling
Gideon Seymour
Harold G. Cant
Richard L. Kozelka
Edgar F. Zelle
G. Aaron Youngquist
Philip F. Sherman
Ellwood H. Newhart
Merrill S. Finch
Willard A. Morse
J. Roscoe Furber
Terrance Hanold
Roland W. Chambers
Alan M. Struthers
Mildred Bowen Bolstad
Bobb Chaney
Catherine S. Lenmark
Lynn G. Truesdell III
Barbara Griswold Laederach
John Sandbo
Jane Houser Pejsa
Charles R. Lloyd

A Hand Always Above My Shoulder

by
Howard Conn

For copies of this book, please write to Aberfoyle Press, 5804 Oak Lane, Edina, Minnesota 55436. The cost is $10.00 per copy plus $2.00 for postage and handling.

Please send a check for $12.00 per copy to Aberfoyle Press. (Minnesota residents please add 6% sales tax.) We cannot process credit cards.

Thank you.

ORDER FORM

Aberfoyle Press
5804 Oak Lane
Edina, Minnesota 55436

I am enclosing a check for $_____ to cover the cost of _____ copy (copies) of *A Hand Always Above My Shoulder*, including shipping.

Name _____

Street _____

City _____ State _____

ZIP Code _____

Telephone _____